Wendell Berry and Higher Education

Wendell Berry
AND HIGHER EDUCATION

Cultivating Virtues of Place

JACK R. BAKER AND JEFFREY BILBRO

Foreword by Wendell Berry

UNIVERSITY PRESS OF KENTUCKY

Copyright © 2017 by The University Press of Kentucky
Paperback edition 2020

Scholarly publisher for the Commonwealth,
serving Bellarmine University, Berea College, Centre College of Kentucky, Eastern Kentucky University, The Filson Historical Society, Georgetown College, Kentucky Historical Society, Kentucky State University, Morehead State University, Murray State University, Northern Kentucky University, Transylvania University, University of Kentucky, University of Louisville, and Western Kentucky University.
All rights reserved.

Editorial and Sales Offices: The University Press of Kentucky
663 South Limestone Street, Lexington, Kentucky 40508-4008
www.kentuckypress.com

Library of Congress Cataloging-in-Publication Data

Names: Baker, Jack R. | Bilbro, Jeffrey.
Title: Wendell Berry and higher education : cultivating virtues of place /
  Jack R. Baker and Jeffrey Bilbro ; foreword by Wendell Berry.
Description: Lexington : University Press of Kentucky, [2017] | Includes
  bibliographical references and index.
Identifiers: LCCN 2016058958| ISBN 9780813169026 (hardcover : alk. paper) |
  ISBN 9780813169033 (pdf) | ISBN 9780813169040 (epub)
Subjects: LCSH: Berry, Wendell, 1934- | Education, Higher—Aims and
  objectives—United States. | Education, Higher—United States—Philosophy.
Classification: LCC LB885.B373 B35 2017 | DDC 378.00973—dc23

ISBN 978-0-8131-7914-8 (pbk. : alk. paper)

This book is printed on acid-free paper meeting the requirements of the American National Standard for Permanence in Paper for Printed Library Materials.

Manufactured in the United States of America.

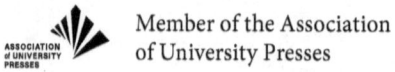

Member of the Association
of University Presses

To Shelby, Michigan, and Stehekin, Washington—
places that call us home—
and to Kelly, Owen, Silvia, and Griffin Baker
and Melissa and Hannah Bilbro—family members
with whom we are grateful to dwell in "the room of love."

[Western settlers'] grand ambition for their children, is to send them to school in some eastern city, the measure most likely to make them useless and unhappy at home. I earnestly hope that, ere long, the existence of good schools near themselves, planned by persons of sufficient thought to meet the wants of the place and time, instead of copying New York or Boston, will correct this mania.
　　　　　—Margaret Fuller, Summer on the Lakes, in 1843

Education in the true sense, of course, is an enablement to serve—both the living human community in its natural household or neighborhood and the precious cultural possessions that the living community inherits or should inherit. To educate is, literally, to "bring up," to bring young people to a responsible maturity, to help them to be good caretakers of what they have been given, to help them to be charitable toward fellow creatures. . . . And if this education is to be used well, it is obvious that it must be used some where; it must be used where one lives, where one intends to continue to live; it must be brought home.
　　　　　—Wendell Berry, "Higher Education and Home Defense"

Contents

Foreword xi

Introduction: An Education for Health and Homecoming 1

Part 1. Rooting Universities

1. Imagining the Tree of Wisdom: The Recovery of the University 25

2. Standing by Our Words: Learning a Responsible Language 47

3. Doing Good Work: Enacting Our Imagination 70

Part 2. Cultivating Virtues of Place

Introduction to Part 2 91

4. Tradition: Remembering Our Story 95

5. Hierarchy: Practicing Gratitude and Respecting Limits 116

6. Geography: Reaping the Fruits of Fidelity 140

7. Community: Learning to Love the Membership 166

Conclusion: Doing Work that Sustains Hope 191

Afterword: The Authors and Their Stories 195

Acknowledgments 199

Notes 201

Bibliography 231

Index 245

Foreword

In 1978 Wendell Berry delivered a commencement address to the graduates of Centre College. Although it was given almost forty years ago, its vision of placed education remains as important as ever. In this speech Berry outlines the ecological and moral order to which humans are responsible, and he points to the ancient virtues that can sustain us in our proper place within this order. Berry quotes from Milton's Comus *to critique gluttony and challenge the graduates to practice the virtue of temperance. The epilogue of* Comus *concludes with the Spirit telling his listeners that the love of virtue is the pathway to true freedom:*

> Mortals that would follow me,
> Love vertue, she alone is free,
> She can teach ye how to clime
> Higher than the Spheary chime;
> Or if Vertue feeble were,
> Heav'n it self would stoop to her.[1]

The love of virtue, as we argue in the following pages, is the fruit of an education rooted in place, and this love forms the basis for "a healthful economy that is at once physical and spiritual." In describing this economy as physical and spiritual, Berry reminds us that the ecological crisis we face today provides pragmatic, physical reasons for us to practice those virtues traditionally understood as moral and spiritual. As Berry tells the graduates, this is an "old truth that a new generation must now try to learn in a new way." This address has not yet been published, and after hearing us present our work at a conference and visiting with us at his home, Berry graciously granted us permission to print it here as the foreword to our book.[2]

I have been asked to say to the graduates, briefly, what I most wish had been said to me at my own graduation. It is hard to think of anything in the way of good counsel that had *not* been said to me either at or by the time of my graduation. The same truths are told in one form or another to every generation. Inexperience doubts them as it must, as perhaps it should, and experience proves them true; the benefits being that the old truths thus remain fresh, and each new generation thus learns something about humility.

And so I think I was probably told everything I wish I had been told. What I wish I had paid closer attention to and understood sooner is what we are now being taught more urgently than ever before by the study of ecological systems: the inescapability of connections and of dependences. Wherever we turn, we are up against order—order that we did not make, that we cannot fully comprehend, that includes and sustains our lives, and that we cannot too radically change without destroying ourselves. There is an order of cause that far outreaches memory; there is an order of consequence that far outreaches prediction.

It is still assumed by some knowingly, by some unknowingly that the Creation is a "fluke" that depends upon humans to put it in order. This doctrine is obviously useful to anyone who wishes to damage the world for profit. But it is equally obvious, thanks to the ecologists, that we can no longer afford the luxury of that oversimplification. Order was here long before we humans were, it will be here long after we are gone, and within that order all creatures "are members one of another." Within that order the ecological axiom always holds: you can't do one thing; each event invariably compounds itself in others. Order ramifies in order; disorder ramifies in disorder. And so great is the magnitude of the order of Creation that no one ever understands the ultimate cause or foresees the ultimate consequence of any act.

The human meaning of this is that we are not, have never been, can never be, alone. There is clearly some comfort in that. But I hope I am making equally clear the difficulty and even the fearfulness that also are in it. No one can act simply in his or her own behalf. Escape either into specialization or into solitude is illusory. If we live in an order that we cannot escape, if we creatures are all "members one of another," then we cannot act except in each other's behalf, and indeed in behalf of the whole densely woven globe of connections that we call the Creation or the Universe.

This is really only a way of saying that life in this world is a moral problem, and that the solution is not easy. That is not news. Or perhaps you could say that it is old news, old truth that a new generation must now try to learn in a new way. For what ecological insight has done is reveal again the practical foundations of ancient morality. If, for instance, the order that I have described is a fact, which it is, and if it surpasses human comprehension, which it does, then temperance is not just a spiritual discipline, but a practical necessity, no less so than food or water or air; and we have an infallible standard by which to measure the sinfulness of gluttony.

But this insight carries us farther than that. It doesn't leave us stranded on the dry ground of moral distinctions. Finally it shows us the possibility of a healthful economy that is at once physical and spiritual. Gluttony is not sinful merely because it consumes too much and leaves too little for others; it is also sinful because it belittles what it consumes, and belittles the source: "... swinish gluttony / Ne'er looks to heaven amidst his gorgeous feast ..." That is John Milton, writing in 1634 a perfectly apt criticism of the "consumer society" of the 1970's. Gluttony gives only the soon-jaded pleasure of the little we can consume; temperance gives the joy of inconsumable abundance.

And so, as it has been for many another graduating class, the old is news for this one of 1978, of which I am honored to count myself a member.

Introduction

An Education for Health and Homecoming

Our current university system caters to Americans' most consumerist, selfish tendencies: universities promise to deliver lucrative employment and "upward mobility," and for these sought-after commodities they can demand ever-higher tuition. As Wendell Berry has been arguing for decades, however, an education founded upon such a reductive economic exchange cannot expect to form healthy, virtuous community members. As the ecological and human costs of our hollowed-out rural communities and destructive agricultural practices mount, the need for graduates who have been educated for "responsible membership in a family, a community, or a polity" becomes even more pressing.[1] Our hope is that this book will contribute, in however small a way, toward mending our damaged places and communities by encouraging universities to begin educating students for health.

Tell the Stories Right

An education for health begins by forming the imaginations and affections of students so that rather than desiring upward mobility, they can imagine healthy, placed lives. Over the last few years, we have been teaching Wendell Berry's novel *Hannah Coulter* in various courses. Told from the perspective of an elderly woman looking back at her long life with its many joys and travails, the narrative leads readers through the arc of Hannah's emotions as she gradually learns to be content. Contentment is a virtue that is particularly difficult for those of us in higher education to practice; universities exist to prepare students to lead better lives in better places, and this obsession with something better erodes our ability to be content. In the opening pages of the novel, Hannah says, "This is the story of my life, that while I lived it weighed upon me and pressed against me and filled all my senses to overflowing and now is like a dream dreamed. . . . This is my giving of thanks."[2] As the narrative unfolds, the reader begins to understand the deep wisdom that lies behind Hannah's proclamation that this story is her "giving of thanks." She has been twice widowed, her children have moved away, and many of her close friends have died, yet in spite of these sorrows, Hannah does not desire a better life. She is grateful for the life she has lived.

One narrative thread in Hannah's life that speaks to educators in particular concerns what is perhaps the greatest challenge in higher education today: the failure of universities to imagine and serve the health of their places. This thread is woven into Hannah's story as she cultivates love for people and place, even as they are significantly altered—often negatively—by the academy. As she sends each of her three children off to college, she has hope that they will return home and settle nearby, but the education they receive encourages them to move away. Hannah reflects on this loss with a poignant metaphor: "After each one of our children went away to the university, there always came a time when we would feel the distance opening to them, pulling them away. It was like sitting snug in the house, and a door is opened somewhere, and suddenly you feel a draft."[3] In this way, the university and its way of life came to be one of her great sorrows.

Her sorrow has its origin in the destructive ideology of the university as part of an industrial economy—an economy in which schools bring in customers and send out displaced individuals with immense debts, having taught those individuals that the good life can be found anywhere but at home. After all her children have left home to pursue better knowledge in better places, Hannah reflects on the danger of such a vision and the salutary example of her husband Nathan: "Most people now are hoping for 'a better place,' which means that a lot of them will end up in a worse one. I think this is what Nathan learned from his time in the army and the war. He saw a lot of places, and he came home. I think he gave up the idea that there is a better place somewhere else. There is no 'better place' than this, not in this world. And it is by the place we've got, and our love for it and our keeping of it, that this world is joined to Heaven."[4] At the heart of our book, then, is a desire to confront the contemporary academic ideology that claims the university should prepare students and faculty alike for a "better place" than home. Our hope is that the university might encourage us to love and keep our places and so participate in joining them to heaven.

It is significant that when seeking to understand why all her children left home for better lives elsewhere, Hannah questions whether she and Nathan told the right stories. One night, realizing that the prospect of any of the children returning is unlikely, Hannah begins "mourning over them" to Nathan, concluding that she has somehow failed her beloved children: "I just wanted them to have a better chance than I had." Nathan, a wise man of few words, responds to Hannah, "Don't complain about the chance you had."[5] Struck by Nathan's response, Hannah finally senses the dreadful thing she has said without knowing it: the stories we tell about the chances we have will shape the lives of the people we love. Hannah then recounts her life—the loss of her mother and the arrival of her cruel stepmother, the loss of her young husband Virgil in the war when she was pregnant, her marriage to Nathan and the birth of their sons—and concludes, "The chance you had is the life you've got. . . . You mustn't want to be somebody else. What you must do is this: 'Rejoice evermore. Pray without ceasing. In every thing give thanks.' I am not all the way capable of so much, but those are the right instructions."[6]

Do students at universities learn the goodness of rejoicing evermore, the wisdom of ordering their lives toward prayer and service, the beauty of giving thanks in all things? What stories are we telling our students during the years they spend in the prime of their youth within these communities?[7] Are these stories speaking to our students about health, contentedness, the goodness of human limits, love? Perhaps we ought to be asking ourselves the same question that preoccupies Hannah in this passage: "But did we tell the stories right? It was lovely, the telling and the listening, usually the last thing before bedtime. But did we tell the stories in such a way as to suggest that we had needed a better chance or a better life or a better place than we had?"[8] Though Hannah is uncertain whether she and Nathan told the right stories, she is certain that telling the right stories is not only possible but also necessary. These stories are threads woven into the garment of our lives, and if we always imply that our students should never return to their previous lives, aren't we tugging at the "loose thread that unravels the whole garment? And how are you ever to know where the thread breaks, and when the tug begins?"[9]

Hannah's musings on the central importance of the narratives we tell have inspired us to begin this book by asking some difficult questions about the university: How might education lead students to practice healthy contentment with people and places? What are appropriate ends for a university education? In what ways can universities shape their graduates into affectionate, virtuous members of their places? It is our hope that this book will continue a conversation about the purpose of higher education by focusing on the important connections among the stories we tell and embody, the language we rely on, the work we accomplish together, and the virtues we cultivate in our communities.

Part of this educational effort entails helping students see how stories shape their affections and imaginations, thus helping them become more virtuous inhabitants of their places. Alasdair MacIntyre, in his seminal book *After Virtue,* argues that one of the requirements for sustaining virtues is a coherent cultural narrative that gives context and purpose to our lives and to community practices. James Smith draws on this connection between narrative and right practices in his three-part Cultural Liturgies series.[10] In his first volume, *Desiring the Kingdom,* Smith outlines an "anthropology that emphasizes the primacy of love and the priority of the imagination in shaping our identity and governing our orientation to the world." He also argues "that education is primarily about the formation ('aiming') of our love and desire, and that such formation happens through embodied, communal rituals we might call 'liturgies'—including a range of 'secular' liturgies that are pedagogies of desire."[11] In other words, the stories we tell shape our actions, and our actions—in turn—shape the stories we tell. Thus, our reliance on Berry's fiction and poetry in the pages that follow stems from our agreement with Smith that stories are integral to a re-visioning of what universities are for: "the way to the heart is through the body, and the way into the body is through story."[12] If we hope to reorient hearts and minds to foster healthy places, we must learn to tell the right stories—we must renarrate higher education.

As Berry indicates in his Centre College commencement address (see the foreword), the narratives that shape our lives—and our educational institutions—cultivate particular sets of virtues. The American Dream that celebrates individual success and limitless upward mobility leads to an education in the virtues of personal ambition, dangerous risk taking, and careless transience. Yet this narrative and these supposed virtues are based on a dangerous myth: the belief that we are separate from our communities and places and that there is no ecological and moral order to which we are accountable. In its place, then, Berry offers the narrative of ecological and communal interdependence: "Wherever we turn, we are up against order—order that we did not make, that we cannot fully comprehend, that includes and sustains our lives, and that we cannot too radically change without destroying ourselves." This ecological order imposes physical limits that parallel the moral limits respected by traditional virtues.

Thus the "new" story that ecology narrates parallels the old story embedded in our moral traditions. An education in the virtues of place, then, may involve relearning old truths and old virtues that provide important correctives to the story of individual success and upward mobility that so captivates the American imagination.

Educating "Stickers"

It is common today for universities to tell stories about the need for "upward (and lateral) mobility," which are generated by the broader culture's stories about progress and success.[13] An article in the satirical newspaper *The Onion* captures our culture's dominant belief that mobility is an indicator of success. Titled "Unambitious Loser with Happy, Fulfilling Life Still Lives in Hometown," the article states: "Longtime acquaintances confirmed to reporters this week that local man Michael Husmer, an unambitious 29-year-old loser who leads an enjoyable and fulfilling life, still lives in his hometown and has no desire to leave." Through interviews with Husmer's more successful high school classmates, the man's dreary life comes into focus:

> Former high school classmates confirmed that Husmer has seemingly few aspirations in life, citing occasional depressing run-ins with the personally content townie during visits back home, as well as embarrassing Facebook photos in which the smiling dud appears alongside family members whom he sees regularly and appreciates and enjoys close, long-lasting relationships with. Additionally, pointing to the intimate, enduring connections he's developed with his wife, parents, siblings, and neighbors, sources reported that Husmer's life is "pretty humiliating" on multiple levels.
>
> In particular, those familiar with the pitiful man, who is able to afford a comfortable lifestyle without going into debt, confirmed that he resides just two blocks from the home he grew up in, miles away from anything worthwhile, like high-priced bars and clubs. In fact, sources stated that the pathetic loafer has never had any interest in moving to even a nearby major city, despite the fact that he has nothing better to do than "sit around all day" being an involved member of his community and using his ample free time to follow pursuits that give him genuine pleasure.[14]

Our laughter at this portrayal of a "loser" reveals our awareness that leaving home is associated with "making it," even though the stress and anxiety experienced by Husmer's "successful" acquaintances call into question the desirability of such a mobile life.

Such restless deracination is only exacerbated by new forms of social media and our increasingly pervasive consumer culture. Constant updates on Twitter or Facebook promise us new information or entertainment whenever we want it. And while material consumption may appear to be motivated by an overvaluation of physical goods, what is most striking about consumerism is the relentless desire to obtain something new rather than to enjoy what one already has. As William Cavanaugh observes: "Once we have obtained an item, it brings desire to a temporary halt, and the item loses some of its appeal. Possession kills desire; familiarity breeds contempt. That is why shopping, not buying itself, is the heart of consumerism. The consumerist spirit is a restless spirit, typified by detachment, because desire must be kept constantly on the move."[15] Consumerism and social media are simply further expressions of an American rootlessness typified by the frontier mentality.

Berry has been describing this cultural obsession with restless mobility for decades now, arguing that it causes extensive damage to our land and our character. As he explains, "Upward mobility, as we now are seeing, implies downward mobility, just as it has always implied lateral mobility. It implies, in fact, social instability, ecological oblivion, and economic insecurity."[16] Elsewhere, Berry uses the term *boomers* to describe those who are always on the lookout for better career opportunities in better places. Berry derives this term—and its opposite, *stickers*—from Wallace Stegner's description of the two contrasting types of pioneers who settled the West. Stegner, a twentieth-century author who wrote about the western landscape where he was raised, identifies boomers as those who came to the West looking to get rich; they were willing to damage the land and its existing communities for a quick profit. Once they had extracted all they could easily get from a place—whether a mine, a forest, or a farm—they moved on to a more abundant place. But, as Berry explains, "Not all who came to American places came to plunder and run. Some came to stay, or came with the hope of staying. These Stegner called 'stickers' or 'nesters.'"[17] Stickers came west looking to transplant themselves into a new home. In another essay, Berry describes such people as "nurturers," those whose "goal is health," the health of the land, the community, and the country.[18]

The root difference between boomers and stickers is not simply that one group is mobile and one group is stationary; rather, they are defined by their contrasting narratives, motivations, and affections. As Berry explains in his 2012 Jefferson Lecture "It All Turns on Affection": "The boomer is motivated by greed, the desire for money, property, and therefore power."[19] Berry's title indicates that his emphasis in making this distinction is on one's affections, and this clarifies a common but misguided criticism of his thought. Berry does not say that everyone who leaves home is a greedy, selfish boomer. Rather, he simply insists that our affections are never without consequences. Thus, the individual motivated by "greed, the desire for money, property, and therefore power," is not necessarily the individual who moves to the only state where she can find gainful employment, leaving her loved ones half a nation away. Nor is the boomer the individual who leaves the small town where his entire family lives because he has suffered abuse at their hands. Instead, the boomer is the individual who is guided by wrongheaded affections—affections for power, wealth, or personal success at whatever cost. We must be clear that *boomer* identifies a story—a way of imagining success that leads to a way of living characterized by disinterest in place, limits, and externalized consequences—not a person who leaves a place. So perhaps an important distinction is that a sticker may be forced to leave a place but will nest in a new place, whereas a boomer wants to leave a place and is willing to leave again should a better opportunity arise elsewhere.[20]

Because our affections have such far-reaching influence—shaping the questions we ask and the ways we arrange knowledge—both Stegner and Berry focus on the conflicting internal desires named by *boomer* and *sticker*. They warn against seeing these terms as categories of people, arguing instead that they differentiate between conflicting internal motivations. As Berry writes, "All of us, I think, are in some manner torn between caring and not caring, staying and going."[21] The choice to root ourselves and shape our desires to the limits of our place is not a clear-cut, one-time choice. Rather, it is a long process of refining and ordering our affections, of choosing to serve the health of our place rather than to fulfill our individual desires, and of seeking the kind of knowledge that will enable us to do this restorative work. As Berry explains, "Having chosen one way, one is never free of the opposite way. . . . We must keep on choosing."[22]

Boomerism pervades our educational culture today, such that its effects are evident in nearly all departments and universities. As Wes Jackson claims, "upward mobility" is now the only major that universities offer: "Little attention is paid to educating the young to return home, or to go some other place, and dig in. There is no such thing as a 'homecoming' major."[23] Steven Bouma-Prediger and Brian Walsh extend Jackson's argument, claiming, "Colleges and universities—small or large, public or private, Christian or secular—tend to educate for upward mobility, to alienate people from their local habitation, and to encourage the vandalization of the earth."[24] What such an education forgets is the need for a vocation that subsumes these techniques under a higher purpose: the restoration of health and the flourishing of one's community. As Berry trenchantly observes in "Higher Education and Home Defense":

> Education in the true sense, of course, is an enablement to *serve*—both the living human community in its natural household or neighborhood and the precious cultural possessions that the living community inherits or should inherit. To educate is, literally, to "bring up," to bring young people to a responsible maturity, to help them to be good caretakers of what they have been given, to help them to be charitable toward fellow creatures.... And if this education is to be used well, it is obvious that it must be used some *where*; it must be used where one lives, where one intends to continue to live; it must be brought home.[25]

Graduates can't serve their communities, they can't take care of them, if they don't settle somewhere and bring their education home. Often our educational system seems designed for students who have been told all their lives to "follow your dreams"; what Berry proposes is that we tell students to "serve your place" and then design an education that enables them to do so.

An education for health, one that inspires students to serve their homes, has to begin by reforming students' imaginations so that they ask better questions. As Berry explains, their differently oriented affections lead boomers and stickers to ask different kinds of questions and to operate in different economies. The boomer or "exploiter asks of a piece of land only how much and how quickly it can be made to produce, the nurturer [or sticker] asks a question that is much more complex and difficult: What is its carrying capacity? (That is: How much can be taken from it without diminishing it?)"[26] Berry expressed this contrast even more simply in an interview with Bill Moyers: "The answers will come not from walking up to your farm and saying this is what I want and this is what I expect from you. You walk up and you say 'What do you need?'"[27] These different questions stem from different desires—a desire for quick profit or a desire for health—and result in different complexities of accounting—one values only profit and externalizes costs and damages, and the other seeks to account for all things. Berry draws a similar distinction in "Two Economies" between our industrial economy, which "tends to destroy what it does not comprehend," and the "Great Economy" or the "Kingdom of God," which "includes everything" in its comprehensive "pattern or order."[28]

This fundamental difference between teaching students to get what they want from their places and teaching them to ask "What do you need?" marks not only the difference between boomers and stickers but also the difference between a more unified way of organizing knowledge and the organization (or lack thereof) in modern universities. Asking "What do I want?" simply leads to training in the techniques of extraction that can satisfy personal appetite. But the question "What do you need?" leads to an education in charity that can serve the health of one's place. C. S. Lewis describes this difference in terms of the contrast between medieval learning and the mere technical training increasingly offered today: "For the wise men of old the cardinal problem had been how to conform the soul to reality, and the solution had been knowledge, self-discipline, and virtue. For . . . applied science . . . the problem is how to subdue reality to the wishes of men: the solution is a technique."[29] The work of conforming our souls to reality via knowledge, self-discipline, and virtue is long and arduous, but if we hope to be responsible members of our places, this is the work we have to take up.

The contrast between boomers and stickers—the different desires they have, the different stories they tell, the different questions they ask, the different economies they participate in, and the contrasting models of the university they propose—should now be clear: the boomer wants to isolate knowledge from its origins in order to maximize its utility and profitability, whereas the sticker values a rooted kind of learning whose branches connect as much as possible. Thus, the way we organize knowledge stems from the kinds of questions we ask, which in turn arise from the orientation of our desires.

By pointing to desires and motivations as the source of a fragmented and rootless educational system, we return to where we started, with the importance of telling the right stories. Perhaps a rooted education, then, could begin by teaching students how to trace the interconnections of wisdom and health through an emphasis on language, imagination, and narrative; such an education might cultivate in students the affections they need to care about the health of their places. While boomers tend to allow their desires to form their questions, Berry argues that mature, nurturing people shape their desires and questions to the limits of their place: "We have, in fact, no right to ask the world to conform to our desires. Sooner or later, if we hope to grow up, we have to confront the opposite imperative: that our rights and the realization of our desires are limited by human nature, by human community, and by the nature of the places in which we live."[30] Teaching students to be stickers, to be nurturers, involves teaching them to patiently and faithfully ask their neighbors and places, "What do you need?"

What Does Wendell Berry Have to Do with the University?

We recognize that these sticker, agrarian ideals are unfashionable in academic circles. In discussing Berry's vision, we use terms that aren't "acceptable" in the academy—terms such as *health, imagination, love, affection, virtue, hierarchy, fidelity*. We do so because we want to resist writing in what Hannah Coulter calls the "Unknown Tongue" of academia.[31] As Berry puts it in one of his essays, "The middling, politically correct language of the professions is incapable either of reverence or familiarity; it is headless and footless, loveless, a language of nowhere."[32] By keeping its feet and its head, Berry's language offers an antidote to the disembodied language of the university, so in drawing on his vision, we retain his embodied language in spite of its unfashionable grittiness. Though some academics may be suspicious of the terms and ideas he employs, this suspicion may stem more from the deracinated culture of the modern university and the jargon such a culture fosters than from any inherent flaws in Berry's agrarian vision. Given that many of the criticisms leveled at Berry seem to be based on misunderstandings, part of our goal is to translate his vision into the context of higher education.[33] We address potential concerns readers might have at various points throughout the book, but in an effort to clear the ground at the outset and gain a fair hearing for Berry's ideas, here are four of the most common misgivings expressed by our colleagues and students when we articulate Berry's vision for higher education.

Berry's vision only applies to farmers. It doesn't have anything to offer urbanites or suburbanites. The practice of farming is indeed central to Berry's writings, and he argues that we need more farmers in the countryside, carefully tending the land. Yet even though he supports policies to resettle rural America, he has a habit of warning enthusiastic young readers *not* to leave the city and take up farming. As he told one interviewer, "It would be wrong to assume that every person is called to be a farmer. . . . I have never, ever said that everybody ought to be a farmer."[34]

Part of our aim in this book is to develop Berry's agrarian thought in order to consider how students might be educated for nonagrarian vocations—hence our emphasis on the need to tell the right stories and our definition of boomers and stickers according to the contrasting orientations of their affections. These insights come from Berry's roots in his rural farming community, yet they apply to students in any academic discipline. So while we agree with Berry that we all need to take more responsibility for the food we eat and the land practices we support, this responsibility doesn't mean that everyone needs to become a farmer. Rather, an education inspired by Berry's ideas would help students seek imaginative ways to serve the health of their communities and places in a variety of vocations and avocations.

Berry's notions of hierarchy and health are an oppressive holdover from the Middle Ages, and his view of "nature" is hopelessly romantic. Adherents of hierarchy and health are not likely to win many votes in an academic senate, and they are certainly not cutting-edge terms in contemporary academic discourse. But perhaps allowing Berry to define these concepts will at least help critics understand why they are essential to his vision of education. He articulates his understanding of hierarchy when he defines education as an ordering process: "A proper education enables young people to put their lives in order, which means knowing what things are more important than other things; it means putting first things first."[35] Berry's insistence on putting first things first—which, as we show in the next chapter, flows from his medieval vision of knowledge as a flourishing tree—stands in stark contrast to the chaos that characterizes the "information economy": we are awash in accessible data, yet we often lack the discernment to interpret and act on these data. As Berry argues, "Until the information is shaped into knowledge in some particular mind and applied with or without harm to an actual place, we will not know whether or not it is an asset or how valuable an asset it is."[36] Unmoored information can be used for good or ill, so Berry urges educators to form people who are capable of ordering knowledge in ways that serve their places. People may certainly disagree about how knowledge should be ordered or which particular things should come first, but Berry thinks these discussions are indispensable to the sustenance of a healthy community.

Health depends on properly ordered knowledge because health itself is a description of a kind of order. Berry has a high view of health, arguing in one essay that "the life and health of the world" is the one standard to which we should hold ourselves accountable.[37] This standard is not significantly different from Aldo Leopold's famous land ethic: "A thing is right when it tends to preserve the integrity, stability, and beauty of the biotic community. It is wrong when it tends otherwise."[38] If anything, Berry defines health more broadly, including not just its aesthetic dimension but also its religious connotation: "the concept of health is rooted in the concept of wholeness.... The word health belongs to a family of words, a listing of which will suggest how far the consideration of health must carry us: heal, whole, wholesome, hale, hallow, holy."[39] Wholeness, like Leopold's beauty, gestures toward the aesthetic quality of health: health is like beauty, in that we can perceive its presence even though we cannot exhaustively describe it. Health names the complex harmony that characterizes natural ecosystems and sustainable human cultures, and it is this harmony that Berry enjoins Centre College graduates to respect through the practice of virtues such as temperance.

Contemporary academic theorists remain skeptical of the concept of health, but the shortcomings of the medical industry and industrial agriculture suggest that Berry may be right to insist on its importance.[40] It may be impossible to completely categorize the conditions present in a healthy human body, but when disease causes things to go wrong, we know that we want the pain to go away and our bodies to function normally again. The current medical-industrial complex operates by treating isolated diseases, and although this works wonders in certain cases, its failure to deal with obesity, diabetes, and other chronic disorders has led to a growing reassessment of the way we approach public health. Similarly, while industrial agriculture led to impressive short-term increases in productivity, its failure to account for the health of the land has resulted in topsoil loss, polluted watersheds, herbicide-resistant "superweeds," morally repugnant concentrated animal feeding operations, and hollowed-out rural communities. Such costs have been described by an increasing number of authors and critics, from Wendell Berry to Wes Jackson, Michael Pollan to Vandana Shiva.[41] Such examples indicate the consequences of replacing health with more simplistic, quantifiable standards.

When Berry urges us to submit to nature's standards and work toward "the life and health of the world," he is arguing that humans need to respect the limits of a formal pattern we do not control. As Berry warned students graduating from the College of the Atlantic in 1989, "And so, graduates, my advice to you is simply my hope for us all: Beware the justice of Nature. Understand that there can be no successful human economy apart from Nature or in defiance of Nature."[42] Our fantasy of nature as an endlessly malleable resource that we can manipulate for our own pleasure is becoming increasingly difficult to maintain in the face of mounting ecological crises. Therefore, Berry argues that rather than educating students in the latest wish-fulfillment techniques, universities should educate students to conform their souls to reality through virtue and wisdom (we expand on these ideas in chapter 5).

Berry is too Christian (or not Christian enough). The moralistic tone of Berry's writing leads some readers to suspect that he is merely smuggling in his Christian faith dressed in the language of virtue and health. In fact, however, Berry's complex relationship to Christianity earns him equal criticism from those who think he's not Christian enough. Liberal environmentalists, who commend his strong stance against corporate exploitation, coal mining, and industrial agriculture, tend to overlook his explicitly Christian essays, and many of Berry's conservative Christian readers were outraged when he declared his support for legalizing gay marriage in 2013. Yet as Berry wrote at the time, he wants to defend the shrinking "middle ground" occupied by "communities and families" who are standing against the "destruction of land and people, of life itself."[43] In his efforts to defend life, he manages to be an equal-opportunity offender, criticizing the cherished issues of Left and Right alike.

What makes Berry's work challenging to both groups is his insistence that religion is economic, that Christianity obliges its adherents to follow a "right livelihood": "a valid spiritual life, in this world, must have a practice and a practicality—it must have a material result."[44] This stance goes against the grain of our post-Enlightenment society that strives for pluralism by privatizing religious faith; people can believe whatever they want, as long as it remains a personal, spiritual matter and doesn't spill over into public life. This arrangement absolves churches of the responsibility to consider economic matters, and it frees everyone to go about the business of making money without worrying about pesky questions of justice or health.

Even if readers may not agree with the particular ways Berry works out the material results of his faith, they can value his efforts to break down this divide between religion and economics. We teach at a small, Christian, liberal arts institution, and although we find much wisdom in Berry's writings about the failures of American Christianity, our focus in this book is how his work influences education more broadly, whether Christian or secular. His place-based vision is certainly informed by his faith, but Berry's broad, diverse audience proves that even those who don't share his faith can learn from him. In chapter 4 we discuss the reasons why Berry chooses to remain within his faith tradition, despite its flaws, but for now, we simply urge readers to remember that people with differing religious convictions (or none at all) can collaborate on educating students to care for their places.

Berry's insistence on the local and the small is unrealistic in our global, interconnected society, and a university guided by such principles cannot be financially sustainable. We certainly recognize that these are difficult financial times for universities and that many institutions are compelled to try to attract more students, whether through expanding online classes, building fancier amenities, or launching flashy new programs. In this rush to grow, however, most universities seem to be following the same blueprint, seeking to become "world-class" institutions that prepare students to be "leaders in the global economy." In an essay published in the *Chronicle of Higher Education*, Patrick Deneen critiques this model of growth in the context of massive open online courses (MOOCs):

> The assumption that knowledge is neither produced nor transmitted in local contexts leads, inevitably, to the conclusion that institutional identity is purely accidental—that every institution is, at its essence, a global content-delivery system. The result? Higher education is more monocultural than ever before. . . .
>
> Colleges and universities are like the once-ubiquitous department stores in every city—Filene's in Boston, G. Fox in Hartford, Woodward & Lothrop in Washington—which, while enjoying distinct locations and histories, became increasingly similar. When consumers grew to value uniformity over a local market culture, those local stores were susceptible to the challenge from a truly universal competitor that

could offer the same wares, produced cheaply, at low, low prices. Those stores are all now out of business. MOOCs are the Wal-Mart of higher education.[45]

The solution Deneen proposes is for small schools to become more "artisanal" and emphasize their unique characteristics. If the future of higher education is online, then the Harvards and Yales will survive and smaller institutions will close their doors. If, however, local schools can make a clear case that what they offer is *different*, that their students will be formed in local and distinctive ways, then small schools stand a chance of bucking the broader trends that spell doom for so many US colleges. In many ways, Deneen's argument parallels that of Clayton Christensen and Henry Eyring, who claim that in light of disruptive innovations in higher education, universities can no longer merely emulate wealthy, prestigious schools like Harvard but must develop according to their own unique, institutional "DNA."[46] Their genetic metaphor indicates the importance of local adaptation if universities are to thrive.

One example of a school that has taken such an approach is Paul Quinn College. When Michael Sorrell became its president in 2007, he shut down the financially struggling school's football program. Given that Paul Quinn is located in Dallas, Texas, the heartland of football, this wasn't a popular move. But Sorrell noticed something else about the school's location: it was in a food desert. The absence of grocery stores made it difficult for residents to eat well, and when Sorrell failed to convince any grocery chains to open a branch in the area, he decided to convert the unused football field into a farm. Now, students work on the farm as part of the school's social entrepreneurship program and sell the crops to local businesses, including the nearby Dallas Cowboys' stadium.[47] This college president saw a need in his community—a need for fresh, healthy food—and eliminated a generic program that many schools have so that his school could meet that specific local need. As a result, the college's financial situation has also improved.

If the success of Paul Quinn College is any indication, perhaps other schools should stop following consultant-lemmings toward the precipice that lies beyond the promise of online information delivery. Instead of trying to be like everyone else, universities should be responsive to their unique locations and histories. They could convert their football fields to gardens, stop building fancy dormitories and student centers, cut tuition and require students to work, and stop trying to churn out world leaders and instead educate students to meet local needs. Judging from the wry humor at the end of his essay "Why I Am Not Going to Buy a Computer," these are the kinds of creative "innovations" that Wendell Berry might urge university administrators to consider. Berry responds to several critics who wrote to him after he published a shorter version of the essay in *Harper's*: "None of my correspondents recognizes the innovativeness of my essay. If the use of a computer is a new idea, then a newer idea is not to use one."[48] Similarly, if online education is a new idea, then local education is a newer one.

Our Approach

To state our intentions simply, one of the goals of this book is to encourage and challenge students of all ages to cultivate the disciplines and virtues that will enable them to love their homes. Our argument may encourage anyone who wants to dwell more fully in a place, but our focus is on how universities can contribute to this kind of placed education. Within universities, we are addressing students, teachers, and administrators in the hope that they might take up the hard work of local adaptation. Of course, we'd be delighted if institutional changes—like those that happened at Paul Quinn College—occurred as a result of individuals working for the health of their places, but we don't propose any big solutions that would have to be imposed from the top by institutional fiat. In fact, waiting for such a big solution only exemplifies the wrongheaded belief that change has to come from the top, that power is centralized. So our solutions are quite intentionally *not* big. Students will be educated for homemaking not when leaders establish some ideal college but when individual university members foster a tradition and a culture that value places and inspire its members to participate actively in their various communities: to tell the right stories, to order their affections, to ask the right questions, and to do good work where they are.

Although we refer to "universities" in the abstract at various points throughout this book, we do so as a useful shorthand, not to imply that all universities are the same. In fact, their diversity is one of the reasons we're hopeful that Wendell Berry's voice might lead to positive change in the landscape of American higher education. Rather than proposing some monolithic program that all universities need to implement or some new curriculum that all schools should follow, we hope that individuals at universities across the nation will work with their colleagues to ask: What does our place need? How can our university better serve its community? What do our students need to be better members of their places? The answers will be unique to each university. As Berry explains, "I don't like or trust large, official programs of improvement, and I don't want to appear to be inviting any such thing. But perhaps there is no harm in making suggestions, if I acknowledge that the suggestions are only mine, and if I make sure that my suggestions apply primarily to the thinking, work, and conduct of individuals."[49] When we give practical examples, then, we intend them as models to spark readers' imaginations rather than as "best practices" that can be implemented uniformly.[50]

Berry isn't particularly hopeful about the future of higher education, but we are—although our hopes are admittedly modest. In some of his essays Berry seems to argue that modern universities are beyond hope of recovery. In "The Work of Local Culture," Berry considers and then rejects the idea that universities can provide the healing learning we need: "May we look for help to the universities? Well, the universities are more and more the servants of government and the corporations." Thus he concludes "that one resurrected rural community would be more convincing and more encouraging than all the government and university programs of the last fifty years, and I think that it could be the beginning of the renewal of our country."[51] We certainly concur that healthy rural communities are incredibly important; in fact, both of us trace our desire to be homemakers to the years we spent in such communities in our youth, and we are now faculty members at a university situated in a rural community. So on the one hand, we agree that families and communities can contribute to the formation of placed virtues in their members. On the other hand, we think that universities, with their rich intellectual and cultural resources, can also play a crucial role in this formation. Indeed, our local community includes the small university where we work, and many young people from rural communities attend this school. Furthermore, most people today don't live in rural communities, so it's imperative that we consider how urban and suburban places can be more responsibly tied to their sources of agriculture, and universities can aid in this vital work. Thus we believe that although universities cannot be the whole solution, they can at least work to form their members into more rooted, healthy inhabitants of their communities.

In other words, we contend that—in spite of Berry's dim hope for universities—his vision can guide higher education toward health. We take Berry at his word when he writes: "An essayist not only has no right to expect complete agreement but has a certain responsibility to ward it off. If you tell me, dear reader, that you agree with me completely, then I must suspect one or both of us of dishonesty."[52] So while we certainly don't dismiss Berry's valid critique of the university, we do think that we can look to universities for help. Universities can shape citizens who care about their places and the people who inhabit them, and (perhaps ironically) we think Berry's essays, fiction, and poetry can guide universities in this endeavor. Berry himself seems to have renewed hope that some universities can provide a placed education, as evidenced by the Berry Center's collaboration with St. Catharine College to offer a BA in farming and ecological agrarianism.[53] Although regulatory disputes later caused St. Catharine to close its doors, the Berry Center plans to continue this program in collaboration with other colleges. Many other universities and colleges are likewise seeking to serve their local places, and throughout this study we examine some of these encouraging examples.

But before universities can hope to be part of the solution rather than the problem, they need to do some soul-searching to determine their raison d'être. In the first chapter, we briefly narrate how universities arrived at their current disoriented and fragmented state wherein they no longer know what they are educating students for. Yet an even more fundamental question is what students themselves are for, because education always implies an anthropology, an account of what people are for.

Berry's body of work extends a tradition that teaches us to imagine that our human purpose entails being properly placed, learning *where* we are. Berry traces this tradition through the Bible, Homer, Augustine, Dante, and T. S. Eliot, and he sums it up by saying that a full understanding of place leads to the axiom that "to be in place is good and to be out of place is evil." Berry justifies this stark claim in the remainder of his sentence: "for where we are with respect to our place both in the order of things and on earth is the definition of our whereabouts with respect to God and our fellow creatures."[54] As Berry's phrase "in the order of things and on earth" indicates, this understanding of place includes a geographic dimension, but it also includes the dimensions of hierarchy, community, and tradition. So in the following pages we explore how a university might educate students to be properly oriented in all these dimensions.

To accomplish this task, we have divided the book into two parts. Part 1, "Rooting Universities," lays out the means by which we begin to desire and know our place. We suggest that imagination, language, and work are the three interdependent means by which we come to care for our places. Today, most universities fail to foster such placed knowledge because of their disorientation and fragmentation. Following Berry, we suggest that such universities would do well to return to a medieval vision of knowledge as a rooted tree. This metaphor reminds us to pay attention to the ways that knowledge coheres, a particularly important reminder in our highly specialized age. Thus, the first step toward a healthier university is to reimagine the organization of knowledge.

The two central means by which we work out our understanding of this imagined coherence of knowledge are a responsible, common language and physical work. Jargon—a specialized language that allows its speakers to hide from the consequences of their words—is one of the chief symptoms and perpetuators of our cultural fragmentation, so in order to know our place, we need to cultivate a better language, one that allows us to come together and make sense. Nevertheless, our language remains abstracted from our place and so always falls short of its complex realities. The chief way that language is sharpened and made more accurate is through work, through getting our hands dirty and confronting the gritty nuances of our situation, and then letting this work refine and sharpen our language. Such work—carried out in the context of a coherent imagination and an accountable language—rises to the level of what Alasdair MacIntyre terms a "practice," on which virtues depend.[55]

In part 2, "Cultivating Virtues of Place," we look at four key dimensions in which humans ought to be placed—tradition, hierarchy, geography, and community—and consider virtues that are appropriate to these dimensions. In a recent conversation at Yale, when Berry was asked about the problems with higher education he responded, "The intellectual structure that's represented by universities is probably wrong, awry, somehow. It would be interesting to just raise the question like this: 'Where are we?'"[56] He goes on to note that asking this question would disrupt the current departmental structure of universities, as this basic question of place can't be answered within the walls of any one department. In focusing on these four dimensions of place, we seek to provide an alternative structure by which we might pursue this question.

We are certainly not proposing these four dimensions as an alternative organization for universities; rather, all members of universities can consider these dimensions as they ask themselves, "Where are we?" To pursue answers to this question, departmental boundaries need to be more porous to encourage collaboration across these arbitrary academic divisions. Ultimately, these four dimensions can't be separated; indeed, understanding these four aspects of place as dimensions reminds us that they all intersect and interrelate—for instance, one can't be rightly placed in community if one is displaced geographically. Looking at them in turn, however, allows us to articulate the importance of each and then to imagine how we can cultivate our proper place along each dimension.

As we examine these four dimensions, we suggest four virtues that students ought to cultivate in order to properly work toward the health and flourishing of their places. The theological and cardinal virtues are certainly vital, but in our deracinated culture, we are especially in need of virtues that reorient and plant us; we thus recast two of these traditional virtues (fidelity and love) and offer two additional virtues (gratitude and memory) as arts that are particularly important to students who want to be stickers. It is our hope that practicing the virtues of memory, gratitude, fidelity, and love will aid students who strive to be rooted homemakers, people who are placed.

We generally follow a three-part structure within each chapter, moving from imagination to language to work as we consider how Berry's ideas might provide hope for higher education. Therefore, each chapter begins with an examination of one of Berry's fictional narratives. Then, to clarify our thinking and language, we consider the ideas presented in the narrative in the context of higher education. Finally, we offer a few practical suggestions for how students, teachers, and administrators might implement these ideas.

We conclude this introduction, as we conclude each chapter in this book, with one of Berry's poems. By framing our argument with stories and poems, we hope not only to persuade readers rationally but also to convince them on the level of imagination and affection. We believe that literature not only delights and instructs us but also moves us to moral action. And so we tell these stories of place and contentment and gratitude to offer an alternative to the prevailing stories of upward and lateral mobility and to encourage action. In this Sabbath poem, Berry voices hope for stability and health, inviting us all to come and learn from our places, to come and treat them well.

XI

The need comes on me now
to speak across the years
to those who finally will live here
after the present ruin, in the absence
of most of my kind who by now
are dead, or have given their minds
to machines and become strange,
"over-qualified" for the hard
handwork that must be done

to remake, so far as humans
can remake, all that humans
have unmade. To you, whoever
you may be, I say: Come,
meaning to stay. Come,
willing to learn what this place,
like no other, will ask of you
and your children, if you mean
to stay. "This land responds
to good treatment," I heard
my father say time and again
in his passion to renew, to make
whole, what ill use had broken.
And so to you, whose lives
taken from the life of this place
I cannot foretell, I say:
Come, and treat it well.[57]

Part 1

Rooting Universities

1
Imagining the Tree of Wisdom
The Recovery of the University

The poem that concludes the introduction invites us to come to our places and learn how "to renew, to make / whole, what ill use had broken." Our ability to imagine wholeness even in the midst of brokenness is central to the task of renewal. Unfortunately, contemporary universities generally fail to form students' imaginations in any holistic manner, choosing instead to focus on narrow, specialized training. Berry's novella *Remembering* powerfully depicts the importance of the imagination in healing the dismemberment and displacement caused by our contemporary mode of life and education.

Imagining a Way Home

The story opens in San Francisco, where Andy Catlett is scheduled to speak at a college. But when he arrives on a plane after attending an agricultural conference in the Midwest, his frustration at the displaced, peripatetic life he is leading causes him to evade his speaking commitment and instead wander the streets of the city, trying to piece together the fragments of his life. Eight months previously, his right hand had been chewed up by a corn-picking machine, and ever since his dismemberment, Andy has struggled to recover his role in his family and community.

Earlier in his life, Andy had given up his place by succumbing to the narrative of lateral mobility taught by his college education. After graduating, Andy "resigned himself to living in cities. That was what his education was for, as his teachers all advised and he believed. Its purpose was to get him away from home, out of the country, to someplace where he could live up to his abilities. He needed an education, and the purpose of an education was to take him away."[1] Andy, following these expectations, got a job as a journalist in San Francisco and then got a better job writing for a magazine based out of Chicago. He was moving up in the world. But then Andy was assigned to write a story about a "successful" farmer named Meikelberger, who grew corn on 2,000 acres. As Andy interviewed the farmer, he came to realize the emptiness of that life: Meikelberger was permanently in debt, he and his wife worked constantly just to keep solvent, and the stress had given him a stomach ulcer. By following the "get big or get out" logic of industrial agriculture, "Meikelberger's ambition had made common cause with a technical power that proposed no limit to itself, that was, in fact, destroying Meikelberger, as it had already destroyed nearly all that was natural or human around him."[2]

This destruction left Andy uneasy with Meikelberger's version of success, but he couldn't imagine an alternative way of defining success. Then, on his way to a meeting in Pittsburgh, he drove past an Amish farm. The farmer was plowing his field with horses, and Andy pulled off the road, drawn by the beauty of the horses working the land. The man, Isaac Troyer, stopped his team and offered to let Andy take the reins. As Andy plowed a few furrows, his boyhood memories of farming returned, and he began to envision a version of success quite different from Meikelberger's. Andy spent most of the day on the Troyers' place, meeting the family, sharing a meal, and hearing about the neighborly economy of their community, an economy that didn't require them to go into debt in an attempt to buy up the surrounding farms. His day with the Troyers enabled Andy to imagine that he and his family could leave Chicago and return home. So as he walks around an old farm for sale near where he grew up, Andy realizes that he "had begun to dream his life" on this place, in this community. When he shares his dream of returning home and buying this rundown farm with his wife, Flora, she responds, "'Well, it's about time.'"[3]

After Andy and Flora return to their hometown and take up farming, Andy thinks he has finally rejected the narrative of success he had learned in college. But the bitterness and frustration caused by the recent loss of his hand have cut him off from Flora, his neighbors, and his land, and he is once again pursuing deracinated success. Wandering the streets of San Francisco, however, Andy begins to remember his community's narrative, a narrative that includes loss and hardship but also healing and joy. As Andy gradually recalls his place in this story and commits himself to returning home and taking up the difficult work of asking for forgiveness and reestablishing himself there, he remembers his father's similar decision to go home.

After college, Wheeler Catlett had worked in Washington for a congressman while attending law school. When he graduated, his boss advised him to accept a good job he had been offered in Chicago. After all, this would enable Wheeler to fulfill his "destiny," which was "that of thousands of gifted country boys since the dawn of the republic, and before: college and then a profession and then a job in the city. This was the path of victory, already trodden out and plain."[4] But it wasn't that easy for Wheeler; he was torn by conflicting desires. Finally, he asked himself:

> "Do I want to spend my life looking out a window onto tarred roofs, or do I want to see good pastures, and the cattle coming to the spring in the evening to drink?"
>
> Elation filling him, he answered, "I want to see good pastures and the cattle coming to the spring to drink." For suddenly he did imagine what he could be. He saw it all. A man with a law degree did not have to go to Chicago to practice. He could practice wherever in the whole nation there was a courthouse. He could practice in Hargrave. He could be with his own....
>
> Andy knows how firmly ruled and how unendingly fascinated his father has been by that imagining of cattle on good grass. It was a vision, finally, given the terrain and nature of their place, of a community well founded and long lasting. Wheeler held himself answerable to that.[5]

So like his father, who went home to be faithful to his imagined vision of wholeness, Andy returns home to be restored to his place in the community.

The crucial parallel between Andy and Wheeler is that both return home when they can imagine a healthy, successful, rooted life. Wheeler's vision of cattle on good grass includes, by implication, the health of his whole place; such a vision is possible only if small farmers maintain healthy pastures with small herds, which is possible only if they are not under financial duress. As Andy knows, it is a vision "of a community well founded and long lasting." But these are also specific visions. Andy doesn't read about the Amish in the abstract; he gets to know an Amish family. Wheeler doesn't crave some abstract rural community defined by its statistics; he envisions cattle grazing on good grass. An education, then, that hopes to form students to serve the health of their communities must offer them particular, complex images of health that they can desire and work toward. Without the ability to imagine what such a healthy, placed life looks like, students will be at the mercy of the standard narrative of success; they will be drawn by the vision of an upwardly mobile life, and they will always be on the lookout for better opportunities in better places.[6]

Yet for both Andy and Wheeler, this imagined wholeness comes in opposition to the formation they received in college. This isn't surprising, given Berry's rather dim view of universities. American schools, and particularly universities, are structured to prepare students for mobile careers that must be pursued away from home and that, in all likelihood, reduce the possibility of achieving Wheeler's vision of healthy cattle grazing on a hill. This orientation stems, in large part, from the fact that many contemporary American universities are fragmented institutions that are fundamentally confused about their purpose. This has led to increasing specialization at the expense of any sort of unified course of study; universities no longer know what they're educating students for. Recently, however, ecological degradation, the declining availability of good jobs, and skyrocketing college costs have led to a spate of books and essays bemoaning the state of higher education and its failure to address our contemporary needs. Wendell Berry's diagnosis that the "modern university . . . more and more resembles a loose collection of lopped branches waving about randomly in the air" leads us to argue that the first step toward a placed education must be to cultivate an imagined vision of wholeness.[7] Our current fragmented way of organizing knowledge cannot hope to form such a vision, but a university organized more like a tree than like a collection of branches might cultivate such a vision and better prepare students to serve the health of their places. If, like Wheeler Catlett, we are guided by a vision of health, then it is at least possible that education can serve this health rather than contributing to its destruction. Therefore, one of the primary tasks of a placed university must be to cultivate a vision of health and teach students to judge their lives against such a standard: this is the work of imagination.

What Does the University Serve?

The typical modern university is much too fragmented to coherently guide its students. In keeping with the fragmented nature of our age, different parts of this conglomerate institution serve different ends: student development helps students socialize, athletic programs keep students entertained, academic departments provide career training in whatever area a student chooses, and a smattering of required courses may suggest a cultural, national, or possibly religious tradition. As likely as not, however, these various divisions of the university lead students in different, conflicting directions. This is the consequence of an institution that has succumbed to competing pressures so that it is no longer a university but what Clark Kerr has aptly termed a "multiversity."[8]

Many others have provided comprehensive histories of the university in order to better understand the current state of higher education, and there is no need to rehearse this complex narrative here. But in reading these histories, an important fact gradually emerges: universities always serve some extrinsic purpose. Education literally means "to lead out from," so it is always directional: it always aims to bring students from one state to another. Education always has an end. In Athens and Rome, proto-universities like those led by Socrates or Plato served to educate young men for civil or social service: the university served the polis. However, after the rise of Christendom, the earliest ancestors of our modern universities were established in Europe primarily to serve the church. Other subjects were taught, of course, but theology was the "queen of the sciences," the most prestigious discipline and the mode of inquiry that structured all other learning. The first colleges in America were likewise founded to educate church leaders, so they also served a religious end. Over time, however, as America became more religiously pluralistic, this religious purpose shifted to a broader civic and humanitarian one: the university strove to make good citizens.[9] In some ways, then, universities returned to the classical model.

Today another shift has occurred, and the primary purpose of most universities, at least in the eyes of their students and the general public, is to train students to get good jobs. The university now serves the economy. This can be seen most clearly in the rise of technical or vocational schools and for-profit schools that promise their students greater marketability. Yet even agricultural institutions that were founded ostensibly to serve farming communities actually function to either train rural youths to get jobs elsewhere or train farmers to turn their land into factories for industrial agriculture. Serving the health of their communities is not one of their goals.[10] Even purportedly liberal arts schools often follow suit, justifying their high costs by promising remunerative employment for their students. This leads to an inability to justify either moral formation or the liberal arts as a means of leading a healthy life, and too often these schools resort to focusing on specialization and career training.

So while the landscape of American higher education is quite diverse, Andrew Delbanco concludes that this crass economic training has led to a broad sense of disease and dissatisfaction: "One generalization, I think, applies across the board: there is a sense of drift. Before the financial crash, students were fleeing from 'useless' subjects such as literature or the arts, and flocking to 'marketable' subjects such as economics. Now, in the lingering aftermath of the global financial crisis, the flight continues; many students are also wondering what, in fact, is useful for what."[11] Kerr concurs with this assessment when he writes, "The ivory tower of old has become an arm of the state and an arm of industry, and the students inside reach out toward the labor market and toward political influence."[12] Berry perceived this problem in the early 1970s when he stated flatly that in America, "the purpose of education is the mass production of producers and consumers."[13] The institution that began with the purpose of leading students out of ignorance to better serve their communities and the church now primarily serves the nation-state's industrial complex. In the absence of any higher purpose, the multiversity defaults to serving the economy, to training students to be effective cogs in a capitalist machine.

Some people seem to think this isn't a problem; they would argue that a university doesn't have to educate, to lead out of ignorance, the whole human person but only certain parts of it. For instance, maybe universities should concentrate on transferring the information and skills students need to obtain good careers. This is the thinking behind many recent public proposals such as Virginia's "Top Jobs Act," which, among other priorities, aims for "increased degree production in high-demand areas such as Science, Technology, Engineering, Math, and Healthcare (STEM-H)."[14] Florida's Blue Ribbon Task Force goes even further, recommending that public universities offer a "differentiated tuition model" that charges less for "specific high-skill, high-wage, high-demand (market determined strategic demand) degree programs."[15] These programs are simply the outworking of a belief that universities should serve the market economy.

Although career preparation is not a bad thing, such an education is a limited one, particularly at a time when our market economy is rapidly destroying the health of our land and communities; our market fails to properly value our homes and land, the sources of our life, so it seems unwise to educate students to perpetuate this destructive system. Perhaps even more insidiously, such an education contributes to a functional anthropology that treats humans merely as participants in an industrial economic machine. As Neil Postman observes of the typical American school, "The curriculum is not, in fact, a 'course of study' at all but a meaningless hodgepodge of subjects. It does not even put forward a clear vision of what constitutes an educated person, unless it is a person who possesses 'skills.' In other words, a technocrat's ideal—a person with no commitment and no point of view but with plenty of marketable skills."[16] Graduates of such a university will be trained to operate as producers and consumers in an industrial society, but is this what people are for? Is this really the highest purpose for which we can educate humans—to make and spend money?

Dissatisfaction with our culture's de facto affirmative answer to these questions has motivated a spate of books on higher education. Many public intellectuals such as Delbanco, Anthony Kronman, Harry Lewis, and C. John Sommerville recognize these dangers and seek to redeem universities from their economic utilitarianism by recovering some higher humanist or civic purpose.[17] Others work from within the Christian tradition—including David Lyle Jeffrey, Alasdair MacIntyre, and Stanley Hauerwas—and argue for the need to recover a theological grounding that can unite the fragmented disciplines of the modern university.[18] We too are Christians, working within the Christian tradition at a Protestant university, so we are sympathetic with such projects to rearticulate the way the university can serve the church by making theology once again the queen of the sciences. Yet while this is an important and viable response for religious institutions, our society is no longer held together by the church, as it was when the first modern universities were developed. So we think it is appropriate to look elsewhere for a way to articulate the kind of unitive wisdom that modern education so desperately needs.

Thus, we propose an education rooted in and united by place. One of the insights in Berry's Centre College commencement address (see the foreword) is that the moral or theological order and the ecological order harmoniously overlap, and given Berry's rich, multidimensional understanding of place, educating students in the virtues necessary to maintain our membership in the order of Creation provides a common ground where civic, ecological, and theological ends can meet. As Berry argues:

> What ecological insight has done is reveal again the practical foundations of ancient morality. If, for instance, the [ecological] order that I have described is a fact, which it is, and if it surpasses

human comprehension, which it does, then temperance is not just a spiritual discipline, but a practical necessity, no less so than food or water or air; and we have an infallible standard by which to measure the sinfulness of gluttony.

But this insight carries us farther than that. It doesn't leave us stranded on the dry ground of moral distinctions. Finally it shows us the possibility of a healthful economy that is at once physical and spiritual.

An education in the virtues of place has the potential to unite these differing educational ends and train students to be members of the "Great Economy."

While the idea of educating students to serve their places is comparatively underdeveloped in contemporary work on higher education, it is beginning to gain more attention. And, given Berry's penchant for gaining a hearing in disparate communities, his call for an education oriented toward homecoming has been taken up by those on both the political Left and Right. As early as 1994, Madhu Suri Prakash wrote an essay on Berry as the introduction to a special issue of *Educational Theory* on ecology and education. She concludes that such an education would need to "focus on community-supported agriculture, student apprenticeships to local exemplars in dwelling, and other activities that relink the practice of education with local ecology and agriculture."[19] Her work continues to inspire conversations in the field of ecopedagogy, as educators look for ways to teach students about issues related to ecojustice, environmental crises, and sustainable agriculture.[20]

Such interests also animate educators who come from more conservative, religious perspectives. Writing to teachers at small Christian colleges, Steven Bouma-Prediger and Brian Walsh argue that in the postmodern context, these colleges ought to educate students for "homemaking."[21] Similarly, Richard Gamble draws on Berry's fiction to emphasize the need to recover a narrative of homecoming. Gamble points out, however, that this doesn't easily translate into abstract institutional or pedagogical principles: "It would be a mistake to distill anything so abstract as a 'philosophy of education' from the stories of the Port William membership."[22] Gamble is certainly right that we ought to avoid simplistic, prescriptive declarations, yet Berry's vision does have practical implications for how we teach. Matthew Bonzo and Michael Stevens consider some of these as they conclude their book on Berry, reflecting on how Christian universities could look more like workshops where students serve as apprentices, learning the knowledge and skills needed to dwell faithfully in their homes.[23]

Currently, these two conversations surrounding Berry and education seem to exist largely in isolation from each other; there is much common ground between them, however, and we engage both throughout this book. What is most striking about these conversations is their limited scope; despite Berry's increasing reputation and the growing awareness of our ecological and communal crises, no full-length book has explored Berry's potential contributions to education.[24] Thus we hope to extend these conversations and bring them together to inspire and guide others toward a placed vision of education, an education in the service of health.

Such an educational vision founded on the health of our places can inform and guide both religious schools and secular institutions. Perhaps theological wisdom can essentially be expressed as the ability to know where we belong—within a physical location, within a community, within a tradition, and within a hierarchy. In an age in which acknowledging religious authority sounds "alarming," place might better fulfill this role of grounding and orienting education.[25] Even Hauerwas, while advocating an increased role for theology in universities, points out how the current organization of universities corrodes place: "Modern universities, whether Christian or secular, have been servants of the emerging nation-state system. That nation-state system, moreover, has been the enemy of locality."[26] So rather than serving the economy or the nation, perhaps universities should serve primarily the health of their places and communities, preparing students to do the same in whatever place they will someday call home.

Affections and the Organization of Knowledge

If we want an education that shapes students to serve their places and local communities, universities will have to stop genuflecting before the industrial economy and the motives of personal success and affluence. It may seem trivial to state this, but we seem to forget that the only value a money economy recognizes is money; it justifies any technique that brings in more money. Techniques of division and specialization have been the most lucrative methods employed by modernity, and universities have adopted them in their quest for economic profit. Yet if we commodify education, dividing it from other sources of value, Berry argues that we will turn it into a weapon that can be wielded to consolidate power:

> When educational institutions educate people to *leave* home, then they have redefined education as "career preparation." In doing so, they have made it a commodity—something to be *bought* in order to make money. The great wrong in this is that it obscures the fact that education—real education—is free. I am necessarily well aware that schools and books have a cost that must be paid, but I am sure nevertheless that what is taught and learned is free. . . . To make a commodity of it is to work its ruin, for, when we put a price on it, we both reduce its value and blind the recipient to the obligations that always accompany good gifts: namely, to use them well and to hand them on unimpaired. To make a commodity of education, then, is inevitably to make a kind of weapon of it because, when it is disassociated from the sense of obligation, it can be put directly at the service of greed.[27]

Berry's claim about the ultimate freedom of education implies that whenever education is made to serve the industrial economy, it becomes an education in the service of individual greed rather than communal health.

The connection between greed and the modern fragmentation of knowledge in the multiversity may not be immediately apparent, but the two are directly related. The desire to use knowledge for power and money contributes to the fragmentation of the disciplines. To shift metaphors, if we wanted to control and manipulate reality, we would organize knowledge into a map, but if we wanted to conform our souls to reality, we would understand knowledge as taking us on a pilgrimage toward a more intimate relationship with truth.[28] As Paul Griffiths argues in *Intellectual Appetite*, "There is a direct genealogical link between the seventeenth-century aspiration toward a *mathesis universalis*—of, that is, mapping all knowledge onto a manipulable grid and providing clear principles of method that would permit the attainment of certainty about any topic—and the late-nineteenth and early-twentieth century hope for institutions of higher education free of commitments to value."[29] This *mathesis universalis,* or universal knowledge, leads to the strict departmental divisions within modern universities, divisions that Berry decries as arbitrary and opposed to our understanding of the true interconnections between all knowledge.[30] Knowledge that has been divided into discrete bits and arranged in a scheme is much easier to use; therefore, if all we care about is knowledge that we can use or knowledge that gives us power, we tend to organize our universities in these fragmented ways.[31] This desire for knowledge as power lies behind the Foucaultian panopticon, the techniques of categorization and control that characterize modernity.[32] Specialization is good and powerful, but taken to an extreme, it becomes irresponsible (because it renders its practitioners unable to respond to their broader context) and dangerous.

Indeed, the same desires that contribute to the fragmentation and specialization of knowledge in universities can have similarly damaging effects in other areas of modern life: diverse, healthy neighborhoods with residences, businesses, and stores are replaced by segregated zones that isolate each function;[33] complex farming patterns with polycrops and integrated animals are replaced by monocultures and factory farming; family doctors who know their patients are replaced by specialists who treat one particular disease; jobs requiring diverse skills are replaced by assembly-line jobs where each person fulfills only one function. Division leads to the illusion of control, and so we divide madly: "The first principle of the exploitive mind is to divide and conquer."[34] With the mounting ecological and social costs, however, it seems more and more clear that the "divide and conquer" mantra leads only to Pyrrhic victories. As C. S. Lewis argues, this greedy desire for control characterizes applied science; it does not pertain to those who want to conform their souls to a reality that is, in fact, interconnected in endlessly complicated and interesting ways.[35] If we demand that our places provide what we want, then we will organize and divide knowledge as we have done in our modern research universities. If, however, we want to learn how to ask of our places, "What do you need?" we will organize knowledge differently. Thus, as we explored in the introduction, different desires lead to different questions and, finally, to different ways of organizing knowledge.

The Tree of Wisdom

In his essay "The Loss of the University," Berry proposes that we might recover a true *uni*versity by remembering that the task of such an institution is to form good human beings: "Underlying the idea of a university—the bringing together, the combining into one, of all the disciplines—is the idea that good work and good citizenship are the inevitable by-products of the making of a good—that is, a fully developed—human being."[36] Berry explores what such a unified education would look like in the rest of the essay. Although he doesn't lay out his argument in quite this way, we find it helpful to think of his hope for the university's recovery as resting on three requirements: an imagination guided by a unified organization of knowledge, a communal language, and responsible work. A university that embodies and unites these three practices might provide students with a rooted education, one that forms fully developed humans capable of serving their places. In the next two chapters, we examine the latter two characteristics—language and work—but in the remainder of this chapter we consider how our imaginations might be formed by a unified vision of knowledge.

If we desire to serve the health of our places, Berry argues, we should return to the ancient understanding of knowledge as a tree. Reimagining knowledge through this metaphor reminds us to pay attention to the ways that knowledge coheres, a particularly important corrective in our highly specialized age:

> This Tree, for many hundreds of years, seems to have come almost naturally to mind when we have sought to describe the form of knowledge. In Western tradition, it is at least as old as Genesis, and the form it gives us for all that we know is organic, unified, comprehensive, connective—and moral. . . . If we represent knowledge as a tree, we know that things that are divided are yet connected. We know that to observe the divisions and ignore the connections is to destroy the tree. The history of modern education may be the history of the loss of this image, and of its replacement by the pattern of the industrial machine, which subsists upon division—and by industrial economics ("publish or perish"), which is meaningless apart from division.[37]

If the history of modern education, and the loss of the university, is a story of the loss of this image, then the recovery of the university should begin with reestablishing this metaphor of knowledge as a tree.

In fact, although Berry doesn't point this out in his essay, one way to understand how knowledge can be imagined as a tree is through the etymological connection in English between the words *tree* and *truth*. Both words come from the Proto-Indo-European root word *drū-*, which means "firm, solid." But *drū-* also means "tree, wood." Trees epitomize rooted strength, which anchors them firmly and deeply in the ground. Their firmness throughout a long life moves us to imagine, even in the midst of the harshest winter, their rebirth and blossoming in the spring. We come to depend on the honesty of trees in their accounting to nature. Thus the ancients turned to the idea of a tree as they began to articulate the importance of being able to trust someone's words and deeds—they considered those things all around them that were strong, hard, hearty, firm, solid; they dared to imagine that a person's word might find its meaning and import in the earth. During the Anglo-Saxon period, the connection between the nouns *truth* and *tree* were still so strong that they were the same word, *trēow*, which has the double meaning of "truth, fidelity" and "tree, wood, beam" and from which we get words like *troth*, *betroth*, and *true*.

If the image of a tree connotes fidelity to both people and the earth, perhaps we ought to give some thought to how such an image might shape the form and content of the work we do at universities. Drawing on this metaphor of knowledge as a tree, we argue that each discipline needs to work out its relationship to both the trunk of truth and the land in which the truth is rooted. Universities must, first of all, provide their students with a coherent trunk of knowledge, a clear sense of how the various disciplines cohere. Hence Berry maintains that the "need for broadly informed human judgment . . . requires inescapably an education that is broad and basic." Such an education begins by leading students up the tree trunk, and only once they have grasped the trunk does it guide them into more specialized knowledge. As Berry argues, "The work that should, and that can, unify a university is that of deciding what a student should be required to learn—what studies, that is, constitute the trunk of the tree of a person's education."[38] Berry acknowledges that determining what constitutes this trunk, or the core curriculum, is a difficult matter, but our current practice of leaving it up to the student is an avoidance of responsibility. How can we expect eighteen-year-old freshmen to know what they need to know if their professors can't even agree on the necessary common knowledge?

Berry suggests that our conversations about what should form this trunk begin with the classic understanding of the liberal arts as the trivium—which involves the study of language—and the quadrivium—which involves the study of numbers: "It cannot be denied, to begin with, that all the disciplines rest on the knowledge of letters and the knowledge of numbers. . . . From there, one can proceed confidently to say that history, literature, philosophy, and foreign languages rest principally on the knowledge of letters and carry it forward, and that biology, chemistry, and physics rest on the knowledge of numbers and carry it forward."[39]

He thinks that further definition of this foundational knowledge should be provided by the local faculty, but what he particularly decries is our current refusal to define the trunk at all: "although it may be possible to begin with a branch and develop a trunk, that is neither so probable nor so promising."[40] Thus, universities have a responsibility to define for their students a common curriculum that anchors their further studies. We explore aspects of such a curriculum in the next chapter, but for now, it's sufficient to understand that if a university community is not rooted in a common narrative and a common understanding of its community, it will wither. And if a university is not unified in reaching toward a shared vision of the good, as a tree stretches toward the light of the sun, then it will sprawl in confusion.

An education unified by a common trunk of knowledge forms students' imaginations to perceive the connections between seemingly disparate fields; in this way, their specialized knowledge remains faithful to the whole tree. Yet while such a liberal arts curriculum is undoubtedly important, it is not sufficient for the formation of healthy imaginations that are capable of judging whether our knowledge and work are serving the health of our places. The standard by which we need to judge all our learning and work is found outside of the university, in the ground where the tree of knowledge is rooted. This rootedness is not only metaphorical but also literal; as Berry explains, the standard to which we must ultimately remain faithful is "the life and health of the world."[41] Elsewhere, Berry calls this external standard the "Great Economy" or the "Kingdom of God." This Great Economy is much more comprehensive than the market economy; in fact, it "includes everything."[42] Of course, the task of making our knowledge and work faithful and responsible to everything is never complete. It requires the ongoing work of judging and correcting our visions, and it ultimately requires a healthy imagination—one that, like Wheeler's, envisions the health of the land (perhaps in the form of cattle grazing on good grass) and sees the complex needs of the community that lie behind this vision. Difficult as this task may be, it is a necessary one, for if the learning that universities foster fails to stem from and contribute to the health of the Great Economy, the university and the communities it exists to serve will wither and die.

Envisioning knowledge as a rooted tree leads Berry to understand this ongoing work of imaginative judgment as mediating between two essential standards: an internal one and an external one. First, we can ask whether an object is good as such, in and of itself. Is this poem good according to the *internal* standards of poetry? Is this computer program an elegant, efficient program? Is this philosophical argument logically valid? These disciplinary questions are important and necessary, but they aren't sufficient for judging whether these artifacts will serve the health of our places; we also need to be able to ask if an object is good according to an *external* standard. Does this poem foster vibrant communities? How will this computer program affect our lives and economies? Is this philosophical argument based on true premises?

Such questions are difficult, and answering them requires both specialization and broadly formed knowledge: specialization teaches us to know whether a given object is good as such, whereas broad knowledge (the tree trunk and the land in which it is rooted) teaches us to judge the effects of this object on its context. Teaching students to judge in this way is essential if a university is to serve the health of its place: "If, for the sake of its own health, a university must be interested in the question of the truth of what it teaches, then, for the sake of the world's health, it must be interested in the fate of that truth and the uses made of it in the world. It must want to know where its graduates live, where they work, and what they do."[43] Without the ability to judge broadly, Berry quips, "a good forger has as valid a claim to our respect as a good artist."[44]

Despite the importance of this work, "Education has tended increasingly to ignore the doubleness of its obligation. It has concerned itself more and more exclusively with the problem of how to make [in a specialized sense], narrowing the issue of judgment virtually to the terms of the made thing itself." So universities teach only how to make a poem that is technically good or how to make a bridge that is well engineered, not how to judge what its effect might be. On the one hand, this increasing specialization may be caused by the burgeoning knowledge in certain fields; it takes a long time to learn how to do surgery, so why waste more time teaching broader knowledge? But, on the other hand, Berry points out that a reason for this specialization might in fact be to avoid the "potentially embarrassing conflict between judgment broadly informed and the specialized career for which the student is being prepared; teachers of advertising techniques, for example, could ill afford for their students to realize that they are learning the arts of lying and seduction."[45]

C. S. Lewis draws attention to another possible reason why the work of judgment has been neglected: in our technocratic age, we increasingly think that only qualified experts can make valid judgments, and we use that as an excuse to abdicate our responsibility to judge for ourselves. Lewis points out the absurdity of saying that only people with specialized skills are capable of judging value:

> Only the skilled can judge the skillfulness, but that is not the same as judging the value of the result. It is for cooks to say whether a given dish proves skill in the cook; but whether the product on which this skill has been lavished is worth eating or no is a question on which a cook's opinion is of no particular value. . . . For who can endure a doctrine which would allow only dentists to say whether our teeth were aching, only cobblers to say whether our shoes hurt us, and only governments to tell us whether we were being well governed?[46]

Neither Lewis nor Berry would say that students should not be educated in specialized fields or that specialized knowledge is not important. On the contrary, they are urging us to recognize that the work of judging requires both specialized knowledge and broad, rooted knowledge.

Teaching Students to Judge Responsibly

In the remainder of this chapter, we consider two ways by which universities might begin forming their students' imaginations to make responsible judgments: telling stories of homecoming and encouraging students to live out their questions. Universities can only do so much in this regard, for even with the best education, one that provides both kinds of knowledge, questions about the effects of our work on the health of our places will never be finally answerable.

Imagining Better Stories

Rooted universities should cultivate healthy, vibrant imaginations, ones capable of relating disparate disciplines to one another and to their likely effects on the world. And our imaginations, Berry argues, should always remain open to further growth and correction:

> The imagination is in the world, is at work in it, is necessary to it, and is correctable by it. This correcting of imagination by experience is inescapable, necessary, and endless, as is the correcting of experience by

imagination. This is the great general work of criticism to which we all are called. . . . One of the most profound of human needs is for the truth of imagination to prove itself in every life and place in the world, and for the truth of the world's lives and places to be proved in imagination.[47]

If this is such a profound need, we ought to reflect on what the imagination is and how it aids in this vital work of judgment.[48] Universities, then, need to pay more careful attention to forming rooted imaginations, ones that can guide us as we attempt to make our language and work serve the health of our places.

We have already touched on the role of the imagination by offering readings from *Hannah Coulter* and *Remembering*. These novels emphasize our need to tell better stories and to follow more beautiful, robust images of flourishing places. These stories and images act as standards by which we can judge our education and even our lives. As we've pointed out, our culture and our institutions of higher education tell stories of upward and lateral mobility, of success gained only by leaving our homes behind. In the United States, our cultural imagination is shaped by figures like Abraham Lincoln, the farm boy who became president, or Horatio Alger Jr.'s heroes, who go from rags to riches often by leaving home for the bustling city. Through these stories, we have imbibed Huck Finn's attitude and, like him, plan to "light out for the territories" if things get rough.[49]

These stories of people moving to "better" places and finding "better" opportunities obscure the fact that our fragmented culture provides only a murky vision of health: today's college students may hope that their education will enable them to get lucrative jobs, modest houses in the suburbs, enviable cars, and ample possessions. Our cultural imagination sees education simply as a means to more refined consumption. With this impoverished notion of health and success, it's no wonder that our universities struggle to articulate what unifies and roots the pursuit of learning.

Berry's response to our eviscerated vision of the good has been to write compelling stories about Port William in which he imagines what a healthy place, with a thriving community and economy, might look like. This is why we repeatedly turn to Berry's fiction to ground and orient the purposes of higher education. Berry's fiction portrays a rich, vibrant vision of health, a vision that includes all members of creation as they seek to live in accordance with the Great Economy.

One of the primary tasks of a rooted education is to tell better stories and provide students with a richer imagination of the good by which they can judge their lives. Consider, for example, the memory of the Shire that guides the hobbits on their journey to Mount Doom, or the flourishing Eden that anchors *Paradise Lost* and *The Divine Comedy,* or the olive tree bed that draws Odysseus home, or the pentangle emblazoned on Sir Gawain's shield toward which all his affections tend. We desperately need these visions of rich health, of *shalom,* to guide and motivate us, just as Wheeler's vision of cattle grazing guides his work as a lawyer. Embedding this vision of health into students' memories should be the foundation of a well-rooted education: it gives students a common standard when they ask, "What are the effects of my work?" "Does my work tend toward health?" "What is my education for?"

Such a rooted imagination can lead us home even when our journeys have taken us far away. This power is illustrated by the scene near the end of Peter Jackson's movie version of *The Return of the King,* when Frodo and Sam are making the arduous climb up Mount Doom to destroy the ring once and for all. When their strength fails and they stop climbing, Sam claws himself over to Frodo, takes him in his arms, and asks him this poignant question: "Do you remember the Shire, Mr. Frodo? It'll be spring soon, and the orchards will be in blossom; and the birds will be nesting in the hazel thicket; and they'll be sowing the summer barley in the lower fields; and eating the first of the strawberries with cream. Do you remember the taste of strawberries?"[50] Frodo weakly replies that he can't, but Sam's recollection of the Shire's goodness and beauty gives him new determination, and he puts Frodo on his back and begins once more to climb the steep slope. "Do you remember the taste of strawberries?" Sam's vivid memories of the Shire hearten him and give him hope, even during the darkest moment of their journey. This vibrant image of the goodness that the hobbits are fighting for guides them on their difficult journey and eventually leads them back to the Shire.

Stories of journey and return were once common—the archetypal example is *The Odyssey*—but they have largely fallen out of favor in the past two centuries. Berry dates this shift to Wordsworth's *Michael,* and he mourns the loss of this narrative of return.[51] Yet, as the popularity of Jackson's adaptations of *The Lord of the Rings* trilogy suggests, perhaps our culture is recognizing the need to recover a more rooted identity. Indeed, stories of return are gaining a hearing even in the deracinated cultures of academia and journalism. Two writers who acknowledge their debt to Berry narrate in their memoirs how they were educated to leave their rural homes and find success in the city; both authors, however, eventually moved back. In *Belonging: A Culture of Place*, a book that is part memoir and part cultural analysis, bell hooks narrates her journey away from the Kentucky Appalachians to Stanford University and a successful career in academia. Eventually, however, hooks returned to Kentucky, taking a position at Berea College and embracing her agrarian roots.[52] Similarly, in *The Little Way of Ruthie Leming: A Southern Girl, a Small Town, and the Secret of a Good Life*, Rod Dreher recounts his personal journey away from small-town Louisiana to various big cities as he pursues a successful career in journalism. But when his sister is diagnosed with cancer, Dreher realizes that her rooted, communal life is what enables her and her family to navigate this devastating disease. After his sister's death, Dreher and his family return to his hometown and root themselves in that place, with all its flaws and joys.[53] Dreher's continued advocacy for his "Benedict option" emphasizes the importance of healthy, local communities in shaping the next generation to desire the health of their places.[54]

Neither of these books portrays rural, small-town life in a romanticized, idyllic way; rather, both stories attest to the power of a healthy imagination to guide people back to their homes, warts and all, where they can take up the difficult work of serving their places and communities. These are examples of telling the story right (as Hannah Coulter hopes she and Nathan have done). And these stories of the complex, difficult work of homecoming can help shape students' imaginations so that they will use their education to serve the health of their places. Students whose lives are rooted in an imagined vision of health will be prepared to employ their learning in the service of their places, for as they proceed up the tree of wisdom, such students will remember the standard of health by which they should judge their work and their lives. Perhaps only if our studies are rooted in our desire to serve our homes, to taste spring's first strawberries, to see cattle grazing on good grass, will we perceive knowledge to be like a tree. And it is these desires and this tree of wisdom that will enable students to put down roots and use their wisdom to serve their places.

Living Out Our Questions

Of course, the work of imagination is difficult—it often requires us to abandon our dreams, to rethink our hopes, to acknowledge our limits. We have found that our students struggle with imaginative work because it doesn't provide neat, tidy answers; in fact, it acknowledges that some, perhaps many, of their questions will remain unanswered. One semester, while teaching a senior-level seminar called Agrarian Literature and Theology with another colleague, we found that some of our students kept coming back to what they saw as the basic problem with agrarianism: it's a beautiful vision of the world, but it isn't "practical." What we were able to discern from the students who expressed this concern is that they wanted practical advice on how to live their lives well in a community, and by practical advice, they meant specific answers to the big questions of their lives. Our conversations went something like this:

"Can I live in a city and still live an agrarian lifestyle?"

"Yes."

"But what, exactly, would that look like? How can I become a part of a healthy community?"

"By living in it and caring for its people and its land."

"But what, exactly, would that look like?"

Similarly, a common response our students have to Wendell Berry is that his works aren't "practical" enough for them, which we interpret as meaning that these students want a template for living, a litmus test for their decisions; they are caring people who fear making the wrong choices in their lives. Perhaps we owe this fear to a culture that co-opts personhood with romantic ideas like "destiny," "purpose," and even "vocation": Look into the crystal ball and you will see what your life is going to be. Do these ten things sequentially and you will achieve your desired result. Such claims lack context and thus remain abstract. Ironically, though, our students see these general bromides as practical, and they are frustrated when Berry refuses to provide them. But how can they expect Berry to provide specific answers to their very particular lives? In many ways, what our students desire is impossible: an answer to their specific questions that is also broad enough to be applicable to any other person or context. Berry confounds them by not answering their questions in the way they want him to. And sometimes they don't know what to do when they put his works down.

Recently, I (Jack) met with a student who had just finished reading *Jayber Crow* as an extra-credit assignment for one of my classes. This young man is no slouch of a student—after all, he accepted the challenge of reading a nearly 400-page novel and writing an essay about it for extra credit. He told me he was moved by the novel, but also conflicted: "Berry is great in the abstract," he said, "but he isn't practical enough." What moved him was Berry's vision for community and land, but what troubled him was how the book's main character could be content leaving the seminary and moving to a small, rural town to become a barber. "How does a person get to the place where he can make such a decision? How does that person know whether or not he's made the right decision?" But the very fact that this student was asking these questions speaks to the power of Berry's works; by imagining characters who undergo a transformation of their affections, Berry invites his readers to consider how their own affections may need to be transformed. As professors, we believe that we are called to model for our students ways of living with such questions and ways of working them out slowly and patiently. Thus, when our students look for more practical answers from Berry, we respond by asking them to sit with their questions and allow them to transform their imaginations. In so doing, we cite a passage in *Jayber Crow* in which Jayber works through his own difficult questions.

Early in the novel, Jayber is attending a seminary with a view to becoming a preacher. But his studies lead him to ask many questions about the core of the Christian faith, such as how prayer works and how we can love our enemies. These questions trouble him so deeply that he finally does something he's been avoiding—he musters the courage to go to the one professor who will be pointedly honest with him. Dr. Ardmire listens patiently as Jayber rattles off the list of questions troubling him; in response, the professor simply says to the confused young man, "You have been given questions to which you cannot be given answers. You will have to live them out—perhaps a little at a time."[55] Jayber is shaken, but he knows that Dr. Ardmire is an honest and exacting man, so he believes the truth of his words. Jayber leaves the seminary, eventually returns to his hometown, and doesn't pray again for many years. By living with and living out his questions, Jayber's image of prayer is radically altered; he finally comes to a place where he can pray again, not with the vending-machine mentality of his childhood faith but with a sober, terrifying awareness that even Jesus's most fervent prayer—that the cup be taken from him—was not answered.

Perhaps the downside to using a term like *imagination* to articulate a vision for the health of universities is that our critics, like our students, might claim that it's not practical enough. However, we believe that imagination is, in fact, the foundation of the process by which individuals in a community work toward truly practical solutions; good work must be guided by an imagination that mediates between the particular and general, the internal and external. Thus, while our focus on the imagination may not be practical in the sense that it doesn't provide immediately applicable answers to specific problems, it is an essential starting point to get us to a place where we can *work out* practical solutions. In other words, we need to be careful to emphasize the process that leads to practical solutions, not the solutions themselves, which are ends, not means. And although a renewed, healthy imagination may not be sufficient for the required work of healing and restoration in a deracinated age, it is nonetheless necessary to form the roots of healthy, placed lives. Because imagination alone is not sufficient, we explore how our language and our work also need to become more responsible and placed in the next two chapters. Indeed, one of the most powerful ways that we can live out our questions faithfully is through the hard work of articulating them with precision and faithfulness.

We close this chapter with the invocation printed at the beginning of *Remembering*. This poem is a prayer for the healing that comes from a renewed imagination—the healing Wheeler experienced by working to preserve cattle grazing on green grass and that Andy experienced when walking in the furrows on an Amish farm. And as the poem's conclusion suggests, such a renewed imagination enables us to return home.

> Heavenly Muse, Spirit who brooded on
> the world and raised it shapely out of nothing,
> Touch my lips with fire and burn away
> All dross of speech, so that I keep in mind
> The truth and end to which my words now move
> In hope. Keep my mind within that Mind
> Of which it is a part, whose wholeness is
> The hope of sense in what I tell. And though
> I go among the scatterings of that sense,
> The members of its worldly body broken,
> Rule my sight by vision of the parts
> Rejoined. And in my exile's journey far
> From home, be with me, so I may return.

2

Standing by Our Words
Learning a Responsible Language

In order to judge our knowledge against the dual standards of the tree of wisdom and the health of our place, we need to learn to speak a more responsible language. This is part of Berry's prayer in his invocation to *Remembering*, that he would "keep in mind / The truth and end to which my words now move / In hope." So in this chapter we consider two related questions. First, what does this responsible language look like? And second, how might universities begin to cultivate such a language?

Andy Catlett's Accountable Language

Universities are rather notorious for using discipline-specific jargon that is incomprehensible to outsiders; Hannah Coulter calls this language the "Unknown Tongue."[1] Near the beginning of *Remembering*, Andy Catlett attends an academic agricultural conference where such language enables the professional attendees to forget how their speech affects the health of real places and communities. The title of the conference is "The Future of the American Food System," and with the exception of Andy, all the speakers seem to be "old farm boy[s] who ha[ve] made good."[2] In other words, the *future* of the American food system doesn't involve them getting their hands dirty growing anything. As the keynote speaker offers his paean to the growth of industrial agriculture, Andy laboriously scrawls a shorthand transcript of the main points. Andy's left hand obeys him awkwardly, so he manages to write down only the gist of the speaker's claims: "4%. Grvlng in rth. Big biz. Amnty of lf: TV. Trd-offs: fam, cmmnty, nghbrs, soil, wtr. Prc of prg. Adpt or die. Gt bg or gt out. Fr mkt. 1 to 70. Fd wld. Weapon."[3] Andy's shorthand may be cryptic, but its bald translation of the flowery language parodies the reductive view of efficiency espoused by the speaker and renders these claims absurd. The old farm boy is proud that millions of people have been freed from groveling in the earth and that now only 4 percent of Americans work in the big business that agriculture has become. These big farmers enjoy the amenities of life, such as TVs. In exchange, this large-scale agriculture has damaged families, communities, neighbors, soil, and water, yet all these things, the speaker insists, are merely the price of progress. In a free-market economy, the remaining farmers must adapt or die; they must get big or get out. Each farmer feeds seventy other people, and this efficiency enables the American farmer to feed the world. This control of the food supply is the American government's most powerful weapon.

The speaker views these changes as great progress and believes the future is even brighter than the present. Yet boiled down in the form of Andy's shorthand, they appear less promising. Are any amenities of life worth the harm to healthy families, communities, neighbors, soil, and water? Should food be wielded as a weapon? By keeping his words abstracted from their real context, the speaker suppresses such questions; thus his language inhibits him from putting first things first. Andy's cryptic abbreviations emphasize the failure of such language to make sense. As Andy listens to the other speakers at the conference, he is bombarded with sentences like this doozy: "A model will be recursive in structure when two conditions prevail: the matrix of coefficients of endogenous variables must be triangular, and the variance-covariance matrix of structural equation disturbances must be diagonal."[4] These professionals, Andy concludes, are "speaking in the absence of the living and the dead a language forever unintelligible to anyone but themselves."[5]

When it is finally Andy's turn to speak, he links the flaw in such language with the architecture of the conference facility: "This room [is] an image of the minds of the professional careerists of agriculture—a room without windows, filled with artificial light and artificial air, where everything reducible has been reduced to numbers, and the rest ignored. Nothing that you are talking about, and influencing by your talk, is present here, or can be seen from here."[6] Andy continues by identifying the core issue, which is that such displaced language inevitably affects real people and real places: "I don't believe it is well understood how influence flows from enclosures like this to the fields and farms and farmers themselves." To illustrate his claim, Andy recounts a story from his own family's history. In 1906 the income from his grandfather's tobacco crop was $3.57 less than the warehouse commission. In other words, his grandfather "had carried his year's work to the warehouse and had come home *owing* the warehouse $3.57." Andy places the blame for this tragedy on the kind of language spoken at the conference: "I think that bill came out of a room like this, . . . where a family's life and work can be converted to numbers and to somebody else's profit, but the family cannot be seen and its suffering cannot be felt."[7]

The flow of Andy's memories suggests another effect of such reductive language: dismemberment. Amidst Andy's memories of the academic conference, his mind recalls the horrible farming accident in which his hand was mauled in a corn-picking machine. As he fought the machine's terrible power that slowly sucked his hand in, he "heard the long persistence of the noise of the machine that did not know the difference between a cornstalk and a man's arm."[8] Of course, the conference did not directly cause this accident, but the kind of language spoken there—a language unable to discriminate properly between the amenities of life and the essentials of life, between quantities of profit and this economy's effect on families and communities—is analogous to a machine that is unable to discriminate between a cornstalk and a hand. And like this machine, such language tears apart real bodies and real communities. While this indiscriminate language promises to free individuals from the constraints of particular places, it ends up dismembering both its speakers and their communities.

Yet also woven into Andy's memories of the conference is his knowledge of another kind of language, one spoken by his community and made responsible by its resistance to abstraction. As he listens to the conference speakers drone on, Andy wonders to himself what his friend Elton would say if he were here: "He would've said, 'If you're going to talk to me, fellow, you'll have to walk.'" Elton's quip is not original. Old Jack Beecham, the previous owner of Elton's farm, had said the same thing to anyone whose talk grew too abstract. As Berry puts it:

> Elton's mind had been, in part, a convocation of the voices of predecessors saying appropriate things at appropriate times, talk-shortening sentences or phrases that he spoke to turn attention back to the job or the place or the concern at hand or for the pure pleasure he took in some propriety of remembrance; and he was a good enough mimic that when he recalled a saying its history would come with it. When he would tell Andy, "If you're going to talk to me, you'll have to walk," it would not be just the two of them talking and listening, but Old Jack would be saying it again to Mat, and Mat

to his son-in-law, Wheeler, Andy's father, and Wheeler to Elton, and Elton to Andy all the times before; and an old understanding and an old laughter would renew itself then, and be with them.[9]

This communal conversation, extending through time and rooted in the landscape, maintains lives that are responsible to their place. It is a talk kept accountable to its place by walking.

The kind of language that Andy learns from Elton, Old Jack, and the rest of his Port William community stands in contrast to the irresponsible language that is often spoken in the academy. Abstracted academic language fails to be responsible to—able to respond to—its objects because either it focuses primarily on the speaker's internal feelings or it takes on a falsely objective tone and focuses only on the object itself. Thus it fails to relate inner and outer, speaker and object, in a way that enables them to respond to each other. By making this needed accountability more difficult, the language typically spoken in universities corrodes community rather than contributing to healthy places. A language that holds individuals in responsible relationships with their places can be maintained only by a love for particular places and objects, a love that motivates speakers to use a careful, accurate language.

Speaking a Responsible Language

In "Standing by Words," Berry links the sort of abstract language Andy hears at the agricultural conference to the destruction of its speakers and its communities: "My impression is that we have seen, for perhaps a hundred and fifty years, a gradual increase in language that is either meaningless or destructive of meaning. And I believe that this increasing unreliability of language parallels the increasing disintegration, over the same period, of persons and communities." "My concern," he goes on to explain, "is for the *accountability* of language—hence, for the accountability of the users of language":

> To deal with this matter, I will use a pair of economic concepts: *internal accounting*, which considers costs and benefits in reference only to the interest of the money-making enterprise itself; and *external accounting*, which considers the costs and benefits to the "larger community." By altering the application of these terms a little,

any statement may be said to account well or poorly for what is going on inside the speaker, or outside him, or both.

It will be found, I believe, that the accounting will be poor—incomprehensible or unreliable—if it attempts to be purely internal or purely external. One of the primary obligations of language is to connect and balance the two kinds of accounting.[10]

Berry proceeds to argue that there are two ways that language fails: first, by being overly subjective, or concerned only with internal accounting and therefore failing to be intelligible to its hearers; and second, by purporting to be objective and thus denying the speaker's position and responsibilities. These two kinds of failure, Berry points out, are mutually reinforcing. Significantly, language that properly accounts for both sides of this ledger parallels the two-part judgment that universities should be teaching their students to make: to preserve the health of our places, we must be able to judge whether our work is good in itself (an internal or subjective standard) *and* whether it is good for the larger community (an external standard). Thus, while the rooted imagination discussed in the previous chapter is an essential part of a healthy education, universities also need to teach their students a language that can responsibly account for these internal and external standards.

Such language guards against the two dangers that Berry identifies. The first danger is language that is merely subjective, language that aims to communicate one's inner emotions or thoughts but does so without adequate attention to conveying this inner experience to one's community: "Any accounting that is *purely* internal will be incomprehensible. If the connection between inward and outward is broken—if, for instance, the experience of a single human does not resonate within the common experience of humanity—then language fails."[11] Berry sees this error in much Romantic poetry, and it continues with a vengeance in the sentimental language of our day—just read any Hallmark card at the grocery store. Such language is a denial of our embodied existence, for by taking refuge in sentiment and ambiguity, it fails to acknowledge that our actions cannot be undone. As Berry puts it, "I do not believe that it is possible to act on the basis of a 'tentative' or 'provisional' conclusion. . . . [W]e must act . . . on the basis of *final* conclusions, because we know that actions, occurring in time, are irrevocable."[12] In other words, if we are going to speak a responsible language, we have to walk in the particular place affected by our speech. Such walking forces our language back into the context of our lives and communities and makes it possible for our language to be understood and acted on.

The second danger is language that takes on a tone of apparent objectivity and detachment. Such language, however, also denies our bodily existence, our inevitable relationship with what we are talking about. Thus, although "objective" language shares a similar presupposition with overly subjective language—the belief that speakers can be abstracted from the context and object of their words—Berry explains that objectivity sees itself as a corrective to subjectivity: "In supposed opposition to this remote subjectivity of internal accounting, our age has developed a stance or state of mind which it calls 'objective,' and which produces a kind of accounting supposed to be external—that is, free from personal biases and considerations."[13] Berry exposes the problems with such language by examining the transcript of scientists' discussion of the unfolding of the Three Mile Island nuclear disaster. In crafting the language for a press release about the accident, these scientists cannot acknowledge themselves as members of a threatened place and community; the best one of them can muster is the statement that, "in the unlikely event that this [meltdown] occurred, increased temperatures would result and possible further fuel damage."[14] As Berry says, "What is remarkable, and frightening, about this language is its inability to admit what it is talking about. Because these specialists have routinely eliminated themselves, as such and as representative human beings, from consideration, according to the prescribed 'objectivity' of their discipline, they cannot bring themselves to acknowledge to each other, much less to the public, that their problem involves an extreme danger to a lot of people.... Public responsibility becomes public relations, apparently, for want of a language adequately responsive to its subject."[15]

These scientists' inability to articulate the real consequences of the accident exposes the way such "objective" language fails to relate speakers to their objects responsibly and accurately. Yet scientists continue to train their students to write lab reports in the passive voice, as if the experiment is conducting itself, and this language conditions them to think of themselves as removed from their experiments. Similarly, economists continue to talk about "job creation" and "workforce realignment" without acknowledging the people and communities affected. For instance, when a casino was built near our town a few years ago, the developers touted the number of jobs it would create, as if this casino would be a boon to the community. Not once did they acknowledge the damaging effects gambling would have on our place. This is the sort of abstract, irresponsible language Andy hears at the academic conference, language spoken in the absence of its objects and in ignorance of its consequences. On the contrary, Berry argues, "Scientists and artists must understand that they can honor their gifts and fulfill their obligations only by living and working as human beings and community members rather than as specialists."[16] How do we do this? By relying on a language that adequately relates our specialties to our common identity as humans.

Such a responsible language is a prerequisite for the work of imaginative judgment that Berry thinks universities should be preparing students to carry out. The specialized talk of experts, therefore, can and must be judged by its effects on the community of which they are a part. I may have no idea how to describe the intricate biological and chemical processes that make a pill an effective medicine for a particular malady, but if I'm suffering, I know whether or not the aspirin is numbing my pain. I can't begin to describe how pushing the buttons on my keyboard makes letters appear on my computer screen, but I know that something is wrong if all I see is a blue screen. I may not be able to explain with the precision and nuance of an art expert why one of Rembrandt's paintings is beautiful, but I know that the work moves me. Specialized language can certainly elucidate each of these apparent mysteries, but it should be intelligible to those nonspecialists who are affected. Berry's claim is simply that nonspecialists are qualified judges of specialist work and that specialists who hide behind incomprehensible language are failing to be responsive to those who are affected by their actions. They aren't walking where they talk.

Such a lack of responsibility to those who are affected by our actions ultimately stems from a lack of love. This is why Berry believes that one way to love our neighbors is to speak a language that is responsive to them. What is it, Berry asks, that might turn our language back to a responsible accounting between ourselves and others?

> I think it is love. I am perforce aware how baldly and embarrassingly that word now lies on the page—for we have learned at once to overuse it, abuse it, and hold it in suspicion. But I do not mean any kind of abstract love, which is probably a contradiction in terms, but particular love for particular things, places, creatures, and people, requiring stands and acts, showing its successes or failures

in practical or tangible effects. And it implies responsibility just as particular, not grim or merely dutiful, but rising out of generosity. ... [L]ove makes language exact, because one loves only what one knows.[17]

Thus a responsible language would be an articulation of affection for those to whom we relate; it would be faithful, honoring, and careful; and it would enable us to judge more accurately whether we are serving the health of our place. As we have seen, such love is shaped and guided by our imagined visions of wholeness, of cattle grazing on green grass or of the taste of the Shire's spring strawberries. Ultimately, only love for such places will motivate us to keep our language responsible.

How to Teach a Responsible Language

We return to the foundational role of love in the final chapter, but for the remainder of this chapter, we consider how students might be educated to speak a language capable of responding to their places. Universities often fail to teach such a language, allowing different disciplines to hide in their own jargon rather than fostering a common, community-wide language that encourages individuals to be more broadly accountable. So we propose several ways by which universities might break down these corrosive divisions and teach their members to speak a common tongue. The classical trivium offers one model of a language that precisely designates its objects and is oriented toward a particular audience. In addition, students could be taught a more responsible language by reading literary texts not as mere reflections of ideologies but rather as works of beauty that can judge and correct our imaginations and affections. If students experience the ways that language can hold speaker, hearer, and object in responsible relationships, they might learn to speak in ways that allow them to serve the health of their places.

Teaching Language through the Liberal Arts

Although Berry lays out the requirements of a healthy language, he seems to fear that universities cannot cultivate such a language. Perhaps this is because much of his experience as a student and educator has been at large research institutions such as the University of Kentucky and Stanford. Part of the reason we remain hopeful that some universities can cultivate a responsible language stems from our experiences as both students and educators at small liberal arts colleges. Health-giving educational communities can and do exist, albeit in small pockets, and many of them are working toward the sort of responsible language Berry imagines.

Of course, we are not arguing that only liberal arts schools can embody healthy language. In fact, such schools too often give lip service to the liberal arts while failing to actually practice them. At our current institution, which describes itself as a Christian liberal arts university, we are working to reimagine how we teach the liberal arts so that they become the trunk of our general education curriculum, but our school (like many others) has much work to do in this regard. As Mark Mitchell points out, liberal education has lost its way and "too often amounts to little more than an overpriced means of creating cosmopolitans of the worst sort: people who have little interest in or concern for real communities, customs, stories, or places."[18] The liberal arts are worth recovering, however, because they offer a way to educate students to be people who have *great* "interest in or concern for real communities, customs, stories, or places."

Perhaps the first challenge to the formation of this healthy vision is clarifying what the term *liberal arts* actually means. When we ask our students what they think it means, some reply that it has something to do with left-leaning politics; others point to classes such as art, music, and literature to define the phrase. Even those creating and teaching the curriculum at so-called liberal arts institutions fall back on the abstract definition of the liberal arts as a broad education that prepares students for an increasingly diverse workforce. But we can initiate a recovery of the liberal arts by recalling the phrase's etymological richness related to liberty or *freeness* in the pursuit of knowledge. We agree with Mitchell when he identifies a "liberal education [as] one that equips free citizens to integrate the various aspects of their experience into a coherent whole."[19] At its best, a liberal education enables students to join the dance in which the abstract and particular, the external and internal, are united. As Mitchell rightly concludes, "Education, in short, must never find itself so attracted to the abstract universals that it neglects the concrete particulars of human life."[20] In the remainder of this chapter, then, we define a vision of the liberal arts that can free students to speak a language that enables them to responsibly care for their places.

An education founded in the liberal arts necessarily and somewhat paradoxically frees humans to be accountable. While our culture tends to emphasize freedom *from* unwanted restrictions, the liberty offered by the liberal arts is freedom *for* generous service. Indeed, the etymological link between "liberty" and "liberality" points to the traditional belief that generosity and concern for others constitute the proper posture of a free person.[21] In other words, a liberally educated person is responsible to exercise her freedom in a way that serves the health of her place and community.[22] Although the agricultural academics at the conference Andy attends thought they were free from the hard work of farming and the constraints of rural life, in reality, and as their language revealed, they were enslaved to unhealthy, dismembered places. As Andy eventually learns, true freedom comes when he commits to working for the health of his place, to walking with the people he talks to. Learning how language ought to make meaning within a community is essential for practicing this responsibility, and it is for this reason that a liberal arts education begins with the trivium, or the study of language.

The liberal arts teach students how language orders our thoughts and our lives, thereby freeing us from the oppression of the unimportant things that so often preoccupy our time. This is why Berry argues that the proper task of contemporary education is to teach students how to responsibly order their lives:

> The complexity of our present trouble suggests as never before that we need to change our present concept of education. Education is not properly an industry, and its proper use is not to serve industries, either by job-training or by industry-subsidized research. Its proper use is to enable citizens to live lives that are economically, politically, socially, and culturally responsible. This cannot be done by gathering or "accessing" what we now call "information"—which is to say facts without context and therefore without priority. A proper education enables young people to put their lives in order, which means knowing what things are more important than other things; it means putting first things first.[23]

In order to learn "what things are more important than other things," we must cultivate a responsible, common language—especially at a time when the role of language in universities is understood as just one more piece in the puzzle of a student's education. Providing an education founded on a common language is nothing new; it was, in fact, the methodology of medieval universities steeped in Latin and Greek literature. But the world is a different place now, and we must translate the classical model into a viable vision for liberal education today.[24]

One of the challenges in teaching a coherent, common language is that in today's universities, language is often conflated with "English Composition," which is typically understood as a "skill" one either possesses or does not. Considered one of the first skills a student needs, learning to write becomes a necessary hurdle in every student's early college education. In fact, we often hear students and faculty alike speak about "getting writing out of the way," as if writing were a box one must check off before moving on to better things. Most students are required to take a 100-level writing course, but many are exempt from this basic requirement because a standardized test has confirmed that they already possess adequate writing skills.

While we certainly agree that students need to be skilled in writing, the conflation of language with what is generally taught as "English Composition" is not healthy. Indeed, language is not something one can pass a test on and opt out of—it is something one must live into. It is not a skill we obtain but a way of thinking that we embody, and it involves head, heart, and hand. As Berry argues, "When we reflect that 'sentence' means, literally, 'a way of thinking' (Latin: *sententia*) and that it comes from the Latin *sentire*, to feel, we realize that the concepts of sentence and sentence structure are not merely grammatical or merely academic—not negligible in any sense. A sentence is both the opportunity and the limit of thought—what we have to think with, and what we have to think in."[25] Since language undergirds all thought in this manner, it seems reasonable to consider carefully how we should teach it.

The trivium provides both liberal arts and research institutions with one possible model of embodying language that precisely designates its objects and is oriented toward a particular audience—a language that is healthful and accountable both internally and externally. We must acknowledge, however, the fear expressed by some of our colleagues that the liberal arts are antiquated, exclusionary, slow moving, or ineffective in our increasingly complicated and progressive world of technology. Some surely feel that an appeal to the liberal arts is an appeal to an archaism—to a time when the world was flat and the church oppressively controlled education in the West. The current academic culture is perhaps too easily enamored with technological progress and its promise to make education easier by making it faster. Indeed, technological innovation obscures facts of the human condition—for instance, that we're not so far removed from the predicament of Orestes or the lamentation of Andromache or the requirements of wisdom and health in Proverbs. Turning to the past necessarily requires us to slow down—we can't move forward too quickly if we're looking at what's behind us. In fact, this orientation toward the past is at the heart of the liberal arts. As Berry explains, "A liberal education rests on the assumption that nature and human nature do not change very much or very fast and that one therefore needs to understand the past."[26] And so we echo Berry's Centre College address by arguing that the old truths are not, by virtue of their antiquity, irrelevant. Instead, we need to find ways to translate, or "bear across," these old truths to today's students. And by turning to the wisdom of the past, we may even learn humility: "The same truths are told in one form or another to every generation. Inexperience doubts them as it must, as perhaps it should, and experience proves them true; the benefits being that the old truths thus remain fresh, and each new generation thus learns something about humility." We turn to the past, therefore, so that we may understand how it has formed us and how it might enable us to proceed with wisdom and humble care.

The liberal arts have traditionally been composed of two broad sets of questions or pathways: the trivium and the quadrivium. The trivium, or the "three ways," consists of *grammar*, the art of order, or questions about the structure of language; *logic* or *dialectic*, the art of thinking with language, or questions about truth; and *rhetoric*, the art of soul leading, or questions about how to use language to persuade others of truth.[27] The quadrivium, derived from a belief in the intelligibility and coherence of the created world and built on the questions asked in the trivium, consists of four ways by which one can investigate and describe ordered relationships: *arithmetic*, the art of pure number, or questions about quantifiable relationships; *geometry*, the art of number in space, or questions about how these relationships extend through space; *music*, the art of number in time, or questions about how our senses perceive these relationships; and *astronomy*, the art of number in space and time, or questions about how these relationships shape the created order.[28]

Given the ways the arts of exploring language and number have expanded in recent years, the work of translating the trivium and quadrivium from the medieval into the modern university is difficult and fraught with political and economic implications. Indeed, as the rest of this book evinces, we do not think the classic liberal arts are a panacea for all the maladies of higher education; instead, we focus here on how the trivium in particular might teach students not only to "understand the past" but also to recognize how the trivium's pathways and questions shape the way we understand all academic disciplines. These first three liberal arts remain foundational for any institution of higher education because they investigate the very powerful human faculties of order, sound thought, and wisdom through persuasion. The fruit of these arts is a liberated thinker and doer who wields a precise language with which to describe and promote the value of people and places and to address and solve problems.

Reimagining Grammar, Logic, and Rhetoric

Earlier in this chapter we unpacked Berry's concern that language fails us when we neglect internal and external accountability; this failure causes our speech to become either overly subjective and concerned only with internal accounting or ostensibly objective, in effect, denying the speaker's position and responsibility. A university ought to teach its students a language that can make this two-part judgment: is my work good in itself (an internal or subjective standard) *and* is it good for the larger community. The health of our places depends on such internal and external accounting, and the trivium can prepare students to practice this dual accounting. Thus, combined with an education rooted in a healthy imagination, the trivium cultivates proper accountability through the arts of order, sound thought, and persuasion.

By delving into the structure of a language (be it ancient or modern), students learn the art of order. It is important to note that the art of *grammar* is not simply learning the rules of a language. Instead, grammar is the linguistic study of the inner workings of a language, which is only partially achieved in most modern language courses that aim for basic spoken proficiency. By focusing on ancient languages, the study of grammar provides a healthy distance between students and their subject; although the language's culture may resonate with them in certain ways, it is necessarily "other" and demands a certain level of respect and humility from them. In other words, students cannot possess the language; they must come to it as guests, as foreigners hoping to be welcomed to its feast.

In particular, grammar teaches students to be accountable to a foreign order, an external system that specifies the way sense must be made. Grammar offers little room for subjective preference. If you want to read a language, you must understand the actual function of each grammatical case and be able to accurately decline words. And when students submit to these strict grammatical rules, they find themselves welcomed into the rich world of a human community, into the life of the people who ordered, spoke, and wrote the language. Through the study of structure and form—declensions, conjugations, kennings, charters, lais, riddles—students begin to encounter the character, desires, and history of the people who breathed that language. They learn that Achilles's desire for imperishable fame is not unlike their own desire to be known in posterity, that Odysseus's struggle to subordinate his desire for honor to his desire to return home is similar to the struggles they face, and that Beowulf's responsibilities to his kin and his people require him to exercise discernment. In other words, studying the structure of language holds students accountable to the internal order of a language and to the wisdom of the human community in history. All students ought to be trained in grammar, turning their vision away from themselves and making them conform to a standard beyond their own making, thus healing the myopia they suffer when they believe their own language is the center of the world and of history.

Students should also be trained to practice *logic*, or the art of soundness of thought and meaning. When students discover the beauty of a sound argument, they are moved by both its internal consistency and its external effects. As they study logic, students learn that their arguments have the power to persuade for good or for ill; they become accountable to their thoughts and words and must stand by them once they are spoken or written. And when they stand by their words, they learn to acknowledge that they are responsible for the patterns and implications of their thoughts. The study of logic demonstrates how sound argument lives in community with grammar: it grows out of the order found in grammar and thus continues a history of patterns and ways of making sense. What patterns and order did the pre-Socratics imagine to be in the world? What arguments did they form? Were they sound? What can we learn from such arguments? The student who learns to navigate the soundness of some of the greatest arguments in the Western tradition (to name only one) is surely being prepared to navigate the soundness of a town's sanitation policy that is built on false premises and that, in the end, threatens the health of a rural community's water supply. In this way, the study of logic should ultimately turn us from the study of soundness in an abstract sense back to the matter at hand, to the particular needs of our place.

Building on the foundation of grammar and logic, *rhetoric* teaches students to assess the consequences of language in a community, demonstrating the damage wrought by inarticulate, unordered language as well as the benefits brought by loving, wise language. Taught well, rhetoric leads students toward language as the art of suasion or, as Scott Crider eloquently argues, the art of soul leading. Drawing on Richard Weaver, Crider explains that the art of soul leading "educates one in a particular liberty, the 'liberty to handle the world, to remake it, if only a little, and to hand it to others in a shape which may influence their actions.'"[29] Rhetoric is always contextual; it focuses on the particular circumstances of speech and the particular conditions of the audience. Students learn to eschew abstraction—there is no universally applicable argument that will convince everyone; instead, the practice of rhetoric teaches students to craft arguments that lead their particular audiences' souls toward a more intimate relation with a specific truth. In this way, rhetoric teaches us to consider the needs of our place and our neighbors and to speak in such a way that serves those needs.

This sort of rhetoric requires us to care for our audiences in a way that acknowledges their personhood and our connection and responsibility to them. In other words, it requires us to speak within a placed community. But rhetoric cannot be taught on its own, and it must be understood within its proper context in the trivium. Because rhetoric is often not understood as building on grammar and logic, many use the term *rhetoric* as a pejorative, referring to the stuff of Sophists who desire to manipulate and deceive rather than "discovering the most convincing *logos*."[30] When we remember that rhetoric is built on sound arguments and a respect for external order, however, rhetoric regains its proper role as the faculty that enables us to lead others toward truth and health. We believe a university can be one place where students, faculty, staff, and administrators have the opportunity to live in a robust community, practicing a language enriched by all three arts of the trivium and carrying on a conversation that leads toward truth. Thus we agree with Crider when he writes that "the best university is a rhetorical community of friends" where we can learn "how to live within such a community with words so full of care that they release the light of brilliance."[31] Surely universities are not the only such communities, but they offer us the unique opportunity to apprentice students in careful, loving language during a formative period of their lives.

If we imagine, then, a student who has been trained in the trivium attending a town meeting along with other citizens from various socioeconomic and educational backgrounds, we can imagine this student's responsibility to these people and their place. She feels a moral obligation to share her concerns about the proposed sanitation policy and is unafraid to do so. She knows that if her thoughts are unordered, or if she argues unsoundly or articulates her words poorly, she will likely fail to adequately communicate the truth of her concerns. In essence, she will struggle to persuade the town board if she has not practiced the arts of the trivium. If her university community has indeed prepared her—through the order of grammar, the soundness of logic, and the persuasive force of rhetoric—to stand by her words and to speak a healthy language that responds clearly and wisely to the problem at hand, then her whole community will benefit.

Incorporating the trivium more deeply into university curricula could take different forms at different institutions. Revising the general education curriculum to require students to take a foreign language might be one way, and Berry has advocated for this requirement at the University of Kentucky.[32] Students might also benefit from composition courses that attend more carefully to logic and to the relationships among speaker, audience, and context. But even without such curricular revisions, faculty and students can find more immediate ways to practice caring, responsible language. For instance, when Berry taught at the University of Kentucky in the late 1980s, he posed a question about the day's reading at the beginning of each class. He then gave the students twenty minutes to write their responses to this question. The catch was that they had to do so in a single sentence. As Morris Grubbs, one of Berry's former students, recounts, this assignment was quite challenging:

> The first quiz was a disaster for most of the class, including me, mainly because we were not accustomed to writing, much less thinking, so directly and precisely. His quizzes demanded archer like strength and accuracy, and we had to get in shape and practice. Focusing our minds to make every sentence and every word matter, we tried our best to rise to our teacher's challenge. Some of our sentences even came close to the mark. Of all of the skills I practiced as a graduate student, this skill of achieving directness and accuracy—this astonishingly practical but difficult skill—is the single most valuable one to me as a writer and a teacher.[33]

This sort of simple assignment may not seem very significant, but it clearly made a difference in the life of at least one student, and it represents the kind of small steps that faculty and students can take toward cultivating responsible language.

Learning from Literature

Berry's essay "In Defense of Literacy" suggests another seemingly simple method to cultivate a healthy language: "We must speak, and teach our children to speak, a language precise and articulate and lively enough to tell the truth about the world as we know it. And to do this we must know something of the roots and resources of our language; we must know its literature."[34] As professors of literature, we predictably agree with Berry about the importance of reading literature. So although we want to avoid thinking that our own discipline has an outsized role in teaching responsible language, we believe literature courses can provide opportunities to cultivate a language "precise and articulate and lively enough to tell the truth about the world." Unfortunately, the way literature is taught at many universities often fails to achieve this end.

With the rise in disciplinary specialization within the academy (as discussed in the previous chapter), literature has increasingly become just one more specialized area of study. Yet Berry argues that understanding literature as something one can specialize in is a "perversion" of this discipline.[35] When Berry explains that such "specialization is of the nature of the applied sciences," he is not decrying the necessary and specialized training of the applied sciences: he is making an Aristotelian distinction. The applied sciences require specialization by their nature, not by accident. Berry's statement, then, is a critique of what happens when we take what is natural in one discipline and try to make it natural in all others. If literature is not a specialty, questions of its truth can no longer be ignored.

Specialization in language and literature, which brackets questions of truth, is a perversion for two reasons: First, it reduces what should be shared by all educated people to a skill needed only by those who hope to teach or write literature, the result of which is that language and literature become superfluous to the majority of students. Second, specialization obscures their very nature as disciplines that teach us to cast our vision outside of ourselves. In other words, these disciplines are essentially moral: "language and literature are always *about* something else. . . . They are about the world. We will understand the world, and preserve ourselves and our values in it, only insofar as we have a language that is alert and responsive to it, and careful of it."[36] Too often the study of literature is perceived as a burden that impedes the "practical" education students need; it then becomes either an "ornament" to display at cocktail parties or a kind of specialized knowledge by which professional academics support their careers. Berry condemns this view with biting irony in his list of a "few simple truths" needed to understand modern education: "The so-called humanities probably do not exist. But if they do, they are useless. But whether they exist or not or are useful or not, they can sometimes be made to support a career."[37] Because university faculty have increasingly "failed to ask the question of the external placement of [their specialized] knowledges with respect to truth and to the world," university curricula have moved further and further away from concerns of moral, external truth and settled for merely discussing questions of factual, internal truth.

One of the damaging results of teaching literature as a specialization is that students are trained to think that literature "is to be learned *about;* to learn *from* it would be an embarrassing betrayal of objectivity."[38] As an example, Berry critiques those who think the Bible can be taught merely "as literature": "It is conceivable that the Bible could be well taught by a teacher who believes that it is true, by a teacher who believes that it is untrue, or by a teacher who believes that it is partly true. That it could be well taught by a teacher uninterested in the question of truth is not conceivable."[39]

Indeed, at its core, literature teaches us to make connections, to understand relationships, and to discern moral truth. We have already seen this understanding of "truth" in its etymological connection to "tree": truth entails making faithful, responsible connections between an object and the network of implications and effects that root it in its place. As Berry writes in regard to the kind of truth that literature can teach, "The issue of truth rises out of the comparison of one thing with another, out of the study of the relations and influences between one thing and another and between one thing and many others."[40] And since the truths of literature are not "objectively provable as are the truths of science," in an academic environment that privileges scientific knowledge there is an "embarrassment about any statement that depends for confirmation upon experience or imagination or feeling or faith."[41] This embarrassment, in turn, leads to the reduction and impoverishment of literary studies. Professors of literature often try to distance themselves from the texts they teach, to position themselves as "students of the behavior of a species to which they do not belong, in whose history and fate they have no part,"[42] and in doing so, they fall back on a language that is as irresponsible as that used by the nuclear scientists trying to explain the potential consequences of the Three Mile Island disaster. Both these scientists and literary "specialists" fail to acknowledge their membership in the community about which they are speaking; thus they cannot speak a language that is responsible to their community.

George Orwell critiques this failure of professionals to speak a common, understandable language in his well-known essay "Politics and the English Language," in which he surveys the incoherent writing of several professors:

> Each of these passages has faults of its own, but, quite apart from avoidable ugliness, two qualities are common to all of them. The first is staleness of imagery; the other is lack of precision. The writer either has a meaning and cannot express it, or he inadvertently says something else, or he is almost indifferent as to whether his words mean anything or not. This mixture of vagueness and sheer incompetence is the most marked characteristic of modern English prose, and especially of any kind of political writing. As soon as certain topics are raised, the concrete melts into the abstract and no one seems able to think of turns of speech that are not hackneyed: prose consists less and less of *words* chosen for the sake of their meaning, and more and more of *phrases* tacked together like the sections of a prefabricated henhouse.[43]

Orwell carefully argues that the "fight against bad English is not frivolous and is not the exclusive concern of professional writers."[44] As Berry argues, everyone is responsible to use clear, accountable language because the community suffers when any member hides behind vague jargon that evades its real consequences. To be accountable in this way means that our attention must be focused in every sentence we compose, such that the "scrupulous writer" will ask at least six questions: "What am I trying to say? What words will express it? What image or idiom will make it clearer? Is this image fresh enough to have an effect? Could I put it more shortly? Have I said anything that is avoidably ugly?" The writer who fails to ask such questions will find imprecise and incoherent writing performing "the important service of partially concealing your meaning even from yourself."[45] These questions set a high standard for writers, but if we accept our interconnections and inevitable dependence on one another, this is the standard for which we will strive.

Lying behind Orwell's insistence on clear language is a recognition that language connects us with those we converse with, so that the quality of our language influences the quality—the health—of our communities and places. Imaginative literature in particular draws on this connective power of language to probe the ways in which we relate to one another and our world. This vital work of remembering connections is modeled for us in the writing of authors like J. R. R. Tolkien. Tolkien understood the power of stories to provoke self-reflection that leads to corrected vision, and we have already seen how his narrative foregrounds the role of imagination and affection in enabling the Fellowship to faithfully serve their homes. Like Berry, Tolkien creates a world in which moral agents work together toward the health of their places, and his stories reveal to readers their own responsibilities. In his poem "Mythopoeia," Tolkien praises the intrinsic storytelling nature of humans, proclaiming the mythmakers and storytellers to be blessed because of the moral order they offer us:

> Blessed are the legend-makers with their rhyme
> of things not found within recorded time.
> It is not they that have forgot the Night,
> or bid us flee to organized delight,
> in lotus-isles of economic bliss
> forswearing souls to gain a Circe-kiss
> (and counterfeit at that, machine produced,
> bogus seduction of the twice seduced).[46]

Odysseus's men repeatedly forget their responsibilities to their home, both when they eat the lotus fruit and when Circe drugs them and transforms them into pigs. The "bogus seduction" of higher education today, a seduction that likewise causes students to forget their responsibilities to home, is that we can study something with pure objectivity, divorced from any responsibility to use our knowledge for our home and not for "organized delight" or selfish "bliss." Yet the "legend-makers with their rhyme" seek to reweave the web of life, to remind us of our broader responsibilities.

So how can literature be taught not as an academic specialty but as if it carries important truths about our place in the world? Although this sounds simplistic, one rather revolutionary way would be to read works of literature as if they were indeed about the world. In one class he taught at the University of Kentucky, Berry assigned works by Shakespeare, Spenser, and Milton alongside agriculture texts by Albert Howard, F. H. King, and Wes Jackson. As Grubbs recounts, Berry read these literary works both "for pleasure and instruction," both for their beauty and for their truth: "What he watched for in his reading, and taught us to watch for, are the ways a text intersects with the practical and ethical life."[47] This is why throughout this book we turn to Berry's fiction and other works of literature for instruction. Imaginative literature can teach us truths about the world and about our responsibilities in it.

Yet for us to learn such truths from literature, we must read with an openness to how literary works might reveal and reform our affections and imaginations. What this means is simply that when we encounter works of art, we both see and are seen by them. To give one example, consider the Old Testament story in which King David commits adultery with Bathsheba. Bathsheba is the wife of Uriah, one of David's loyal soldiers, yet David kills Uriah in an attempt to cover up his sin. When the prophet Nathan arrives at court to confront David, Nathan does not immediately condemn him but rather tells him a story about two neighbors: One was wealthy and had a huge flock of sheep, and the other was poor and had one lamb that the family treated as a household pet. When a traveler came, the rich man took the poor man's lamb and killed it to feed his guest. David's anger is "greatly kindled" on hearing this story, and he tells Nathan that the rich man must pay restitution for the lamb and then be executed. It is at this point that Nathan says to David, "Thou art the man," turning the judgment David has delivered back upon David himself.[48] As David Jeffrey and Gregory Maillet observe, "David's impulsive interpretation and rush to judgment regarding the story of the purloined lamb constitutes much more than a literary interpretation. His response reveals that Nathan's parable has been diagnostic of the heart of its hearer; the story has interpreted the interpreter."[49] This is literature's highest power, to hold a mirror to the reader's heart and provoke change. In Rilke's famous poem about the broken statue of Apollo, the poet shifts abruptly from describing the statue's appearance to voicing the statue's claim upon the viewer: "there is no place at all / that isn't looking at you. You must change your life."[50]

This has been our own experience as readers of Berry's fiction. When we read Berry's stories about the beautiful but damaged community of Port William, we learn to long for its health and restoration. Yet when we read the last page of a story and look up from the book, we ask ourselves, "Why don't I care this way about the place where I live? What does my place need from me to grow healthier?" If we let it, literature can reshape our imaginations and affections and teach us how to love our places. In this way, literature is language made responsible—language that challenges us to consider how we can better respond to our place in the world.

At its best, then, literature reads us and interprets our desires, helping us become more accountable dwellers in our world. Engaging language and literature is a moral practice that can lead us toward healthful relationships with our communities. All students, no matter their academic major, need to learn a language that can hold their specialized knowledge responsible to their place. Perhaps chemists can learn from *Brave New World* to consider how their research might affect their communities. Farmers might learn from *Remembering* to treat their animals not as units of production but as fellow creatures. And hospice workers might learn from *Sir Gawain and the Green Knight* to sympathize with those facing the inevitable and imminent end of life.

Universities must take seriously their task of educating students to be moral beings concerned with truth. Rather than being communities where the "Unknown Tongue" allows researchers to call food a weapon and polluted soil and water the price of progress, universities should cultivate a "precise and articulate and lively" language that holds their members responsible to their communities. Faculty and students can learn to speak such a language through studying grammar, logic, and rhetoric and through reading literature with an openness toward how it teaches us to live. But ultimately, if universities want to talk with their communities, they will also have to walk with them. They will have to start doing good work.

In one of his Sabbath poems, Berry imagines a language that literally talks while it walks. He figures a stream near his home as a "book" whose words compose an ever-changing song out of water and stone. The stream sings a language precise and sensitive to its place, one whose music is formed by its walk down the hill. From this stream, the poet learns "A language that is a stream flowing / and is a man's thought as he / walks and thinks beside the stream." This language stands in sharp contrast to the language damaged from the abstractions of war, salesmanship, and power, for it is a language intimately responsive to its place.

> A changing song,
> a changing walk,
> a changing thought.
>
> A sounding stone,
> a stepping stone,
> a word
> that is a sounding and a stepping
> stone.
>
> A language that is a stream flowing
> and is a man's thoughts as he
> walks and thinks beside the stream.

His thoughts will hold
if the words will hold, if each
is a stone that will bear weight,
placed by the flow
in the flow. The language too

descends through time, subserving
the false economy, heedless power,
blown with the gas of salesmanship,
rattled with the sale of needless war,

worn by the mere unhearing
babble of thoughtlessness,
and must return to its own
downward flow by the flowing
water, the muttered syllables,
the measureless music, the stream
flowing and singing, the man
walking and thinking, balanced
on unsure footholds
in the flowing stream.[51]

3
Doing Good Work
Enacting Our Imagination

Work keeps our imaginations and words accountable to the real needs of our places; it is the way we walk as we talk. Work thus provides an important corrective to our dualistic culture in which we tend to privilege mind and soul over body. Universities too often institutionalize this dualism, promising their graduates "freedom" from manual labor. Yet this dualism causes great damage to ourselves and to our places, denying our embodied existence in a physical world. An education in the service of health must lead students toward lives of good, caring work, work that enacts their love for particular places and people.

Old Jack's Love and Work

We have already quoted Jack Beecham's apt saying: "If you want to talk with me, you'll have to walk."[1] He says this repeatedly because he has learned this lesson the hard way. For much of his life, Jack's words remained at odds with his hands; his loves remained divided from his work. When he was a young man, he scraped together enough money to buy the farm he had grown up on. Once he owned the land, Jack had his first taste of the satisfaction of working out the healthy order he imagined his place could embody:

> After the full responsibility of [the farm] fell to him, he saw it with a new clarity. . . . The work satisfied something deeper in him than his own desire. . . . When he stepped into the first opening furrow of a new season he was not merely fulfilling an economic necessity; he was answering the summons of an immemorial kinship; he was shaping a passage by which an ancient vision might pass once again into the ground.

He remembers those days for their order, the comeliness of the shape his work made in each one of them as it passed.[2]

Jack's legal responsibility for this piece of land gives his work a wholeness and a beauty that go far beyond the "economic necessity" his work used to fulfill. This link between his vision and his work enables him to participate in the "immemorial kinship" of those who have cared for this place. Jack's hands are giving shape to his love for his farm.

Jack soon begins to court a young woman named Ruth, but shortly after they are married, their love becomes strained. Ruth is disappointed at Jack's lack of ambition; she wants him to become someone important, someone who doesn't have to work in the fields all day. She is repulsed by his hands that grasp "whatever filth or dirt or blood his life required. . . . They did willingly and even eagerly what, before, she had seen only black hands do reluctantly."[3] As Jack feels Ruth's disapproval, his desires gradually shift, and he becomes discontent with his small farm and hard work. He begins to believe the cultural message "that no place may be sufficient to itself, but must lead to another place, and that all places must finally lead to money; that a man's work must lead not to the health of his family and the respect of his neighbors but to the market place, to that deference that strangers yield to sufficient cash."[4] And so Jack takes out a mortgage and buys more land.

Jack can't handle his expanded holdings by himself and is forced to hire a black man to live on his new farm and help him with the work. The desire to profit from more than one can responsibly care for leads to destruction and loss. In this case, Jack's hired hand, Will Wells, is the one who suffers from Jack's greed. Will works hard, and he and Jack labor together to mend the ill use the land suffered in previous years. Will and his wife even fix up the old house they live in and make themselves at home there: "Working at odd times, . . . Will had elaborated around his little house the design of a neat homestead. . . . Except that it was not his place, except that he had to hold himself answerable to Jack, he was at home there."[5] Even though Jack and Will work side by side, their work is not equal: "A vast difference lived between them even while they worked together—the difference between hopeful and hopeless work."[6] Their hands make the same motions, but Will's work is doomed to frustration because he has no vision of the wholeness that his work serves: "his labor formalized and preserved no bond between him and the place; he was a man laboring for no more than his existence."⁷ So when Jack and Will quarrel and Will leaves, Jack knows he cannot ask another man to suffer this drudgery, this work divorced from love and responsibility. Jack sells the extra land at a loss and returns to working only what his own hands can care for. His renewed fidelity to his farm, his care for this place "that was rightfully his, not because it belonged to him so much as because, by the expenditure of history and work, he belonged to it," restores his affection for the land and his satisfaction with its wholeness, and now his "healing" work serves "the health of his place."⁸

Discouraged by Jack's lack of ambition and his failure to make something of himself, Ruth turns away from her husband. Nevertheless, when Jack has an affair with a neighbor named Rose, Ruth is deeply hurt, and Jack acknowledges that she has a right to feel that way:

> He saw that his infidelity had touched her as his love had not. . . . After that he was torn. He felt the insult and shame that he had given Ruth, and he felt it, he knew, because he cared for her, because he would be forever yearning and grieving after the loss of what perhaps they never could have had. And with Rose too he was beginning to feel an incompleteness. His love for her led to nothing, could lead to nothing. . . . It was as though he bore for these two women the two halves of an irreparably divided love. With Ruth, his work had led to no good love. With Rose, his love led to no work. . . . [H]e felt more and more the futility and uselessness of being out of place.⁹

This division remains Jack and Ruth's tragedy. Even after Rose dies, Jack and Ruth's marriage never unites love and work. So although Jack learns from his mistaken ambition for more land and finds satisfaction working within the limits of his abilities, he never achieves a similar union in his marriage. This failure is a constant reminder of the need to join our talk with our walk, our words with our deeds, our love with our work. Jack knows all too well that unenacted desire isn't real love and that work without love quickly becomes dehumanizing drudgery. Jack's hard-earned knowledge should serve as a warning to universities to value work and the practical arts: if students are to serve the health of their places and communities, they need to submit their imaginations and desires to the corrective discipline of work.¹⁰

While our dualistic culture devalues work, incorporating manual work into higher education reminds students that love must be enacted.

An imagined vision of health and a language that accounts for the broader context of our work are vital to leading a placed life. But unless these are enacted and clarified by physical labor, they will remain irresponsible, detached from reality, and ultimately damaging to ourselves and our places. The liberal arts, therefore, remain insufficient unless they are joined with the practical arts, as advocated by the medieval Scholastic Hugh of St. Victor and by the original charter of land-grant colleges. After examining the damaging effects of our culture's dualistic denigration of work, we propose three benefits of manual work: work puts us in contact with external standards, it corrects false or naïve ideas by adapting them to local realities, and it is one way we participate in bringing about healthy order. Although the current structure of universities may make it difficult to incorporate manual work into the curriculum, a first step is to understand even academic work as embodied. And some colleges have found creative ways to make their students work, whether through tuition waivers, service learning, or community gardening. Challenging students to do physical work in their local economies encourages them to continue this practice when they graduate and establish their own households.

Working Past Dualism

In our contemporary economy, industrial specialization tends to divide thought and work. As already discussed, disciplinary overspecialization leads to fragmentation of the different forms of knowledge that universities pursue. This fragmented form of thought inhibits the different disciplines from speaking to one another or relating their particular spheres of knowledge to any common external standard. Yet perhaps an even more damaging result of the industrial mantra to "divide and conquer" is that our economy reinforces the division between thought and work. To an increasing extent, manual work is done by employees who are little more than hired hands. These "hands" are guided by consultants and think tanks that provide abstract guidance regarding best practices.

It is certainly true that not all specialization is bad; both of us have PhDs, so at some point in our lives we saw value in pursuing the most specialized degree available. But as we noted in the first two chapters, healthy judgment mediates between internal and external standards, between specialized knowledge and the effects of this knowledge in particular places.

Yet our contemporary division of labor means that fewer persons are in a position to make judgments based on the best available knowledge *and* practical, local experience. Universities focus almost exclusively on the former, overlooking the vital role that work plays in putting ideas into action and allowing knowledge to be judged by its effects on our places. Specialization that divides thought from work, then, is particularly hazardous, damaging both our thinking and our places.

The distance between work and thought continues to grow due to our cultural aversion to work. Americans seem to think that work is a terrible burden to be avoided at all costs.[11] The irony is that work is a burden largely because our culture has divorced it from meaning and affection. Berry pins much of the blame for this division on industrialization and, more particularly, on the false anthropology upon which a globalized, industrial economy is based. Despite modern industry's promise to eliminate dehumanizing drudgery, thus far it has tended to increase the prevalence of such work. Its logic of specialization and mechanization is oriented toward an ideal world in which all work is done by machines, yet it fails to recognize that work is intrinsic to the human condition and can be a great joy. This failure to discriminate between kinds of work devalues all work, and as a result, more and more humans either become obsolete or are given mindless tasks that machines can't yet do.[12] Berry deplores this situation because of the damage it does to both people and the world:

> With industrialization has come a general depreciation of work. ...We can say without exaggeration that the present national ambition of the United States is unemployment. People live for quitting time, for weekends, for vacations, and for retirement; moreover, this ambition seems to be classless, as true in the executive suites as on the assembly lines. One works, not because the work is necessary, valuable, useful to a desirable end, or because one loves to do it, but only to be able to quit—a condition that a saner time would regard as infernal, a condemnation. This is explained, of course, by the dullness of the work, by the loss of responsibility for, or credit for, or knowledge of the thing made.[13]

As Berry identifies at the end of this passage, work becomes degraded when the worker loses responsibility for the thing being made. In his essay, Berry draws on Eric Gill's helpful distinction between making and doing:

the maker skillfully realizes the object that she imagines in her mind, but the doer simply does the narrow task to which she is assigned.[14]

The industrial-based shift from making to doing damages workers, the products of their work, and ultimately the places where these products are used: "When workers' minds are degraded by loss of responsibility for what is being made, they cannot use judgment; they have no use for their critical faculties; they have no occasions for the exercise of workmanship, of workmanly pride."[15] Key here is that *both* thought and work suffer from their division: when work is demeaning to the worker it is likely to become sloppy, and under these conditions, a person's thought grows more abstract and irresponsible. It is for these reasons that Jack Beecham insists, "If you want to talk with me, you'll have to walk."

We ourselves have experienced the drudgery of manual work. When I (Jack) worked on a fruit farm as a teenager, I experienced both the great joy of being present on a piece of land from sunup to sundown and also the great frustration of spending most of that time with my mind "degraded by the loss of responsibility for what [was] being made."[16] Though I have dear memories of the years I spent doing good, hard work—trimming root suckers under every tree in endless apple orchards, pulling cherry tarps during ninety-hour workweeks, picking up stones brought to the surface by the plow in dusty fields under the unimpeded summer sun—these memories are conflicted. This same hard work turned my affections away from farmwork and ultimately away from Oceana County, a place deeply connected to the land in the shared experience of its residents.

Working on a fruit farm taught me the virtue of long-suffering perseverance in the face of seemingly endless tasks, but it could not teach me to love a place that needed nothing more of me than my seasonal work—and so I was given a small glimpse of the migrant worker's plight. In other words, because the farm was not mine, the care of the land ultimately was not mine, and the prospect of living and working on that land could never be a life I embraced. In large part, I could not imagine how the work I was doing was serving anything other than producing a paycheck. And because my work lacked imagination, it was divorced from my mind and affections; therefore, more often than not, it became only drudgery. Berry describes this problem in an interview about how farm labor can become meaningful and enjoyable: "You have to see the whole picture. Nobody comes to farm to dispose of dead livestock or to cope with a disease outbreak. Nobody comes to mend fences, although I happen to like mending fences myself. You have to have some sense of how each task is gathered into the larger pattern."[17]

As Berry's description indicates, not all difficult, physical work has to be drudgery. I (Jeff) have fond memories of the summer I spent digging an outhouse hole. This may seem like a rather onerous task, but I enjoyed digging the hole because I was doing it for friends, I could see (and smell) the need for it, and I knew I would benefit from the work. For several summers I lived with these friends while working nearby to pay for college. Instead of paying rent, I worked a certain number of hours around their homestead. One summer, it had become painfully clear that a new outhouse was needed, so I spent an hour or two each evening digging a hole. It was hard work, but I took satisfaction in watching the hole grow deeper and knowing the good end toward which I was working. When it became difficult to get the dirt out of the hole, it was deemed sufficiently deep. My host, who is more skilled than I am, built a simple but sturdy structure over it, complete with a stained-glass window and a hand-split shake roof. Now, whenever I visit these friends, I can see that my work contributed, in a small way, toward the *making* of a well-ordered and beautiful household. Even hard, messy work becomes meaningful when the worker can envision the "larger pattern" it serves.

This necessary union between thought and work seems to be the point of an old parable: Three stonecutters were working together. A man came up to the first and asked him what he was doing. "Cutting this stone," he replied. The man asked the same question of the second stonecutter: "I'm earning a living for my wife and family." Finally the man asked the third stonecutter what he was doing. "I'm building a cathedral," he said. "This stone I'm cutting will form part of the east transept." The first was simply going through the motions, the second simply wanted the wages, but the third was able to imagine the order of his work and envision its end. To use Gill's distinction once again, they were all *doing* the same task, but only the third man was *making* a cathedral. The first two men were in a similar position to Will Wells, doing the labor of hired hands, but the third was able to see that his daily work served a beloved, imagined whole. This is part of the reason why a liberal arts education is so valuable: teaching students the common language and structures that all disciplines share prepares them to see how their work relates to the whole. If students know they are building a cathedral, they can take pride and joy in their work and perform it thoughtfully and responsibly. If they discover that they are being employed to build a dungeon, they can quit and work elsewhere. The worker who sees only his own task is a slave.

If what we have been saying about work is true, and if work that enacts a healthy imagination is a deeply human good, then why has our culture bought into the industrial division of labor? According to Berry, it's because Western culture suffers from a long-standing dualism that divides mind and soul from body. It is this false anthropology that leads to unchecked industrialization, which is why Berry has been drawing attention to it for decades. The "dualism of body and soul," Berry argues, "is the most destructive disease that afflicts us."[18] This dualism has had many damaging effects, including the mechanization and industrialization of our economy that divides work from home, love, and thought.

Perhaps one of the worst American tragedies caused by this dualism is racial slavery, a result of the racial and class segregation that stems from the segregation of mental and physical labor. Throughout American history we have created different ethnic underclasses to do manual labor—African Americans, Irish Americans, Chinese Americans, Hispanics. This practice not only damages people on both sides of these racial and class divides but also contributes to the damaging of our places. Berry argues that a contributing cause of the exploitation of the land in the South has been the division between white landowners and black workers: "The white man, preoccupied with the abstractions of the economic exploitation and ownership of the land, necessarily has lived on the country as a disruptive force, an ecological catastrophe, because he assigned the hard labor, and in that the possibility of intimate knowledge of the land, to a people he considered racially inferior; in thus debasing labor, he destroyed the possibility of a meaningful contact with the earth."[19] Berry's diagnosis demonstrates that our places will not be healthy until we learn to unite knowledge with the "meaningful contact" that labor provides.

By now, the extensive and destructive effects of our cultural division between soul and body, thought and work, should be clear. Yet in spite of these damaging consequences, the university remains one of the chief culprits in exacerbating these divisions. Most students today view a university diploma as a ticket to a life without manual work. The university encourages this belief in its very structure. As Berry notes, "The present organization of intellectual and academic life . . . formalizes the differences between knowing and doing, the laboratory or classroom and the world."[20] In his 2013 Chubb Lecture at Yale, Berry praises universities for providing students the opportunity to think and learn, but he criticizes the way higher education is "geared toward an indoor, sedentary culture."[21] On their own, universities certainly won't be able to bridge the deep divide between work and thought, but they might at least stop being such egregious offenders.

Uniting the Liberal and Practical Arts

The university has not always educated the mind at the expense of the body. In the twelfth century, Hugh of St. Victor served as the master of a school just outside Paris. In his *Didascalicon*, Hugh lays out a curriculum that unites the liberal and practical arts on theological grounds. As Jim Halverson explains, "Hugh understands all fields of knowledge, from theology to manufacturing techniques, as integral parts of God's redemptive process. According to Hugh, all learning, and all work informed by learning, is the uniquely human response to and cooperation with God's work of restoring a fallen creation. According to this vision, learning contributes to the restoration of the entire Christian person, as well as to the larger restoration of society."[22]

Hugh followed the common medieval understanding of man's "twofold nature"—body and soul—but he did so without falling into the dualisms of Enlightenment thought.[23] Accordingly, his system of education sought to form both parts of the human person. To this end, it included the trivium, quadrivium, and theology, as well as practical and mechanical arts such as economics, politics, agriculture, textiles, hunting, and medicine.[24] The mechanical arts have a long history in classical theories of education, but Hugh's vision united the liberal arts with the practical and mechanical arts by seeing them all as necessary to the restoration of humans and communities.[25]

Although Berry doesn't seem to be influenced by Hugh directly, he has written in favor of linking the liberal and practical arts more closely. Berry finds a model for this in the Morrill Act, the law that established land-grant agricultural colleges. This 1862 act stipulated that the funding should support colleges "where the leading object shall be . . . to teach such branches of learning as are related to agriculture and the mechanic arts . . . in order to promote the liberal and practical education of the industrial classes in the several pursuits and professions in life."[26] Berry thinks agricultural colleges have largely failed to live up to this charge, but he takes hope in the vision of holistic education articulated by the Morrill Act.

Unfortunately, keeping the liberal and practical sides of education connected has proved difficult. Many colleges offer either technical, "vocational" training or more theoretical degrees. In both cases, students are formed into specialists rather than educated as whole persons, and because they have grasped only one branch of knowledge instead of being led up the tree of wisdom, each side devalues the other's knowledge: proponents of vocational programs often critique recipients of liberal arts degrees for being out of touch and useless, while proponents of liberal arts programs tend to view with condescension those they perceive as the uneducated, working-class masses.

Berry acknowledges the need to see "liberal and practical as a description of *one* education, not two," noting that "as long as the two terms are thus associated, the combination remains thinkable: the 'liberal' side, for instance, might offer necessary restraints of value to the 'practical'; the 'practical' interest might direct the 'liberal' to crucial issues of use and effect."[27] What is essential, Berry argues, is to recognize that "the wrong is on neither side; it is in their division. One of the purposes of this book [*The Unsettling of America*] is to show how the practical, divorced from the discipline of value, tends to be defined by the immediate interests of the practitioner, and so becomes destructive of value, practical and otherwise. But it must not be forgotten that, divorced from the practical, the liberal disciplines lose their sense of use and influence and become attenuated and aimless."[28]

Berry continues his criticism, explaining how the separation of liberal and practical damages both kinds of knowledge: "Without the balance of historic value, practical education gives us that most absurd of standards: 'relevance,' based upon the suppositional needs of a theoretical future. But liberal education, divorced from practicality, gives something no less absurd: the specialist professor of one or another of the liberal arts, the custodian of an inheritance he has learned much about, but nothing from."[29]

The necessary union between the liberal and practical arts leads Berry to propose, at the end of his 2012 Jefferson Lecture "It All Turns on Affection," that economy be designated one of the fine arts: "I mean, not economics, but economy, the making of the human household upon the earth: the *arts* of adapting kindly the many human households to the earth's many ecosystems and human neighborhoods."[30] Like Hugh of St. Victor, Berry sees the objective of education to be the restoration and healing of persons and communities, and such an education must be both liberal and practical, forming both mind and body.

The Benefits of Work

The interplay of liberal and practical, their mutual interdependence, is probably irreducibly complex, as is the connection between mind and body in the human person. For purposes of this chapter, though, we focus on three ways that physical work shapes mental understanding: it puts us in contact with external standards, it corrects false or naïve ideas by adapting them to local realities, and it is the means by which we participate in bringing about healthy order. Our goal is to name specific benefits that come from uniting our talk and our walk, to encourage educators and students to consider ways they might better attend to the corporeal dimension of higher education.

Local work puts our ideas in contact with external standards, enabling us to more properly judge those ideas. As we have seen, one of Berry's chief critiques of the university is that it typically insulates disciplinary knowledge from external standards. He explains this problem in the context of agricultural research, arguing that "academic specialists of agriculture tend to validate their work experimentally rather than practically . . . [T]hey would rather be professionally reputable than locally effective, and . . . they pay little attention, if any, to the social, cultural, and political consequences of their work. . . . There is nothing more characteristic of modern agricultural research than its divorcement from the sense of consequence and from all issues of value."[31] Examples of the consequences of such isolation abound. Recently, a professor at the University of Maastricht grew hamburger meat in a lab, touting this success as a breakthrough that will enable us to "raise" meat more efficiently.[32] While our current method of raising beef cows in industrial feedlots is morally and environmentally atrocious, this sort of technocratic solution fails to address the underlying problems of greed, industrial agriculture, and the impoverishment of rural communities. By calling cows "manufacturing unit[s]," we make such solutions imaginable, but if professors thought of cows as "family companion animal[s]" that formed part of humane, integrated land communities, they would ask different questions and work toward different solutions.[33] Perhaps this professor did not know or work with any locals who raised beef, and his lack of accountability to his place and community left him "free" to solve abstract problems in his lab.

Such abstraction from local communities is not unique to agricultural departments, and it has come to define the "objectivity" that universities uphold. But as Berry points out, this sort of objectivity is a vice: "'Objectivity' has come to be simply the academic uniform of moral cowardice: one who is 'objective' never takes a stand."[34] It may be cowardly to refuse to make our knowledge accountable to external standards, but this separation or divorce between knowledge and its effects also stems from our cultural dualism that privileges mind over body. And the antidote to this dualism is to go to work, for professors and students to get their hands dirty so that they are forced to enact their ideas and learn what effects they have on their places.

In this process of working, they may find their ideas and imaginations to be clarified. Earlier, we emphasized the need for universities to cultivate imaginations that envision and desire healthy places. This is indeed crucial, but the imagination, in isolation, tends to weave naïve, romanticized visions of idyllic communities; for this reason, it needs to remain open to correction through work, through getting one's hands dirty in actual places. In his essay "People, Land, and Community," Berry explains this process by narrating a young farmer's relationship with his land. "A farmer's connection to a farm . . . begin[s] in love," Berry claims. "One loves the place because present appearances recommend it, and because they suggest possibilities irresistibly imaginable."[35] These imagined possibilities may not be realistic, given the actual conditions of the farm, but like a young lover, the farmer's affection blinds him to the blemishes of his new farm until he sets to work:

> When one buys a farm and moves there to live, something different begins. Thoughts begin to be translated into acts. . . . One's work may be defined in part by one's visions, but it is defined in part too by problems, which the work leads to and reveals. And daily life, work, and problems gradually alter the visions. It invariably turns out, I think, that one's first vision of one's place was to some extent an imposition on it. But if one's sight is clear and if one stays on and works well, one's love gradually responds to the place as it really is, and one's visions gradually image possibilities that are really

in it. Vision, possibility, work, and life—all have changed by mutual correction.... One works to better purpose then and makes fewer mistakes, because at last one sees where one is.[36]

Berry's description of this process indicates the complicated and reciprocal interconnections between imagination and work, vision and reality.[37]

The absence of such faithful work in a particular place leads to the kind of dangerous abstractions we saw earlier in the language of the nuclear scientists who could not name the danger the Three Mile Island disaster posed to surrounding communities. Such abstract, irresponsible language continues because so-called experts and theoreticians aren't required to stand and work in the presence of their words. Work is needed to adapt our ideas to actual local conditions. Berry emphasizes the importance of local adaptation because he has seen the damage caused by imposing ideas developed in one place onto a different place. Our culture thinks such centralization is efficient, so we talk about "best practices" and not "reinventing the wheel," but often these catchphrases are a cover for the importation of unexamined big ideas that don't adequately meet local, particular needs. Local work makes it possible to correct such naïve imaginations while at the same time allowing outside ideas to inform and inspire our work.

Finally, by actually enacting our desires and ideas, work is the means by which we participate in bringing about healthier places. Enthusiasm, feelings of goodwill, and imagination are worth very little if they do not lead to productive work. Such work may be slow and take many years to come to fruition, but it is the only way we can actually restore our places. In *The Memory of Old Jack*, Berry contrasts Jack's struggles to unite his loves and his work with Nathan and Hannah Coulter's thriving household. Hannah, as we have seen, has known plenty of sorrow and difficulty, including the death of her first husband in World War II. But after she and Nathan marry, they buy an old, run-down farm and make it their home, gradually restoring its order and productivity. In a few years, their farm's "disorder is only in appearance—visible perhaps to a stranger's eye, but not to Hannah's, who knows the deeper order of intention and labor. As long as she and Nathan are here and able to work there will be order, if not in sight, then within reach."[38] This is the great gift of work: it brings order and health within reach. As Berry states in an interview, the hope he has for the future rests "on the willingness of good people to do the right thing now.... [G]ood work, faithfulness, willingness to serve, honesty, peaceableness, and loving kindness will support hope."[39]

But one doesn't have to buy a farm and start a household to learn the satisfactions of good work. In a more recent conversation at Yale, Berry points to washing dishes as a mundane opportunity to experience the pleasures of restorative work:

> [There is] some kind of pleasure connected to cleaning up a mess that everybody ought to be aware of. The best example I know is washing dishes. I'm like anybody else, I don't do it unless I have to, but once I'm in it, I really love washing dishes. You can't imagine a worse mess than a bunch of dishes piled over here on this side, dirty, dripping, ugly, in utter disorder. And you put them through this process of soap, and scrubbing, and scrubbing, and rinsing, and all of a sudden here they are over here in a neat pile, all pleasant to look at.[40]

Washing the dishes may not seem like a very promising way to begin the work of healing our places, but Berry's point is that if we set to work where we are, doing the tasks that need to be done, we will begin to enact the restoration of our place. And as we work, we will experience the satisfaction of seeing our participation lead to healing and order.

Embodying Education

The home and local communities are the best settings for young people to learn how to work toward the health of their places. But in this section we propose a few ways that universities might incorporate work more deliberately into their curricula. The goal should be to organize schools in recognition of the truth that one cannot form minds without forming bodies also. As James Smith argues, universities "should be conceived not just in terms of dissemination of *in*formation but also, and more fundamentally, as an exercise in *for*mation."[41] Students come to universities with both minds and bodies, and when we focus exclusively on their minds, we foster a culture in which the mind is privileged at the expense of the body.

So what would it look like if universities fostered such an attitude toward work? How might we restructure the "present organization of intellectual and academic life" so that it does *not* formalize "the differences between knowing and doing"?[42] As we've noted before, solutions should always be adapted to the particulars of the local context, but here we provide a few ideas about how both professors and students can practice an education that includes work. These ideas entail emphasizing the embodied nature of academic work, incorporating manual work as part of the curriculum, and cultivating communities that value local, diversified work.

The Physicality of the Intellect

It is important to recognize that the "life of the mind" depends on the embodied lives of our places, for whether or not we acknowledge this truth, our intellectual and physical work depend on each other at a very basic level: without work, our thoughts are malnourished. In his poem "Prayer after Eating," Berry expresses this basic and essential relationship:

> I have taken in the light
> that quickened eye and leaf.
> May my brain be bright with praise
> of what I eat, in the brief blaze
> of motion and of thought.
> May I be worthy of my meat.[43]

Berry's poem is a clarion call to give thanks for and to acknowledge the necessary and good relationship among the places where we live—their health, sustainability, and beauty—the work we do in those places, and the work of our minds.

The poem links our intellectual and physical appetites through the embodied imagery of a meal sustained by light. Berry's imagery waltzes with the metaphor of light, which permeates and guides our existence, quickening both our sight and the vegetable and animal lives by which we subsist. When we eat, we take in and commune with the light that has "quickened eye and leaf"; we are light-eaters whose brains glow brightly "with praise / of what [we] eat." The firing of our synapses—that "brief blaze / of motion and of thought"—ought to lead us to a place of thankfulness and humility, to the hope that we might be, in even the smallest way, worthy of consuming the embodied light that allows us to think and to be grateful.

Thus, the poem articulates how the intellectual work we do cannot be divorced from the physical work that we and other creatures have done. In other words, the process we used to write this book is intimately connected to photosynthesis: without light, which we did not make and do not control, grass would not grow; without grass, cattle could not be fed, and they in turn could not be fed to us; without this food, we would lack the sustenance our brains require to do intellectual work. It is a great indictment of higher education today that we have so divorced our intellectual work from the life of the world. And by something so seemingly mundane as giving thanks for our food—imagining how our work might then be worthy of this food—we can begin to recast a vision for the health and interconnectedness of our intellectual and physical work.

What is more, recognizing the analogous satisfactions brought by physical and intellectual work allows university members to break down the wall that is often erected between the two. Such a recognition enables us to remember that even work that seems purely intellectual—like writing—remains deeply embodied. As Berry explains:

> At first glance, writing may seem not nearly so much an art of the body as, say, dancing or gardening or carpentry. And yet language is the most intimately physical of all the artistic means. We have it palpably in our mouths; it is our *langue*, our tongue. Writing it, we shape it with our hands. Reading aloud what we have written—as we must do, if we are writing carefully—our language passes in at the eyes, out at the mouth, in at the ears; the words are immersed and steeped in the senses of the body before they make sense in the mind. They cannot make sense in the mind until they have made sense in the body. Does shaping one's words with one's own hand impart character and quality to them, as does speaking them with one's own tongue to the satisfaction of one's own ear? There is no way to prove that it does. On the other hand, there is no way to prove that it does not, and I believe that it does.[44]

As Berry's reflections on language indicate, it is possible, and quite necessary, to educate our students in such a way that they learn to draw the work of their minds together with the work of their bodies; the intellectual work students do at a university is itself embodied and physical.

Work Colleges

Some smaller colleges practice the belief that body and mind are connected by embedding work requirements into the curriculum. Schools like Berea College, College of the Ozarks, and Warren Wilson College incorporate manual labor into their students' formal education.[45] There is even a Work Colleges Consortium that represents seven such colleges located around the United States.[46] Jane Schreck sees these colleges as offering a healthy model for higher education both in their embodied organization and in their lower cost. Although the number of such schools has declined, Schreck concludes that "the idea they are built on seems universally applicable as both financially practical and educationally effective."[47]

When Berry visited Warren Wilson College in 2011 and took a tour of the campus, he was quite impressed with its manner of combining work and learning: "The faculty and staff people I spoke with seemed totally committed to the college and its idea, and the students were busy and enthusiastic. Their work contributes directly to the maintenance and daily life of the school. This seems to make them extraordinarily aware of the school and the place as the context of their education." Both Warren Wilson College and Berea College challenge their students to actively participate in the work of their place, which makes Berry hopeful: "Both schools, I think, pretty much require the students to be involved in the life of the place, which surely mitigates against passive consumption of a commodified 'education.'"[48] These work colleges provide a model of learning that radically changes the organization of intellectual life by formalizing connections between the education of students' minds and bodies.

Communities of Work

These ways of embedding work into the organization of the university seem promising to us, but we also recognize that they aren't feasible for every school. Yet even if universities do not require all students to do some manual work, individual professors can find ways to include a work component in their syllabi. Many professors and programs incorporate service learning, and this offers an excellent opportunity for connecting coursework with hands-on experience in the local community. When the Berry Center collaborated with St. Catharine College on a farming and ecological agrarianism program, they included farm labor and community internships along with course work so that students learned with both their minds and their bodies.[49]

Even outside of such institutional frameworks, classes can challenge students to see manual labor as part of their intellectual growth. For instance, in our team-taught Agrarian Literature and Theology course, students were required to spend at least ten hours working in a garden and then write a brief essay reflecting on how this work reshaped their understanding of the ideas discussed in class. One of the benefits was that we had lots of "volunteers" to work in our campus garden that spring. This assignment also gave us the opportunity to build connections with nearby community gardens where our students worked as well. Almost universally, the students wrote that actually getting their hands dirty not only enriched their understanding of the readings but also fundamentally changed their relation to food and agriculture. Working in a garden is qualitatively different from reading about gardening; it forms students in tactile, holistic ways that complement and enrich their intellectual formation, bringing them in contact with external standards and limits, correcting their naïve imaginations, and granting them the joy of seeing their hands enact order.[50] Many schools now have campus gardens, from large schools like Yale and Baylor University to small schools like Messiah College and Paul Quinn College. Gardens like these can be started by groups of faculty, staff, and students; often, very little investment or institutional support is needed.

Spending a few hours working in a campus garden won't miraculously transform students. It won't make a college campus "green" or agriculturally self-sufficient. But it may foster the vital work of reforming our imaginations, helping us do good work in the places where we find ourselves. When students, professors, and staff members work side by side, finding creative solutions to mundane problems like building beds, erecting a greenhouse, dealing with pests, and choosing what to grow, it expands the academic culture and the campus conversation to include practical considerations about where our food comes from. In this way, gardening together is one way to cultivate a community that values local, diversified work. It is certainly not the only way, however. The opportunities for informal teaching in this area are limited only by our imaginations.

To prime the pump, here are a few of the practices we've witnessed or heard about. One professor regularly takes students to the local interfaith homeless shelter to spend time with the residents and lead a short worship service. Another professor hosts "Foxfire" days at her home; inspired by the original Foxfire project, she invites students to learn traditional crafts such as baking, spinning, or sewing.[51] One English student worked with an elderly community member to revise and expand a book on the town's history. Another student reads to a man in his late nineties at the assisted-living home across the street from our university and has encouraged other classmates to do the same.

These small ways of practicing good work in local communities won't transform our broken economy, but they can begin to reeducate, to reform our thinking and living. Berry articulates this reformation in the context of how the act of gardening changes our thinking: "if we apply our minds directly and competently to the needs of the earth, then we will have begun to make fundamental and necessary changes in our minds."[52] These changes in our minds will expand our imaginations and sharpen our language, and it is precisely these interdependent relationships among imagination, language, and work that an education for place must foster. In the following poem, Berry elaborates on the ways that gardening can be a type of school, teaching us to inhabit our places more faithfully.

> Let us enlighten, then, our earthly burdens
> By going back to school, this time in gardens
> That burn no hotter than the summer day.
> By birth and growth, ripeness, death and decay,
> By goods that bind us to all living things,
> Life of our life, the garden lives and sings.
> The Wheel of Life, delight, the fact of wonder,
> Contemporary light, work, sweat, and hunger
> Bring food to table, food to cellar shelves.
> A creature of the surface, like ourselves,
> The garden lives by the immortal Wheel
> That turns in place, year after year, to heal
> It whole. Unlike our economic pyre
> That draws from ancient rock a fossil fire,
> An anti-life of radiance and fume
> That burns as power and remains as doom,
> The garden delves no deeper than its roots
> And lifts no higher than its leaves and fruits.[53]

Part 2

Cultivating Virtues of Place

Introduction to Part 2

In the first half of this book we laid out a three-part approach to educating students for homecoming: share stories of habitation and dwelling to form healthy imaginations; study the trivium and read literature for what it can teach us about speaking a common, responsible language; and do work that enacts our love so that university members participate in local, healing economies. For imagination, language, and work to flourish in students' lives, though, students also need to practice virtues or habits that form them for "responsible membership in a family, a community, or a polity."[1] University communities, therefore, have to devote more attention to forming the habits or virtues that membership requires. In the second half of this book, we explore four virtues—memory, gratitude, fidelity, and love—by which students can place themselves along four dimensions—time, or our responsibilities to tradition; hierarchy, or our responsibilities to the created order; geography, or our responsibilities to our physical location; and community, or our responsibilities to the people around us. Thus, in part 2 we develop the work of virtue in four specific directions as a way of articulating a vision for an education that unites persons with their places through habits of membership.

As in part 1, we continue to open each chapter with a reading of one of Berry's stories, not only because of the role stories play in forming our imaginations but also because virtues are inevitably rooted in narratives and practices. To use the terms we've developed thus far, virtues flourish in cultures that foster healthy imaginations and practice good work. Our current educational culture looks for abstracted "skills" to teach students, but virtues cannot be divorced from their embodied, communal practice, so the best way to understand virtues is in such a narrative context. Alasdair MacIntyre carefully works out the way that virtues depend on communal practice and narrative in his seminal work *After Virtue*. Intrinsic to his definition of virtue is that it is an excellence or quality intelligible only within a community's tradition and story, oriented toward a common good. As his "partial and tentative definition of a virtue" states, "A *virtue is an acquired human quality the possession and exercise of which tends to enable us to achieve those goods which are internal to practice and the lack of which effectively prevents us from achieving any such goods."*[2] This is a formal way of stating that virtues are qualities that enable humans to attain goods intrinsic to a community. MacIntyre emphasizes that virtues are dependent on "practices" because, he argues, virtues make sense only within a communal tradition or narrative that defines the goods to be achieved—otherwise, such qualities aren't "virtues" but mere "skills," isolated qualities that may or may not be oriented toward the good.[3]

For instance, MacIntyre states that throwing a football doesn't count as a practice, but the game of football does.[4] What this means is that the ability to throw a football accurately over a long distance isn't a virtue because, by itself, it doesn't achieve any recognizable good. If Tom Brady were to show a group of aliens how far he could throw a football, they might be impressed with his strength (so long as the ball were properly inflated), but they would have no conception of how that ability could result in a beautiful completed pass in a game of football or how such a completion could serve the larger goals of winning a game, advancing to the postseason, or winning the Super Bowl. The only reason we value individuals who can throw a football well is that we are participants in a community where football is practiced, and we have learned from this community the narrative standards by which to judge excellent or virtuous play.

It is this connection between virtue and communally practiced narratives that leads MacIntyre to define humans as "story-telling animal[s]." He claims that our understanding of virtue is dependent on the narrative in which we identify ourselves: "I can only answer the question 'What am I to do?' if I can answer the prior question 'Of what story or stories do I find myself a part?'"[5] James Smith cites MacIntyre's argument to emphasize the importance of the underlying narratives that give shape to our daily rituals and habits. As Smith puts it, "we live at the nexus of body and story," of communal practice and narrative.[6] Smith calls this nexus *habitus*, a term he draws from the French philosopher Pierre Bourdieu to name "the embodied know-how (the 'practical sense') that is 'carried' in a community of practice."[7] It is in this way that virtues are intelligible only within communities. As Berry explains, "A purposeless virtue is a contradiction in terms. Virtue, like harmony, cannot exist alone; a virtue must lead to harmony between one creature and another."[8]

Berry's claim that virtues lead to harmony between creatures corroborates MacIntyre's description of those virtues that are most fundamental. Because MacIntyre understands practices to be inherently communal and traditional, he particularly values those virtues that maintain communities in which people can seek good, healthy lives together. These are the sine qua non of all other virtues—the virtues that foster healthy places and communities:

> The virtues therefore are to be understood as those dispositions which will not only sustain practices and enable us to achieve the goods internal to practices, but which will also sustain us in the relevant kind of quest for the good, by enabling us to overcome the harms, dangers, temptations and distractions which we encounter, and which will furnish us with increasing self-knowledge and increasing knowledge of the good. The catalogue of the virtues will therefore include the virtues required to sustain the kind of households and the kind of political communities in which men and women can seek for the good together.[9]

In fact, MacIntyre argues, "the creation and sustaining of human communities" were understood by the "ancient and medieval worlds" to "be a practice" with its own internal goods.[10] Our argument is simply that memory, gratitude, fidelity, and love are four of the "virtues required to sustain the kind of households and the kind of political communities in which men and women can seek for the good together." They are four of the virtues that sustain healthy places.[11]

Berry's stories invite readers into a narrative of households in which individuals learn the virtues required to sustain their community. After opening each chapter with an episode from Berry's fiction that portrays how a particular virtue contributes to the health of the place, we explore how this virtue might apply to higher education. Finally, we conclude with some specific examples of how students, teachers, and other members of universities might incorporate this virtue into the life of their community. In other words, we begin with a narrative that enables us to *imagine* this virtue, then develop a *language* to talk about the virtue, and conclude with practices that allow us to *work* out this virtue. As we've explained before, these examples are not intended as blanket prescriptions for all institutions; rather, we hope they inspire readers to imagine analogous practices that they can develop in ways that are appropriate to their context.

Memory, gratitude, fidelity, and love are four ways of dwelling in our places such that we participate in the flourishing of those around us. However, as we've argued throughout the first half of this book, educators and students won't see the need for such virtues unless they first accept the narrative of homemaking. In essence, Berry narrates stories about how our places have been deeply damaged by our disregard for their health. American culture has privileged personal success and affluence regardless of the cost to the other members of our ecological communities. These costs are mounting, and we can no longer ignore our shallow community bonds, our polluted rivers and lakes, our impoverished topsoil, and the other cultural and physical consequences of this standard American narrative.

As Berry argues in his 1978 commencement address at Centre College (see the foreword), the study of ecology reminds us of "the inescapability of connections and of dependences." Given these connections, "no one can act simply in his or her own behalf. Escape either into specialization or into solitude is illusory." Or, as he puts it more simply, "life in this world is a moral problem." The proper response to this problem is to develop virtues and disciplines capable of honoring these connections: "what ecological insight has done is reveal again the practical foundations of ancient morality." Recovering this ancient morality might enable us to take our places in "a healthful economy that is at once physical and spiritual." It is in this rooted economy or ecology—both words come from the Greek term *oikos*, meaning "household"—that Berry's narratives invite us to dwell.

Another way of articulating these connections among narratives, virtues, and places is to say that in order to properly *inhabit* our place, we need to cultivate these *habits*, these ways of dwelling. The etymological connections between "habit" and "habitation," between the way we are in the world and the place where we live, indicate the need for students to be educated in ways of being, in virtues, if they are to learn to live where they are: our habits shape the ways we inhabit our habitation. Therefore, an education for health must include narratives and practices that form students to be virtuous inhabitants.[12]

4
Tradition
Remembering Our Story

Memory may be the habit that is most fundamental to the process of education. At its core, education involves handing down cultural memory and wisdom. As Berry describes it, "The inescapable purpose of education must be to preserve and pass on the essential human means—the thoughts and words and works and ways and standards and hopes without which we are not human. To preserve these things and to pass them on is to prepare students for life."[1] While this sounds straightforward, the magnitude of the task of handing down cultural memory dooms the educational effort to inevitable failure: "What must we teach? What do we owe the young? . . . What do we owe them that can possibly prepare them for the experience of living in an unpredictable world? The education industry doesn't accept the inherent tragedy of that. We don't know enough to teach the young. We don't even know enough to decide what they need to know. But we've got to make a gamble. We're going to be surprised, they're going to be surprised; we know that."[2] Given teachers' immense obligation to pass on the wisdom of the past, we want to consider the faculty of memory, how memory functions within communities, and how students might learn to remember their places and so embody the wisdom needed to inhabit and care for those places.

Re-membering a Broken Community

One of the blessings of memory is that its practice encourages us to see the coherent whole, the narrative of which we are a part, and then to love this pattern, serve its health, and pray for its healing in the midst of—and anticipation of—its wrongs. Even while suffering wrongs, we come to a clarifying truth: we are all members in a long story that includes the dead, the living, and those yet to come. Because the living exist only by the former living of those now dead, practicing memory is a virtue that embeds us in a narrative of hope and responsibility. Remembering is thus an act of gratitude and humility.

To be a responsible member of this world is to be a creature who *remembers*—one who sees how the pieces fit together and how they sometimes come apart. But one who remembers is one who desires the good of cohesion, of the joining of members in one body, of stories that narrate our past and our present and that point (however shakily) toward our future. Perhaps the paradox of this virtue of memory is that it binds us both to those who bring us joy and to those who confound us. For instance, as Jayber Crow's visions of the gathered church and the gathered community are clarified in his memory, he comes to know that every community is "imperfect and irresolute but held together by the frayed and always fraying, incomplete and yet ever-holding bonds of the various sorts of affections."[3] The hard truth of Jayber's vision of re-membered community is illustrated poignantly in "Pray without Ceasing," a short story about a dark tragedy in Andy Catlett's past. In this story, Andy is invited to participate in a process of remembering that teaches him not only about his ancestors (some of whom he's never met) but also about himself—that he himself is the embodiment and fruition of his ancestors' forgiveness, love, and hope.

The story's form embodies the healing process of memory: Andy, the narrator, recalls the story in 1990 but shifts between the original events in 1912 and a conversation he had with his grandmother Margaret in 1965. The story centers around the murder of Andy's great-grandfather Ben Feltner at the hands of Ben's best friend, Thad Coulter, but the narrative also re-members the individuals in the community who were torn apart by this murder. As Andy learns, even those who have died still belong to his place; their past choices and actions continue to shape the present-day community.

Looking back at the last days of his grandfather Mat's life, Andy is moved by his grandfather's absence and begins to remember the world of the dead. He observes that he no longer says of Mat, "'He is my grandfather,'" for "he has become the dead man who was my grandfather. He was, and is no more. And this is a part of the great mystery we call time. But the past is present also. And this, I think, is a part of the greater mystery we call eternity." As Andy comes to know, the past forms us whether or not we are aware of it, as do the dead, who—though no longer present in time—are forever present in the memories and stories of the living: "I have in my mind, not just as a memory but as a consolation, his welcome to me when

I returned home from the university and, later, from jobs in distant cities."[4] Our memories are not simply held in our minds like artifacts behind the tempered glass of a museum exhibit, only to be dusted off when we've finally found a use for them. Our memories are in fact alive and formative; this is perhaps part of their paradoxical nature—though they may involve those who no longer walk among us, they shape and form the living who share them. For Andy, the memory of his grandfather's greetings is a consolation to him that remains present.

Thinking about his grandfather's death reminds him of one of the last times he saw him alive. Andy had gone to visit Mat and Margaret, and after spending some time at Mat's bedside, he showed his grandmother a newspaper clipping recounting his great-grandfather Ben's murder; when Andy read the clipping, he realized he had never heard the full story behind this tragic family event. Seeing "how incomplete the story was as the article told it and as I knew it," Andy recalls, "I felt incomplete myself."[5] The memories Margaret shares with Andy are not hers alone but instead a collection of shared memories: "She spoke as if she were seeing it all happen, even the parts of it that she had in fact not seen."[6] Yet the distant nature of these memories does not preclude them from becoming her own. And this seems to be one of her reasons for telling Andy these stories from the past: remembering is both personal and communal. Though Margaret provides a way for Andy to remember the shape of his own familial history, she hopes he will also see this story of betrayal and murder as one thread of a larger narrative history that extends to the beginning: "That was the point. Or it was one of the points—the one, perhaps, that she most wanted me to see. But it was not the beginning of the story. Adam and Eve and then Cain and Abel began it, as my grandmother depended on me to know. Even in Thad Coulter's part of the story, the beginning was some years earlier than the July of 1912."[7] In recounting these memories, Margaret welcomes Andy into a remembered narrative that stretches back to the beginning of time and yet includes and "completes" Andy.

In Margaret's telling, Thad's son Abner had borrowed money against his father's farm to open a store. When the store failed, dashing Abner's ambitions, he fled and left his father destitute. Facing ruin, Thad drank himself into despair before visiting Ben and asking for money, but Ben refused to help Thad as long as he was drunk. Taking Ben's refusal as a permanent rejection of himself, Thad returned home, got his gun, and shot Ben. Realizing the awful thing he has done, Thad surrenders himself to the local jail. Then, even after a visit by his daughter Martha Elizabeth, who offers him forgiveness, he takes his own life in shame and remorse.

While this is a tragic story, the other point Margaret wants Andy to see is that memory enables forgiveness, love, and healing. So while Andy may expect the story to focus on his great-grandfather's death and to single out Thad Coulter as the villain, Margaret relates how Martha Elizabeth followed her father-turned-murderer to his jail cell and sat beside him. Even though he had murdered Ben, Martha Elizabeth continued to love Thad as her father, offering him the opportunity to be re-membered into the family and community he had so violently rejected. Despite Thad's suicide during a solitary night in his cell, his daughter's faithful presence embodies a mercy that Margaret wants Andy to see:

> "You see," my grandmother said, "there are two deaths in this—Mr. Feltner's and Thad Coulter's. We know Mr. Feltner's because we had to know it. It was ours. That we know Thad's is because of Martha Elizabeth. The Martha Elizabeth you know." I knew her, but it came strange to me now to think of her—to be asked to see her—as a girl. She was what I considered an old woman when I first remember her; she was perhaps eight or ten years younger than my grandmother, the red long gone from her hair. She was a woman always near to smiling, sometimes to laughter. Her face, it seemed, had been made to smile. It was a face that assented wholly to the being of whatever and whomever she looked at. She had gone with her father to the world's edge and had come back with this smile on her face. Miss Martha Elizabeth, we younger ones called her. Everybody loved her.[8]

As a child, Andy had known "Miss Martha Elizabeth" without any notion of her connection to his great-grandfather's death. He knew her as a loved and lovely woman, but it is only through Margaret's story, through remembering the graciousness, forgiveness, and humility of Ben's wife Nancy and his son Mat, that Andy comes to see Martha's membership in his community more fully.

Andy must find a way to reconcile the two Martha Elizabeths he holds in his mind, which means he must also find a way to reconcile the two Thad Coulters—the Thad who was Ben's best friend and the Thad who murdered him. Yet he is not left alone to find the way, because his grandmother guides him to view Thad through God's love: "'People sometimes talk of God's love as if it's a pleasant thing. But it is terrible, in a way. Think of all it includes. It included Thad Coulter, drunk and mean and foolish, before he killed Mr. Feltner, and it included him afterwards.'"[9] Margaret's articulation of forgiveness here is astounding, given the suffering she and Mat endured on account of Thad's waywardness and evil. Remembering requires us to reshape not only our minds but also our loves—and reshaping our loves means that we must sometimes agree to hold seemingly contradictory thoughts in our memories; in other words, we may need to learn to love our enemies. Thus, as Margaret comes to the end of her memory of Thad Coulter and his daughter Martha Elizabeth, she reveals to Andy what is at the heart of her memories: "'If God loves the ones we can't,' she said, 'then finally maybe we can.'"[10]

Because Mat Feltner was willing to remember the man his father was and the man that Thad was—which included being Ben's friend—he was able to pursue forgiveness and mend the deep wound between the Feltners and Coulters of the Port William community. As Andy remembers, "My grandfather renewed and carried on his friendship with the Coulters: with Thad's widow and daughters, with Dave Coulter and his family, and with another first cousin of Thad's, Marce Catlett, my grandfather on my father's side. And when my father asked leave of the Feltners to marry their daughter Bess, my mother, he was made welcome." This union between Bess Feltner and Wheeler Catlett—descendants of so much pain and suffering—embodies the profound healing brought by loving memory. And even though no "Feltner or Coulter of the name is left now in Port William," their hope and love are present in Andy himself—the inheritor of their forgiveness: "But the Feltner line continues, joined to the Coulter line, in me, and I am here. I am blood kin to both sides of that moment when Ben Feltner turned to face Thad Coulter in the road and Thad pulled the trigger. The two families, sundered in the ruin of a friendship, were united again first in new friendship and then in marriage. My grandfather made a peace here that has joined many who would otherwise have been divided. I am the child of his forgiveness."[11] The knowledge Andy attains by the end of the story is a knowledge of inclusion, forgiveness, and remembering; he and those before him—the loved and the unloved, the cruel and the kind, the guilty and the innocent—are joined and sustained within this world because they are remembered in the same story.

As Andy discovers, his own ignorance of his community's history didn't prevent that history from forming and shaping his life. Students, then, ought to learn from their cultural past in order to understand more deeply how that past shapes them; understanding history is a precondition for working toward its healing. As students develop the habit of memory, they begin to participate in a rich, ongoing conversation that equips them to attend and tend to their places. This participation is particularly important in an educational environment that values technologies that access information. Such technologies can be valuable, but when they become normative, we outsource knowledge to "the cloud" rather than learning knowledge and forming it via memory into wisdom. Well-stocked memories enable us not merely to access information but to embody wisdom and allow it to form our lives. In addition to exercising a healthy skepticism about the promised benefits of new educational technology, faculty and students can develop simple practices that cultivate the habit of memory: memorizing poems, studying etymologies, remembering their places, and learning the human history of their disciplines. Furthermore, universities, despite the contrived nature of their community, can foster institutional memory as a way of teaching students the importance of participating in communities that remember, that pass down local knowledge to succeeding generations. As Andy discovers, such local remembering lays the foundation for forgiveness, love, and healing.

Remembering Cultural Landmarks

The kind of memory that holds wisdom in place is necessarily local and communal. It is local because each place needs to remember particular lessons and stories that can guide its human community in adapting to their particular place, and it is communal because such memory, if it is to be truly useful in preventing the repetition of damaging mistakes, must exist beyond the lifetime of any one person. Much of Berry's work, then, explores this kind of local memory. For instance, in "The Work of Local Culture," Berry compares healthy memory to healthy topsoil, noting that both take past life, whether plant or human, and form it in ways that can serve future fertility: "A human community ... must collect leaves and stories, and turn them to account. It must build soil, and build that memory of itself—in lore and story and song—that will be its culture."[12]

Universities, especially large ones, are not particularly suited to this work of remembering local culture. Even so, what higher education *can* cultivate is the memory of our broader cultural inheritance, work that is likewise vital to the health of local places. Berry explains this twofold work of memory in a conversation about what schools would teach if they were educating students to live as members of their communities:

> You see that children are taught—not just enough to get them a job or get them a diploma—but taught enough to function as responsible, affectionate members of that community. They'd be taught the community's history. They'd be taught the ecological limits of the local countryside. It would be a matter of great importance that children should know what their grandparents and great-grandparents did. They would be taught what has gone wrong. They would be taught what's worked. All that in addition to the larger cultural inheritance that they're going to need. It's a complex commitment.
>
> And I think the educational system, whatever it would be, should take into consideration the complexity of that local commitment. Of course, our educational system has failed completely to do that. We're educating kids to live anywhere, not somewhere in particular.[13]

We discuss some of the ways universities can help foster local memory later in this chapter, but institutionally, universities are much better equipped to educate students in their "larger cultural inheritance" than in their "community's history." Families, community organizations, and K–12 schools have more opportunities to cultivate the kind of local memory Berry describes here. While this doesn't mean that universities should continue to educate students "to live anywhere, not somewhere in particular," it does mean that their focus should be on passing down a coherent cultural inheritance and on habituating students to remember so that they can work out this virtue in their own particular places.

Berry imagines cultural memory to be a set of landmarks that ought to guide our actions; if nothing else, they tell us where not to go. As he writes at the beginning of *Life Is a Miracle*, "Human hope may always have resided in our ability, in time of need, to return to our cultural landmarks and reorient ourselves."[14] As Andy realizes, his grandmother's story is part of a much longer human narrative: "Adam and Eve and then Cain and Abel began it, as my grandmother depended on me to know."[15] Being able to understand his local history within the context of these cultural landmarks enables Andy to understand the significance of his ancestors' forgiveness. Thus, by passing on a broader cultural inheritance, universities can shape and enrich local memories.

Some readers may fear that by advocating for an education rooted in students' native tradition—which in the United States is generally, though not exclusively, the Western tradition—we are being reactionary or oppressive. Yet as Berry points out, this tradition forms students whether they understand it or not.[16] Andy was a product of forgiveness whether or not he knew the full story of his great-grandfather's murder; likewise, we are inescapably shaped by our cultural landmarks.[17] In addition, Berry points out that the Western tradition underlying much of American culture contains wisdom we would do well to learn from: "If we want to use the world with care, we cannot exempt ourselves from our cultural inheritance, our tradition. This is a delicate subject at present because our cultural tradition happens to be Western, and there is now a fashion of disfavor toward the Western tradition. . . . This tradition obviously involves errors and mistakes, damages and tragedies. But that only means that the tradition too must be used with care . . . and in fact care is a subject about which our tradition has much to teach."[18]

Remembering our native tradition does not mean that we should ignore other traditions. Berry himself acknowledges that he "owe[s] a considerable debt . . . to Buddhism."[19] Nevertheless, because he was born into the Western, Christian tradition, he argues that if he chooses to "turn away from it or against it, . . . that will only bind [me] tightly to a reduced version of it."[20] For those born into this tradition, then, "a better possibility is that this, our native religion, should survive and renew itself so that it may become as largely and truly instructive as we need it to be."[21] So rather than betray his place in this lineage or traduce the wisdom it hands down, Berry strives to translate his tradition carefully to meet the present needs of his own context. The connections between the words *betray, traduce, translate,* and *tradition* indicate the anxiety embedded in our language with regard to properly handing cultural wisdom from one generation to the next.

Berry's understanding of the placed character of the human mind leads him to reject modern understandings of the mind as a disembodied calculating machine that is hermetically sealed off from the world. Berry terms this definition of "mind = brain = machine" the "Tarzan theory of the mind"—that is, the belief "that a human raised entirely by apes, would have a mind nonetheless fully human."[22] On the contrary, human minds develop within particular bodies, histories, and places, leading Berry to propose that a more correct formula would be something like this: "mind = brain + body + world + local dwelling place + community + history."[23] Because all thought, language, and memory are inevitably dependent on place and community, if we care about educating minds, we must also tend to the traditions that form these minds.

Berry expands on this proper stance toward tradition elsewhere, articulating that tradition should be both remembered *and* corrected:

> Outrage and rebellion against the past are undoubtedly human necessities, but they are limited necessities, and they probably should be limited to youth. Things are obviously wrong with the past; young people have the clarity to see them and the energy to rebel against them. But as a general principle, such rebellion is destructive, for it keeps us from seeing that the past, unsatisfactory as it is, is the source of nearly all our good. Maturity sees that the past is not to be rejected, destroyed, or replaced, but rather that it is to be judged and corrected, that the work of judgment and correction is endless, and that it necessarily involves one's own past.[24]

As Kimberly Smith explains, Berry's "goal, then, is to revive and renew the intellectual traditions he has inherited."[25] Many Americans treat their tradition like they treat the earth: they extract whatever resources they can easily get from it and then move on. Berry's decision to tend and care for his tradition, one that has been abused and misused, parallels his decision to nurture a "marginal" farm whose previous owners exploited and damaged it.[26]

Furthermore, there are times when these cultural landmarks provide an indispensable corrective to damaging local traditions that have made such places marginal and threatened. Perhaps the most obvious example is the racism that plagues many communities throughout the United States; universities ought to educate students in those aspects of their cultural tradition that can judge and correct such injustice. In *The Hidden Wound*, his book on growing up within a racist culture, Berry exemplifies this process of using broader cultural memory to correct local memory. He looks at four literary passages "that deal with the meeting and mutual recognition of social opposites": Odysseus and Eumaeus in *The Odyssey*, Jim and Huck in *The Adventures of Huckleberry Finn*, Levin and the peasant he works with in *Anna Karenina,* and the aristocrat Bezukhov and the peasant Karataev in *War and Peace*.[27] By reflecting on these stories, Berry imagines possibilities for interracial recognition and friendship that his own local tradition has largely forgotten. It is precisely this sort of conversation between the broader cultural landmarks and the particular needs of local places for which universities should prepare students.

Building the Treasuries of Memory to Foster Wisdom

This work of internalizing and applying the wisdom within our traditions requires that universities stock students' minds with the riches of the past and teach them to cultivate habits of careful attention that enable them to sift through these riches and use them well. St. Augustine, writing near the end of the fourth century, described memory as an expansive palace complex: "I come to the fields and vast palaces of memory, where are the treasuries of innumerable images of all kinds of objects brought in by sense-perception. Hidden there is whatever we think about, a process which may increase or diminish or in some way alter the deliverance of the senses."[28] Augustine's spatial metaphors imply the extent and the value of his memory. By walking around its vast palaces, he can "alter" or work with the things stored there, whether these things are previous thoughts or the experiences of his senses.[29]

In this way, the ability to think or reason depends on these "treasuries," on having a well-stocked "storehouse"; such treasuries enable one to be thoughtful or, literally, full of thoughts. As Augustine explains, "The process of learning is simply this: by thinking we, as it were, gather together ideas which the memory contains in a dispersed and disordered way, and by concentrating our attention we arrange them in order as if ready to hand, stored in the very memory which previously they lay hidden, scattered, and neglected."[30] Attention and thinking, then, derive the material on which they work from the treasuries of memory. A simple illustration of this is the "learning curve" required by all new subjects. Consider algebra: At first, everything is new, and it takes great effort on the student's part simply to orient herself to the terms and concepts of the new field—the use of x and y, the idea of variables, the patterns by which equations can be reconfigured. But as she stocks her memory with this information, she begins to learn her way around algebra's topography and is able to participate in further explorations of its order, playing with various equations and different ways of solving them. Memory is the place in which we order our knowledge and integrate new ideas. It is this process of stocking and ordering memory that is the path toward wisdom.

In today's cultural and technological context, however, the overwhelming amount of information we can access threatens this kind of rich, well-stocked memory. And as our memory treasuries become depleted, our ability to reason and learn deteriorates; in other words, memory's impoverishment threatens wisdom. If wisdom is the embodiment and prudent application of knowledge, what the Greeks termed *phronesis*, then the proliferation of knowledge does not necessarily increase wisdom and may in fact undermine it. When we access knowledge, use (or consume) it, and then forget it, that knowledge never becomes part of us, but when stories, events, information, and sensations are lodged in our memories, we participate in knowledge. Memory internalizes knowledge, allowing us to participate in its interconnections and gradually grow toward wisdom.

Berry addresses these concerns when he writes about the damage "the information economy and the communications industry" have done to knowledge and to the concept of information itself:

> Let us consider how we have degraded this word *information*. As you would expect, in-form-ation in its root meaning has to do with the idea of form: a pattern, structure, or ordering principle. To in-form is to form from within. *Information*, in this sense, refers to teaching and learning, to the formation of a person's mind or character. But we seem to be using the word now almost exclusively to refer to a random accumulation of facts, all having the one common characteristic of availability; they can, as we are too likely to say, be "accessed." . . . At whatever cost this information is made available to its potential users, it arrives unformed and unexperienced. There is nothing deader or of more questionable value than facts in isolation.[31]

If unformed knowledge is dead, then the remedy is to properly order it within placed memories. Embodied in a person's memory, knowledge can inform from within, leading toward a wise life.

The danger with accessing more and more of the knowledge we rely on is that it remains external to us. When we interact with it only in fragmented segments, we lose the ability to relate disparate kinds of knowledge within our memories. T. S. Eliot describes this loss at the beginning of "The Rock":

> The endless cycle of idea and action,
> Endless invention, endless experiment,
> Brings knowledge of motion, but not of stillness;
> Knowledge of speech, but not of silence;
> Knowledge of words, and ignorance of the Word.
> All our knowledge brings us nearer to our ignorance,
> All our ignorance brings us nearer to death,
> But nearness to death no nearer to GOD.
> Where is the Life we have lost in living?
> Where is the wisdom we have lost in knowledge?
> Where is the knowledge we have lost in information?[32]

Eliot's questions articulate the disorientation caused by the accumulation of information outside any remembered order.[33] As these words attest, wisdom is not something we can manufacture, access, or possess. Rather, wisdom exists only when it is embodied in persons with rich, well-ordered memories.

These threats to memory and wisdom, however dire they may seem, are not new; they extend at least as far back as the invention of writing.[34] One particular historical moment may shed some light on our current situation. In the twelfth century, when the modern university was born, newly available Muslim texts and an increased demand for education created a situation in Paris somewhat analogous to the present, when computers and the Internet make overwhelming amounts of information accessible and a knowledge-based economy creates more demand for higher education.[35] It was in the twelfth century that one of the founders of modern universities argued that the cultivation of memory was the appropriate response to this increase in available knowledge. Hugh of St. Victor identified memory as the faculty that would enable students to order information into wisdom.[36] As Ivan Illich explains, "By reviving ancient architectural memory training, Hugh hopes to prepare boys born around 1120 to read their way toward wisdom in an age in which the new collections could only too easily have scattered their brains and overwhelmed them. He offers them a radically intimate technique of ordering this huge heritage in a personally created, inner spime."[37] Illich borrows the concept of "spime," or "space-time," from Einstein, but as he notes, the spatial metaphor for memory is an ancient one, extending back to St. Augustine and even earlier.

Key here is Hugh's perception that, faced with a proliferation of information, students need an order embedded in their mental space to orient them toward wisdom. Information threatens wisdom; wisdom survives by building memory. This is true because memory requires mental space to relate and organize knowledge into a coherent form. In the case of Andy Catlett, his community's memory slowly arranged the tragic events caused by ambition, greed, loss, fear, drunkenness, and rage into a narrative that also included faithful love, forgiveness, and hope. A student must be able to hold a wide variety of knowledge in her head in order to sort through it, relate various pieces together, and patiently cultivate wisdom. This is why Jayber's professor told him, "You have been given questions to which you cannot be given answers. You will have to live them out—perhaps a little at a time."[38] Yet students can't live out their questions if they don't keep those questions in mind and patiently work on them. Memory is the place where we put first things first. It's the place where we judge new knowledge against our visions of health and goodness—cattle grazing on good grass or the taste of the first spring strawberries. It's the place where we live out our questions in pursuit of healthy places.

Much has been written about the effects of information technology on our brains. Nicholas Carr's books *The Shallows: What the Internet Is Doing to Our Brains* and *The Glass Cage: Automation and Us* have popularized this research, unpacking how our dependence on technology changes our memories, our attention, and even our sense of identity.[39] Two particular examples bring into focus the ways that impoverished memories can damage our ability to inhabit our places well.

First, personal identity, understood in terms of relational and familial networks, has been replaced by personal brand. Without memory, we have no identity at all, no way of knowing that the "I" who is writing this sentence is the same person who raked the lawn yesterday, the same person who graduated from a particular college, the same person who has obligations to parents and siblings. Memory is the faculty by which all these relations are narrated into a coherent whole, a coherent person. In other words, memory enables us to understand ourselves as relational persons; this power is at work throughout "Pray without Ceasing," as Andy is re-membered into his community as a child of his ancestors' forgiveness.

When we off-load our memories to electronic devices, however, we also off-load part of our identity, and in the process, identity is converted into an individual's "brand." Young people are encouraged to build their brands through Facebook, Twitter, and Linked-In, choosing how to make themselves appear attractive through these various mediums. An individual can then be rebranded quite easily by changing a few photos and posting different status updates. Rather than developing an identity through long-standing relationships, an individual's identity becomes more ephemeral and malleable. Such an identity is only shallowly rooted, and such a person is less able to commit to understanding and serving the complex health of a place and its community.

A second consequence of a hollowed-out memory is a loss of attention. Our students routinely tell us that they couldn't understand a particular essay or book, and the cause seems to be their inability to follow a sustained argument. In one conversation overheard in the hallway, a student confided to his classmate that he couldn't read more than a page and a half before getting distracted. Surely students have always struggled to internalize lengthy, difficult texts; nevertheless, this generation has developed a uniquely short attention span through their immersion in text messaging, Twitter, and constant access to amusement. Although diffuse forms of attention certainly have value, deep, focused attention is required to understand and care for the complex relationships that make up healthy places.

The etymology of the word *attention* implies this need to focus deeply. To "attend" to something means literally "to stretch toward" it. The Indo-European stem *ten-* or *tend-*, which we might translate as "to span, stretch, or extend," is the ancestor of our English words *tension, tune,* and *tend*—meaning both "to move toward something," a tendency, and "to care for something," to tend a garden, for example. So *attention* signifies a relation stretched between two different things. And embedded in the connotations of these related words is the suggestion that the quality of our care is related to the quality of our attention; we cannot *tend* to someone if we do not first *attend* to them. So memory is essential to caring for a place because it provides a space where we can organize diverse knowledge and tune it to the needs of a particular person or place. Wheeler Catlett's life is tuned to his remembered vision of cattle grazing on green grass, and he judges possible actions against this standard. Andy's life, as he remembers the forgiveness of his ancestors, becomes tuned to exercise this same love toward the other members of his community. An education for place, then, must consider ways to habituate students in the virtue of memory.

Forming Healthy Memories

We have observed an obsession in higher education with technologies that impoverish memory. The connectivity of the Internet lures universities with the promise of efficiency and profit—institutions can charge tuition to students around the world who want to "access" their information. Yet this process devalues memory by promising to make information easily accessible. The effect of this promise is to deform wisdom into discrete bits of knowledge: as we have seen, off-loading memories to the digital cloud decontextualizes knowledge, rendering it information rather than wisdom. Eliot's resonant questions—"Where is the wisdom we have lost in knowledge? / Where is the knowledge we have lost in information?"—become ever more pertinent. Rather than falling for the promises of educational technology, faculty and students should consider ways to resist practices that impoverish memory and instead cultivate habits that enrich memory.

Reducing Technological Reliance

One simple way to form healthier memories in college classrooms is to shut down laptops and smart phones and make classrooms places of focused attention. This suggestion will come as no surprise to readers of Berry's provocative essay "Why I Am Not Going to Buy a Computer."[40] Although we both use computers to write (which made collaborating on this book much easier), we've largely banished them from our classrooms and we've set limits on when and where we allow ourselves to use computers. Although some teachers may feel that banning computers in class is impractical or hinders learning, a recent study found that students who take notes on their computers remember less of the material than students who take notes by hand, even though computers enable students to record much more information.[41] Researchers surmise that those who take notes by hand have to process the content more thoroughly, deciding what is important enough to write down, while those who type notes transcribe more indiscriminately. The mental processing required to determine what is important enough to write down apparently embeds information more deeply into students' memories.

The use of computers in classrooms tends to erode memory and attention not only because of the way computers encourage students to take notes (indiscriminately) but also because of the way computers encourage students *not* to take notes. Clay Shirky, who teaches classes in technology and new media, explains that after many years of allowing computer use in his classroom, he now bans all technologies. According to Shirky, the problem is that computers have been engineered to be maximally distracting: "Computers are not inherent sources of distraction—they can in fact be powerful engines of focus—but latter-day versions have been designed to be [distracting], because attention is the substance which makes the whole consumer internet go."[42] Anyone who has sat behind someone using a computer in class knows how distracting that luminescent screen can be as the student navigates between his notes and Facebook, e-mail, Twitter, or whatever webpage seems most interesting at the moment. Such "multitasking" inhibits the kind of deep attention that true care requires, whether care for an academic subject, care for the people with whom we are talking, or care for the place in which we live.

Memorizing Poetry

Limiting our reliance on computers may slow the flow of memory from our minds to the disembodied cloud, but individuals can also take steps to replenish their memory treasuries. One simple practice we've adopted both in our classrooms and in our personal lives is memorizing poetry. In addition to the well-formed language and rich wisdom contained in many poems, metered verse shapes our minds on a deep level. Poetry works by setting language in time; it teaches us to count and measure the passing of time so that we participate more deliberately in it. As Alfred Corn explains in his excellent book on prosody, poetry is like music, in that it uses "duration as one of [its] expressive resources."[43] By dividing "passing time into measurable units," poetry removes time from an abstract and amorphous experience and teaches us to experience time in a more ordered way.[44] Such order aids in memorizing poems—there's a reason that poetry and music have long been relied on for their mnemonic function—and it may also habituate or tune our minds to experience time as rhythmic and ordered, thus cultivating the faculty of memory itself.[45]

In addition to their form, many poems contain riches that are worth adding to our memories. Berry supports requiring students to memorize poems, drawing on an Augustinian image of memory as a room when he states, "you've got to *furnish* their minds."[46] Stratford Caldecott speaks from a similar understanding of memory when he calls for "the revival of memory and the discipline of learning by heart (*enlarging* the heart in the process)" as a way of contributing to "the cultivation of imagination and a poetic or musical vision of the interconnectedness of all things."[47] Memorizing poetry, then, can help students furnish and enlarge their memories.

When I (Jack) was in high school, my English teacher, Mr. Lehman, required us to memorize and recite before the class the opening lines of the "General Prologue" to Chaucer's *Canterbury Tales*. At the time, I found the assignment challenging because the language seemed so foreign and the stakes so high. Mr. Lehman was an encourager, so he pushed us to commit the lines to memory and to care about the sound and rhythm of Chaucer's poetry. When I recited the lines—which I'm certain were marked by mispronunciation and error—I felt like I had accomplished a great thing. And I felt a connection to Chaucer's English that would later propel me into graduate studies in Middle and Old English. To this day, the opening lines of the "General Prologue" are etched in my memory. A further joy is that I can now look back (I can remember) and see that this seemingly simple act of memorization was a formative part of my life. And although I understood very little of what I memorized in high school, the poem's sound and rhythm were embedded in my memory. In time, I would grow into the knowledge and beauty of Chaucer's poetry as his rain-dappled world came to settle, vibrant in my mind. To this day, the first spring rain brings to mind these lines.

Studying Disciplinary History

Throughout this book, we've followed Berry's example in turning to the history of language for insight and guidance. Berry often draws on etymological connections—such as the links between *ecology*, *economy*, and *home* or those that unite *health*, *whole*, and *holy*—to discern an order in the communal memory palace that is the English language. While philology is no longer fashionable in academic circles, studying the history of words sheds light on the deep links between seemingly disparate concepts. Philology enables us, then, to participate in our cultural memory and its wisdom.

While philology may seem most appropriate to an English classroom—and we often employ etymologies in our teaching—the kind of historical sensibility it represents can inform all disciplines. Too often the sciences and even some social sciences are taught as established bodies of knowledge, delivered whole and infallible from the sanctified halls of "science." "Research has shown" may be one of the most insidious phrases in contemporary parlance. Historian John Lukacs, in his reflective book *Last Rites*, disclaims objective knowledge and the existence of "facts" themselves: "There is only one kind of knowledge, human knowledge, with the inevitability of its participation, with the inevitable relationship of the knower to the known, of what and how and why and when man knows and wishes to know."[48] Lukacs's claim that all knowledge is participatory is not a denial of objective reality but a recognition that knowing is a human act and that "facts" cannot exist apart from the person and culture in which they are known.[49]

In general, this historical consciousness is more prevalent in the humanities than the sciences. Art professors are likely to discuss the scientific, philosophic, and literary developments that influenced Michelangelo's new portrayal of the human form, but biology professors may be less likely to situate scientific knowledge within its cultural and historical contexts. They may not point out, for instance, that our understanding of DNA as a cellular code is filtered through our culture's immersion in computer code. Yet the available cultural metaphors powerfully shape the kinds of theories and insights scientists develop.[50] For instance, Darwin's theory of evolution depends as much on the metaphors made available by capitalist, industrial nineteenth-century England—individualism, competition, scarcity—as it does on observation of the natural world.[51] This is not to say that these scientific theories are not valuable and true, but students should learn that such theories cannot be abstracted from their personal and cultural histories.

How can this historical memory be incorporated into science classes? When I (Jeff) was a student, my calculus teacher regularly brought in one-page biographies of mathematicians who had discovered theorems foundational to the topics we were studying. This served to humanize and historicize the principles we were learning; it reminded us that even a discipline as seemingly objective as math isn't handed down to us on some golden platter from the sky. Rather, the math we use is a product of human debates and disagreements; it's a system that developed over time as humans tried to find abstract ways to explain the orderly relations they observed in the world. If math and science teachers place their subjects within this historical context, students will be more likely to see these disciplines as part of the broader human conversation, and they will learn to trace the connections between minds, bodies, histories, communities, and places. In other words, by learning how knowledge depends on its place within a historical human community, students may learn to make their own knowledge responsible to the tradition and place on which they depend.

Fostering Institutional Memory

University communities are strange beasts. On the one hand, they have high turnover: students leave after four or five years (hopefully), and administrators seem to move on just as often. On the other hand, although some faculty members transfer to bigger schools with reduced teaching loads, most stay at the same institution for decades, and many staff members have similarly long commitments. This means that within universities there are always tensions between new members with new ideas and old members with longer institutional memories. Navigating this tension by fostering a healthy sense of the institution's history—one that is faithful to the past without being stuck in it—can teach students how to practice a communal memory.

Our own school, Spring Arbor University, serves as an interesting case study, particularly with regard to its agrarian past. Our institution touts certain portions of its heritage—for instance, that it was founded in 1873—yet many fascinating and instructive aspects of its history tend to be overlooked. When we were doing the legwork to start a garden on campus, one of the librarians unearthed old records in the archives about a school farm. At one time, Spring Arbor University housed a seminary, and back in the early part of the twentieth century (and up until the postwar education boom), the school had a farm, including cows and a large garden, across the street from today's main campus. Students worked there, and the produce went to the dining hall to help keep board affordable. In fact, the farm was instrumental in the school's survival during the Great Depression. Today, a McDonald's sits on this site.

A page from the 1926 yearbook includes a picture titled "Seminary Farm Scene" that captures several young men standing alongside cows in a snow-swept field. The farm is referred to as "Our School Auxiliary," and there is a letter from the farm manager seeking support from patrons in Michigan, Ohio, and Indiana.[52] In a 1927 yearbook article, the author describes how the farm has been improved over the previous five-year period: farm buildings were rearranged and remodeled to meet their particular needs, precautions were taken to prepare for the rigorous Michigan winters, and hog houses were carefully placed so that they could be easily maintained. The author states, "In our vision we make our way across the farm and see a field ready for the third cutting of a splendid crop of alfalfa, the wheat and oat fields of the summer are covered with a green coating of sweet clover, the corn is standing with drooping ears, a two acre tract of artificially drained muck land which formerly grew only swamp grass is partially covered with long rows of excellent celery, the remainder with peppermint."[53]

Such a vision for the school farm helped shape the identity of this place of learning, yet few of the university's current employees have any knowledge of this important past. Those involved in the farm, before it was eventually sold to pay bills, believed such work offered a vision of hope and sustainability—perhaps borne out of necessity, but cultivated in love: "This may be a vision but with close management and careful study of the needs it is a possibility." Thus in Spring Arbor, imagination was tied to possibility through farm labor.

We hope for a revival of this agrarian work on our campus in the future, but we know that such a restoration must begin with remembering. Remembering and attending to our past form the foundation for intimacy, for belonging. Thus, memory provides the grounds for a legitimate hope. If we want to be members of our places, their history must become part of us; by remembering that students were once responsible for producing their own food here, we can be thankful for their contributions to this place, and we can imagine how to renew their good work.

Berry imagines this practice of memory as a healing virtue because it enables us to fit the pieces of the past—our past—together in ways that bring wholeness. In his poem "A Vision," he even figures memory as a sacrament, a means of grace, that preserves the abundant health of a place. The vision of health the poet hopes for depends on an active, communal memory that restores what "greed and ignorance" destroyed.

> If we will have the wisdom to survive,
> to stand like slow-growing trees
> on a ruined place, renewing, enriching it,
> if we will make our seasons welcome here,
> asking not too much of earth or heaven,
> then a long time after we are dead
> the lives our lives prepare will live
> there, their houses strongly placed
> upon the valley sides, fields and gardens
> rich in the windows. The river will run
> clear, as we will never know it,
> and over it, birdsong like a canopy.
> On the levels of the hills will be
> green meadows, stock bells in noon shade.
> On the steeps where greed and ignorance cut down
> the old forest, an old forest will stand,
> its rich leaf-fall drifting on its roots.
> The veins of forgotten springs will have opened.
> Families will be singing in the fields.

In their voices they will hear a music
risen out of the ground. They will take
nothing from the ground they will not return,
whatever the grief at parting. Memory,
native to this valley, will spread over it
like a grove, and memory will grow
into legend, legend into song, song
into sacrament. The abundance of this place,
the songs of its people and its birds,
will be health and wisdom and indwelling
light. This is no paradisal dream.
Its hardship is its possibility.[54]

5

Hierarchy

Practicing Gratitude and Respecting Limits

The poet's vision of a community sustaining abundant life in its place through the sacrament of memory also functions as an expression of gratitude for the beauty and richness of this life. It is in this way that memory should lead to gratitude, to recognizing our dependence on the past, on our place, on our community. In fact, as much as thought depends on memory, it also depends on thanksgiving. Drawing on the meaning of the Greek word *logos*, Martin Heidegger links memory and thought as a prelude to his famous identification of thinking and thanking.[1] As one scholar explains, the "Greek *logos*, meaning 'word' or 'thought,' is derived from the Greek verb *legein*, to gather up. Thinking is a matter of collecting, pulling together, assembling, and gathering, and this activity is necessarily an act of memory."[2] Understanding thought as a collecting or remembering should lead us to be grateful for the sources from which we collect. Roger Lundin expands on this in the context of language: "Through our participation in communities of language, we *receive* our very ability to comprehend anything at all. In this most fundamental sense, 'Denken *ist* Danken,' 'thinking *is* thanking,' for without the gift of language—and without the traditions of practice, interpretation, and belief that are embedded in language—the isolated self would be at a loss as to how to comprehend, let alone respond to, its world."[3]

Yet rather than understanding thought as a form of thanksgiving for the gifts of our tradition and community, universities tend to practice thought as a form of conquest and control. Recovering a proper sense of our human dependence might enable us to think gratefully. Such gratitude imposes certain limits on one's thinking and actions: one shouldn't think or act in a way that will damage the sources of life. We explore the connection between gratitude and limits—both of which derive from hierarchy—in this chapter as we seek to discover how practicing the virtue of gratitude can make us more responsible members of our places.

How Andy Catlett Learned Limits

In his short story "Andy Catlett: An Early Education," Berry provides a humorous portrayal of the need to practice proper gratitude by limiting our intellectual pursuits and making them appropriate to our place. Andy, looking back on his childhood, recalls his youthful "infatuation" with various scientific endeavors. First it was chemistry, but when he received his own chemistry set for Christmas, he soon tired of it. Then he investigated "afterimages": "I learned that I could stare at [a] lightbulb for a while, and then, by blinking, send a flock of brightly colored horseshoes flying all over the room." When that line of investigation was cut short by his teacher, he turned to candle making. Andy waited until he was home alone one day and then heated up a pot filled with odds and ends of candles: "How what happened next happened I can't say, for I soon found that I didn't have time just to stand around watching a pot, but it did happen that a fairly spectacular tall flame was standing on top of the stove. Pretty quickly it burnt up all my wax and went out, and I soon got the kitchen back to rights and no harm done."[4]

Andy's good luck couldn't last, however. His mother knew this—although Andy did not—and she attempted to forestall disaster by employing a switch to warn him whenever his behavior went beyond the limits of prudence. This had little effect: "her punishments wrought no significant change in my behavior. Her influence over me at that time did not extend many feet beyond the end of her lilac switch, whereas my quest for knowledge extended limitlessly round about."[5] Andy carried this insatiable curiosity with him to school, but rather than applying it diligently to his books, he directed it toward discovering what he could get away with: "What I wanted to learn was the precise line between what my teachers would put up with and what they would not put up with. And to draw a line of this sort required much experimentation." He describes his quest for knowledge in terms of scientific and geographic conquest: "I probed the contours of [my teacher's] patience and sounded its estuaries like an early navigator mapping the New World."[6] Andy's hubristic desire for indiscriminate knowledge leads inexorably to his downfall.

Andy's limitless quest for "truth" finally lands him in real trouble when he attempts "the scientific debunking" of *The Night before Christmas*. One evening, Andy finds himself contemplating an open fireplace and the seemingly impossible physics of Santa Claus's route to the Christmas tree:

> As a critic, from the beginning I held the text in great honor, and the text did not say that he came down the chimney, left the toys for the children, and let himself out by the door. The text said in plain English: "up the chimney he rose."
>
> In those days I was a true pure scientist. If the subject of my inquiry had been the nature of gravity itself, I would not have minded whether the falling body had been an apple or a bomb, or upon what or whom it might have fallen. I was hard driven in my quest for truth.[7]

As Andy indicates, his methods are indiscriminate and unconcerned with possible consequences, such as who might be beneath the bomb he drops to inquire into gravity. Alone in the house, "and having therefore full intellectual freedom" to conduct his experiment, Andy climbs inside the fireplace and attempts to rise up the chimney. Disappointed at his failure, and at having debunked Santa's mode of travel, Andy wiggles back into the room: "And that, I think, must have been the occasion upon which I discovered soot. Coal soot is exceedingly black and exceedingly light. I was covered with it, which I only found out by using one of the curtains to wipe what felt like a cobweb out of my eyes. I was a living pencil, for on everything I touched I left a mark."[8]

Helplessly watching as the unforeseen ramifications of his experiment make their mark on his surroundings, Andy finally realizes that perhaps his former ignorance was preferable to his current situation:

> The Christmas quandary I had started with . . . began to look like a pleasant sort of ignorance. I would gladly have gone back to it, except that it had now evolved into an insistently present problem for which there was no present solution. In fact, every attempt I made at a solution reliably worsened the problem. Even when I merely rubbed my head the better to study the situation, I loosened more soot. I saw a flake of soot levitate from the top of my head and land on a bedspread, white to match the curtains. When I took a swipe at it to knock it to the floor, I made a broad dark streak. It began to seem to me that I needed to be going.[9]

But as he turns to leave, Andy sees his mother standing, shocked, in the doorway. Darting around her, Andy manages to climb out the hallway window in a desperate attempt to escape the imminent consequences of his actions. To his surprise, his mother quickly shuts and locks the window, stranding him on the roof. Trapped, Andy concludes that he's safe from his mother's wrath as long as he remains on the roof, but as the minutes go by, he realizes he'll get hungry if he doesn't climb down eventually. Contemplating running away from home, Andy decides to climb down the apple tree and make his escape. As he steps onto the tree's upper limbs, however, he makes an unpleasant discovery: "[My mother] was sitting on the ground with her back against one of the tree's three trunks. She looked comfortable. A lengthy switch was lying across her lap beneath her folded hands."[10]

There is something humorous about this image of a mother patiently waiting out her young son's predicament. As an old man remembering this incident, Andy can appreciate its humor: "I am many years older now than she was then, and I can easily imagine how knowingly she was amused. But I could imagine then, for I *saw*, how perfectly she was determined."[11] His vision of his mother's firmness impressed on him a new respect for limits, for the consequences of his inconsiderate and unfettered pursuit of knowledge:

> She looked strange. . . . It took a long time for my education to catch up with the vision of her I had then, for though she was a Christian woman she was sitting down there looking positively Buddhist. She was sitting perfectly still. She was not going to move in so much as I could imagine of the future. She was not looking left or right, let alone up into the tree where I was. But I knew she knew where I was. I felt illuminated by omniscience. She was at peace down there. She was using up all the peace there was. There was none at all up in the apple tree where I was.[12]

Andy contemplates jumping off the roof, but he finally submits to his mother's patience and slides down the tree: "I felt as if I were presenting myself to a bolt of lightning. It was something like that: swift, illuminating, and soon over."[13]

Because of Andy's inconsiderate curiosity, he can't be bothered to contemplate the consequences of his investigations. He isn't aware that he's doing anything wrong, but that's the problem; he thinks and explores with thoughtless ingratitude, heedlessly causing problems for his teachers and his parents. While this may be excusable in a fourth-grader, it causes grave problems when scientists and other intellectuals never learn to conduct their research with humility and a respect for limits that are proper to our human condition. As Andy discovers when he spreads soot throughout the clean room, there can be "a pleasant sort of ignorance." Unfortunately, most modern experimenters aren't subjected to "swift, illuminating" consequences for their reckless choices. And yet experiments that result in atomic bombs, pesticides, and genetically modified seeds have drastic consequences for all of us. As Berry claims, "Past a certain scale, as C. S. Lewis wrote, the person who makes a technological choice does not choose for himself alone, but for others; past a certain scale, he chooses for all others."[14] Thus Berry argues that we should pursue knowledge within limits and apply it within healthy forms. The proper response to our inevitable human ignorance is to pursue learning with humility and gratitude.

Universities can become places where students cultivate an appropriate sense of their place in the world. Academics enculturated in a publish-or-perish environment tend to form similarly driven, ambitious students who aspire to be heroic global leaders solving big problems. But not everyone can—or should—be a leader, so universities should also honor humble vocations that help steward the health of local places. Such stewardship can be an act of gratitude for the good gift of life. Yet this grateful stewardship runs counter to the denial of limits that is embedded in much of our contemporary culture, which believes in scientific progress, in unending technological improvement, in boundless economic growth, and in enlarging individual political rights. The arrogance and ingratitude that cause these various denials of limits are exacerbated by the specialized, fragmented organization of knowledge in higher education. Such isolation allows academics to be unmindful of and ungrateful for their places, the sources of their life and health. And ultimately it is this lack of thought and thanks that permits the research conducted in universities to result in unintended, devastating consequences.

At the conclusion of this chapter we suggest some ways that universities can foster proper gratitude and an acceptance of our limited, embedded place in creation. These include observing the Sabbath, acknowledging our ignorance, and maintaining a local, contextual scope in learning. Such habits can help us recover a grateful intelligence and a responsible language that enable faculty and students alike to imagine the consequences of their research and learning. When we recognize ourselves as finite and limited beings, we will finally be able to think gratefully. And then, perhaps, our stories can become less like Andy's discovery of consequences and more like Hannah Coulter's "giving of thanks."

Thinking with Gratitude

When writing about gratitude and limits, Berry repeatedly turns to the story of *King Lear*. Shakespeare's play has become, as Berry puts it in *Life Is a Miracle,* one of the "principle landmarks" by which he orients his thinking. "The whole play," he writes, "is about kindness, both in the usual sense, and in the sense of truth-to-kind, . . . or knowing the limits of our specifically *human* nature."[15] To illustrate his point, Berry focuses on the subplot involving the Earl of Gloucester. Gloucester, "like Lear, is guilty of hubris or presumption, of treating life as knowable, predictable, and within his control." He has unjustly exiled his loyal son, Edgar, and in an ironic mirroring, Gloucester is blinded in punishment for his loyalty to King Lear. In this state of blindness, Gloucester despairs of life and seeks to kill himself. He asks a beggar, who, unbeknownst to him, is his disguised son Edgar, to lead him to a cliff so that he might jump off it. Edgar agrees, telling Gloucester he is on the brink of a precipice when in fact he is still on level ground. Gloucester falls forward, and Edgar then pretends that he has watched him fall and they are now at the bottom of the cliff. Edgar speaks to Gloucester, marveling at his miraculous survival in an attempt to teach his father to properly value life:

> Hadst thou been aught but gossamer, feathers, air,
> So many fathom down precipitating,
> Thou'dst shiver'd like an egg: but thou dost breathe;
> Hast heavy substance, bleed'st not, speak'st, art sound.
> Ten masts at each make not the altitude
> Which thou hast perpendicularly fell.
> Thy life's a miracle. Speak yet again.[16]

As Berry explains, this final line "calls Gloucester back—out of hubris, and the damage and despair that invariably follow—into the properly subordinated human life of grief and joy, where change and redemption are possible."[17] And Gloucester repents of having given up on life: "I do remember now. Henceforth I'll bear / Affliction till it do cry out itself / 'Enough,

enough, and die.'"[18] Remembering that his life is a miraculous gift teaches Gloucester to steward it rather than cast it away.

Berry reads this story in the context of "the welter of innovation and speculation" that is contemporary bioengineering. "Suicide is not the only way to give up on life," he observes, and many of our attempts to control and dictate life arise from a dissatisfaction with its inherent limitations, most notably death. As Berry goes on to elaborate, "we can give up on life also by presuming to 'understand' it—that is by reducing it to the *terms* of our understanding and by treating it as predictable or mechanical.... [T]o reduce life to the scope of our understanding (whatever 'model' we use) is inevitably to enslave it, make property of it, and put it up for sale."[19] The tragic irony is that in attempting to make life controllable, predictable, and profitable, we destroy it.[20]

The alternative to such reductive thinking—and its mechanistic language—is to foster a grateful mode of thought and language. In fact, as we mentioned at the beginning of this chapter, thinking itself can be a way of practicing gratitude and stewarding life. This is what Heidegger means when he claims that "thinking is thanking": "At its most penetrating, the exercise of thought is one of grateful acquiescence in Being. Inevitably, jubilantly, such acquiescence is a giving of thanks for that which has been placed in our custody, for the light [of Being] in the clearing."[21] In other words, careful thought is the right use of the gift of life. This is the gratitude Berry practices in his poem "Prayer after Eating," in which he prays to be worthy of the food that illuminates his thought; right thinking is one way of stewarding the good gift of food. Such insight leads to Heidegger's meditative questions: "The supreme thanks, then, would be thinking? And the profoundest thanklessness, thoughtlessness? Real thanks, then, never consists in that we ourselves come bearing gifts, and merely repay gift with gift. Pure thanks is rather that we simply think—think what is really and solely given, what is there to be thought."[22] Heidegger sketches a sort of phenomenological account of stewarding the gift of life by careful thought: "As we give thought to what is most thought-provoking, we give thanks."[23]

Heidegger's reflections here stem from an ontological hierarchy: human "being-in-the-world" (*Dasein*) derives from Being (*Sein*) itself. Berry's insistence on proper gratitude likewise flows from an ontological hierarchy, one he inherits from medieval thinkers in the form of the "Chain of Being" and one that he transposes into an ecological key. The Chain of Being, as Berry points out, is first of all a theological or ontological description, one that defines the "human place in Creation ... as a moral circumstance."[24] In "Poetry and Place," Berry develops a defense of hierarchy against nineteenth-century Romantic poets, but his argument applies equally to boomers who assert the absolute freedom of the individual self and reject any imposition of limits. Berry acknowledges that hierarchy can be unjust and oppressive but insists that retaining some hierarchy is essential for responsible, caring action:

> For when hierarchy is destroyed, not just in false or unjust *instances*, but *in principle*, then all the kinds of things, and therefore all things, are by definition displaced. It is the hierarchical principle of the Chain of Being that makes it all-inclusive; Creation is not so bountiful and various as it is because life is copious, but because it is orderly, full of places where an abounding diversity of creatures can be at home.... If all the kinds were equal, all places would be in dispute, to be contended for. The result would be a free-for-all, which in turn could only result either in a restoration of hierarchy or in total annihilation, for the most powerful kind would either destroy *all* the less powerful, and so eventually destroy itself, or it would respect their places in an order which both keeps them alive and implies their right to live.[25]

In other words, by indiscriminately casting off the restrictions of hierarchy, Romantics (and boomers in general) unleash a chaos in which might makes right.

Such libertine notions of "freedom" continue to characterize the kind of thinking practiced at most universities; academic specialization and market pressures to commodify knowledge lead to displaced, abstracted thought. Berry's point is that such displaced thinking—heedless, like Andy's curiosity, of its possible consequences—damages the other beings with whom we share life:

> Implicit in the Chain of Being is the idea that creatures are protected in their various kinds, not by equality, but by difference; and that if humans are responsibly observant of the differences between themselves and the angels above them and the animals below, they will act with respect, restraint, and benevolence toward the subordinate creatures; this is their duty toward the subordinate

creatures, and it is part of, inseparable from, their duty to the higher creatures and to God.... When humans abdicate their proper place, either by pride or self-debasement, they blaspheme God and brutalize nature.[26]

Our thought cannot be free of our condition and our place, and attempts to assert such freedom inevitably damage both ourselves and our places. To put this in the context of Berry's discussion of *King Lear*, thought abstracted from our hierarchical place is thought that has given up on life.

We recognize that some modern readers may be uncomfortable with the medieval, Christian sources of the Chain of Being, but Berry also links his treatment of the human place in creation to ecological insights. As scientists continue to warn us, irresponsible human actions have drastic consequences for the entire planet; the obligations enjoined by the Chain of Being corroborate the scientific observations of ecologists who articulate our interconnectedness with the rest of life. Norman Wirzba draws on these insights when he links the heedless use of goods with ingratitude toward the natural processes that sustain us: "Our temptation is to think that we live through our own effort and that the goods we enjoy are ours because we have earned and deserve them. A moment's reflection can quickly dispel that illusion, as everywhere we look we can see the generosity of others: earthworms aerating and rebuilding soil, plants turning sunlight into energy, family providing for us since birth, teachers looking out for our children."[27] Elsewhere, Wirzba links gratitude and the human condition even more explicitly: "When we forget these gifts, or when we fail to see them *as gifts* and mistake them to be ours by right or by our own effort, we falsify who we are"—or, as Berry might say, *where* we are.[28] So whether one approaches the question of the human place in nature from a theological standpoint or an ecological one, the conclusion is the same: life is not a possession that can be earned; rather, it is a gift we have been given. Humans play a unique role in the ecosystem, and we ought to recognize the responsibility we've been given by exercising our power within proper limits.

Before continuing, we should pause to acknowledge that gratitude, like place, can be stifling. Recognizing life as a gift can appear to burden us with an immense, unpayable debt for existence.[29] This is why Peter Leithart ultimately criticizes Heidegger's account of thought for remaining too bound to tradition and lacking the freedom to critique the past. It is no accident, Leithart suggests, that Heidegger was unable to resist Nazi ideology: "Heidegger's way of thinking about thanking is deeply conservative, even reactionary. Thought is a moment of response to Being's Advent, and this easily becomes acquiescence in whatever is, whatever happens to appear.... There is little or no room for a moment of refusal, no space for critical ingratitude, whether inspired by the Christian gospel or Enlightenment reason. It is dispiriting, but it seems no accident that the greatest modern philosopher of gratitude is also the philosopher of fascism."[30] As an alternative, Leithart praises Christianity, and the Enlightenment development of Christianity, for breaking Western culture free from the closed circle of Pagan gratitude in which a gift obligated the recipient to return the favor: "Christianity displayed 'ingratitude' toward traditions, religions, benefactors, but it was an 'ingratitude' enclosed in comprehensive gratitude toward an infinite God who was the source of all good gifts but who also relativized all those gifts by the self-gift of his Son."[31]

Leithart is right that gratitude should be understood in an open rather than a closed sense. Yet as is evident from the passage quoted above, even Heidegger—despite his other philosophical baggage—conceives gratitude not as a narrow gift exchange but as stewardship of the gifts we've received: "Real thanks, then, never consists in that we ourselves come bearing gifts, and merely repay gift with gift. Pure thanks is rather that we simply think—think what is really and solely given, what is there to be thought."[32] In Leithart's account, this understanding of gratitude originates, at least in Western culture, with Jesus. Prior to Christianity, Roman culture practiced reciprocal gift giving; the proper response to a gift was for the recipient to give back another gift. This leads to political patronage and inbred social communities. But Jesus, and Paul after him, defined "gratitude as *right use* of the gift rather than gratitude as *return*."[33] This is the understanding of gratitude—gratitude as stewardship or usufruct—that Berry develops in essays such as "The Gift of Good Land," "Christianity and the Survival of Creation," and "God and Country." He follows this Christian tradition in directing ultimate gratitude toward the creator for the gift of life, understood both as the particular gift of our own individual lives and as the life we share with all creation.[34]

So the first response to those who think that gratitude unduly constricts or narrows our ability to think and act is to assert that gratitude includes a freedom to correct and improve the gifts of our inheritance. Neither we nor Berry advocate passive acceptance of whatever we are given.

There are certainly times when people ought to reject the ways their places or communities have warped and damaged the gift of life. We *shouldn't* be grateful for abusive places, and in fact proper gratitude for the gift of life entails correcting or rejecting such abuses. The posture of gratitude, like Berry's stance toward tradition, maintains the ability to judge and correct; it is not a passive reception of whatever is.[35] Grateful thinkers can still be inventive and creative, but they seek to create in ways that do not damage the good gifts they have inherited. Indeed, the etymology of *invent* suggests precisely this posture: to *invent* means "to come upon" or "to find." In other words, invention is not *ex nihilo* discovery; it involves working with what has been given.

Our second response to such critiques of gratitude is that our current cultural context neglects proper gratitude by its emphasis on libertine freedom and individual autonomy. Americans like to think of themselves as self-made, beholden to no one, and fully deserving of whatever rewards and benefits they can accrue. Much American innovation seems to be motivated by a desire for individual wealth and acclaim rather than to foster and honor the gift of life. In such a culture, universities ought to remind students to think and act with gratitude for the gift of life. So if we lived in a culture that practiced more constricting, reciprocal forms of gratitude, it would be appropriate to emphasize the need to question this closed circle and to practice critical, personal discernment.

Wilfred McClay makes a similar point about our cultural situation when he addresses concerns people may have about the hierarchical dimensions of place: "'Place' may . . . point toward notions of social hierarchy that Americans generally find anathema. Many of us can still remember when the idea of 'knowing your place' was used to promote racial segregation and the social and legal subordination of women." As McClay points out, however, our most pressing societal problems are not too-rigid hierarchies but a chaotic lack of any order whatsoever: "technological wizardry and individual empowerment have unsettled all facets of life, and given rise to profound feelings of disquiet and insecurity in many Americans."[36] Likewise, Berry links our cultural insistence on personal freedom with the damaging irresponsibility of corporations and our industrial economy: "[The] slang of personal 'liberation' . . . has done little for real freedom (which requires perception of authentic differences and distinctions), but has set many free from their rightful obligations and responsibilities—to, for example, their spouses and their children. . . . But there is too close a kinship between the personal freedom from reverence, fidelity, neighborliness, and stewardship and the corporate freedom to pollute and exterminate. When, if ever, the accounting is properly done, many of our present 'liberties' and 'necessities' will be seen to owe too much to the exploitation of 'cheap' labor, raw materials, energy, and food."[37]

It is in this cultural context that we call for universities to recover a sense of hierarchy and gratitude, not to the exclusion of liberty and discernment but as a corrective to the unfettered pursuit of individual power. The result of grateful thinking, then, would be a more careful, responsible stewardship of the gift of life, both our individual lives and the ecological communities in which we subsist.

Boomer Arts versus Grateful Stewardship

Berry's call to grateful stewardship doesn't play well in a culture that exalts individual success and heroic achievement. In our boomer culture, it "is no surprise that the predominant arts and sciences of the modern era have been boomer arts and boomer sciences."[38] What we suggest is that universities should consider how to educate students in sticker arts and sticker sciences, ones that serve the health of their places. At the root of many of our educational culture's values are a lack of gratitude and a rejection of the limits that such gratitude would entail. These values are expressions of our "inordinate desire to be superior . . . to our condition," and they encourage universities to celebrate prestigious, heroic professions rather than the quiet, humble work that serves the health of our places.[39]

It is now de rigueur to point out the bankruptcy of higher education's publish-or-perish culture—what Berry terms "academic Darwinism"[40]—but Berry's real insight is his ability to see how this academic culture of individual achievement has infected students. When professors tell their students the wrong stories, stories of heroic success rather than quotidian faithfulness, it reinforces the boomer mentality of the broader culture. Students are encouraged to seek high-status professions rather than to consider how they might properly steward the gift of life in their local places:

> To place so exclusive an emphasis on "high achievement" is to lie to one's students. . . . The goal of education-as-job-training, which is now the dominant pedagogical idea, is a high professional salary. Young people are being told, "You can be anything you want to be."

Every student is given to understand that he or she is being prepared for "leadership." All of this is a lie. Original discovery is *not* everything. You don't, for instance, have to be an original discoverer in order to be a good science teacher. A high professional salary is *not* everything. You *can't* be everything you want to be; nobody can. Everybody *can't* be a leader; not everybody even wants to be. And these lies are not innocent. They lead to disappointment. They lead good young people to think that if they have an ordinary job, if they work with their hands, if they are farmers or housewives or mechanics or carpenters, they are no good.[41]

This pressure to succeed in a prestigious career, along with our unwillingness to acknowledge the limited knowledge and experience of eighteen-year-old freshmen, impoverishes their very identities. In some ways, colleges tell students that they *are* their careers. For instance, when we ask students what they want to do with their lives, they rarely say they want to be loving spouses and parents who enjoy tending their small gardens. Instead, they tell us what they want to do for a living: doctor, pastor, accountant, chemist. The fact that they've been trained to describe their specialized careers as a "living" ought to give us pause.[42] Are our jobs the definition of our lives, our existence?

In our own experience, the Protestant Christian tradition encourages young people to think of their life's work as a vocation, or a calling from God. Students at our school are deeply shaped by both the boomer ethic and a sense of divine calling, and the combination has some interesting effects. Students care very much about the work they'll do after college, but they also struggle to sense whether God has indeed called them to some particular work. What happens, then, is that many young Christians believe that the most Christian vocation is a full-time ministry. To help students parse how boomerism has invaded even Christian discussions of vocation, I (Jack) ask them if God ever calls someone to be a plumber. This simple question gets at the flaw of boomer logic—if everyone is a leader, then who does the most basic and good work necessary for any society to flourish?

When universities overhype the leadership potential of their students, they contribute to the warping of vocation in a characteristically boomer way. And students internalize these messages. As David Brooks observes in a recent address, young people today "have tremendous faith in themselves." While American students rank twenty-fifth in the world in math scores, Brooks notes that they rank their own mathematical abilities very highly; Americans have the dubious distinction of being "number-one in the world at thinking we are really good at math." Ours "is an achievement culture," Brooks concludes, one that values "résumé virtues" rather than "eulogy virtues." These are the values of a boomer culture, one that believes firmly in the priority of individual "success."[43]

Such values are naïve, causing students great disappointment when they discover they are not very good at math. Even more dangerous, however, is that these values lead to heedless actions that damage our communities. In opposition to this self-centered careerism promulgated by universities, Berry combines the Judeo-Christian understanding of stewardship with the Buddhist notion of "right livelihood" to encourage the humble, necessary work that tends the health of our places. A university shaped by Berry's agrarian vision would educate students to carry out this work of humble stewardship rather than steer students toward prestigious careers of heroic progress and conquest.

Berry finds guidance for his understanding of right livelihood in the Old Testament account of God's gift of the Promised Land to Israel. In his essay "The Gift of Good Land," Berry argues that this land was a "gift given upon certain rigorous conditions." And remembering this ontological reality—that the land and the life dependent on it are not something humans can own but are divine gifts—warns us against hubris, "which is the great ecological sin." Recognizing the land as a gift reminds us that "people are not gods. They must not act like gods or assume godly authority. . . . We must not use the world as though we created it ourselves."[44] This is the hierarchical principle that guides Berry's call for grateful thinking and working. When humans assume godly authority, they step out of their proper place in the Chain of Being and can cause great damage to the fabric of life.

Rather than heedlessly and arrogantly pursuing knowledge without limits, we should cultivate gratitude for the opportunity we've been given to live, to be here, to participate in this wondrous place. How do we "prove worthy" of this great gift, Berry asks? We must be "faithful, grateful, and humble." We must be "neighborly," and we must "practice good husbandry." These characteristics of "right livelihood" delineate an "elaborate understanding of charity," one that recognizes I cannot love my neighbor if I do not also love "the great inheritance on which his life depends."[45] Berry outlines this elaborate understanding of charity in the form of a list that sounds much like a potential college curriculum:

> Real charity calls for the study of agriculture, soil husbandry, engineering, architecture, mining, manufacturing, transportation,

the making of monuments and pictures, songs and stories. It calls not just for skills but for the study and criticism of skills, because in all of them a choice must be made: they can be used either charitably or uncharitably.

How can you love your neighbor if you don't know how to build or mend a fence, how to keep your filth out of his water supply or your poison out of his air; or if you do not produce anything and so have nothing to offer, or do not take care of yourself and so become a burden?[46]

These are the sticker arts, the arts of right livelihood that universities concerned with educating placed students would include in their curricula.

One of the reasons such humble, charitable arts are neglected is that the Judeo-Christian literary tradition overemphasizes heroic arts, thus devaluing the more mundane vocations that are just as important. As Berry wryly observes, "It may, in some ways, be easier to be Samson than to be a good husband or wife day after day for fifty years." A focus on the heroic obscures two crucial issues: "the issue of life-long devotion and perseverance in unheroic tasks, and the issue of good workmanship or 'right livelihood.'" The Industrial Revolution exploited this obsession with heroism and figured the industrialist as a hero: "For the principle of good work it substituted a secularized version of the heroic tradition: the ambition to be a 'pioneer' of science or technology, to make a 'breakthrough' that will 'save the world' from some 'crisis' (which now is usually the result of some previous 'breakthrough')."[47] And this narrative that upholds pioneering, heroic breakthroughs continues to shape our cultural perception of prestigious professions.

Elsewhere, Berry acknowledges that some "breakthroughs" can be beneficial; some pioneers do serve their places. What is needed to make this normative, however, is a more critical consideration of the consequences of breakthroughs. An obsessive focus on a heroic discovery can lead a researcher to overlook its repercussions. Berry turns our attention to the work of judgment, calling on us to consider the value of a discovery from the perspective of those affected by it: "Intelligence minimally requires us to consider the possibility that we might well have done without some discoveries, and that there might be two opinions from different perspectives about any given discovery—for example, the opinion of Cortés and that of Montezuma. Perhaps intelligence requires us to consider even that some unexplored territory had better be treated as forbidden territory."[48] Andy realized this double-edged nature of discovery as he stood in his mother's white room "discovering" that soot can't be brushed away. Yet the heroic view repeatedly fails to consider how discoveries might affect the contexts and sources of life.

The archetypal figure for such a hubristic pursuit of knowledge is Milton's Satan. Satan's heroism stems from the fact that he is displaced from his "place in the order of creation or the Chain of Being." As Satan claims, he possesses

> A mind not to be chang'd by Place or Time.
> The mind is its own place, and in itself
> Can make a Heav'n of Hell, a Hell of Heav'n.
> What matter where, if I be still the same.[49]

This abstraction of the mind from place, according to Berry, stems from a false sense of its hierarchical position: "Implicit in this is the assumption that one's mind is one's own, and that it may choose its own place in the order of things; one usurps divine authority, and thus, in classic style, becomes the author of results that one can neither foresee nor control."[50] This displaced mind, ungrateful for the lives it depends on and affects, is the mind of the heroic industrialist: "I do not know where one could find a better motto for the modernist or technological experiment, which assumes that we can fulfill a high human destiny anywhere, any way, so long as we can keep up the momentum of innovation; that the mind is 'its own place' even within ecological degradation, pollution, poverty, hatred, and violence."[51] This narrative exults hubris and endangers the health of all places.

As an example of how the heroic and displaced mind thinks, Berry points to global attempts to solve world hunger, which is a problem that "cannot be solved until it is understood and dealt with by local people as a multitude of local problems of ecology, agriculture, and culture." This ongoing, necessary work of local adaptation may not seem heroic or exciting because it is "modest, complex, difficult, and long." Yet it is also "the most important work."[52] This is not the kind of work the young Andy would have found exciting, as it doesn't promise any earth-shattering discoveries. And yet such work, conscious of its sources, might mend the earth shattered by those seeking heroic breakthroughs. Thus, this is the work of right livelihood or grateful stewardship to which placed people should apply themselves. It is work that acknowledges and respects the limits of an individual's knowledge, and it is work done thoughtfully and thankfully.

Trespassing Limits

The tendency of the heroic or boomer arts to transgress proper limits leads Berry to argue that humans should pursue knowledge in ways that respect the limits inherent in our creaturely condition. He terms such a properly humble method of thinking the "way of ignorance" and contrasts it to the dangerous thoughtlessness (and thanklessness) inherent in the methods of modern science and technology.[53] Part of what it means to steward life gratefully is to pursue knowledge within appropriate limits.

Berry's plea for researchers and experimenters to follow this "way of ignorance" is founded on the observation that humans are finite creatures who cannot know enough to foresee the consequences of their actions: "We are creatures whose intelligence and knowledge are not invariably equal to our circumstances. The radii of knowledge have only pushed back—and enlarged—the circumference of mystery. We live in a world famous for its ability both to surprise and to deceive us. We are prone to err, ignorantly or foolishly or intentionally or maliciously." In response to this condition, Berry recommends that rather than trying to increase the *amount* of information we possess, humans should commit themselves to sustainable *forms* of knowing: "Perhaps the most proper, and the most natural, response to our state of ignorance is not haste to increase the amount of available information, or even to increase knowledge, but rather a lively and convivial engagement with the issues of form, elegance, and kindness. These issues of 'sustainability' are both scientific and artistic."[54] As he writes elsewhere, this search for sustainable forms could lead to authentic scientific breakthroughs: "The establishment and maintenance of this limit seems to me the ultimate empirical problem—the real 'frontier' of science, or at least of the definition of the possibility of a moral science. It would place science under the rule of the old concern for propriety, correct proportion, proper scale—from which, in modern times, even the arts have been 'liberated.'"[55] This formal, moral science is Berry's proposed response to our human condition of ignorance, and it suggests a curriculum taught in few, if any, universities.

Instead, universities all too often cultivate an unlimited pursuit of technological capabilities, regardless of the potential consequences. Alan Jacobs calls this the "Oppenheimer principle": "At the height of the Red Scare in the 1950s, J. Robert Oppenheimer, who had directed the American atomic bomb program during World War II, found himself under scrutiny for alleged Communist sympathies. He was interviewed at length, and at one point found himself reflecting on how he and his people had made their decisions.

Oppenheimer said, 'When you see something that is technically sweet, you go ahead and do it and argue about what to do about it only after you've had your technical success. That's the way it was with the atomic bomb.'"[56] We're not suggesting that all scientific investigation is this heedless and dangerous; rather, we're arguing that when knowledge is pursued with ingratitude and a displaced mind, it can lead to tragic, unintended consequences. So we would like to ask, along with Leithart, whether we can imagine a healthier form of science: "Modern science depends on a willingness to probe and manipulate nature, but this can come at the cost of gratitude for [the] good of nature as it comes to us. Can we preserve the advances of science while trying to restore a sense of grateful wonder at the natural world?"[57]

Practicing Grateful Thinking

We conclude this chapter by suggesting some practices that might lead those in an academic culture to be more grateful thinkers, more properly placed people. These suggestions are meant to inspire teachers and students as they consider what habits they might incorporate into their own lives to pursue knowledge within appropriate limits.

Keeping the Sabbath

When we observe the Sabbath, we acknowledge that our work and knowledge aren't essential. The world will survive without our work. In addition to fostering proper humility, a day of rest gives us the space to take delight in the miracle of life. In the Judeo-Christian tradition, the Sabbath remembers both the creator's rest after creation and Yahweh's deliverance of Israel from bondage in Egypt. It's a day to remember that life and liberty are gifts, not possessions we can earn or control. As Walter Brueggemann writes, "Sabbath is the practical ground for breaking the power of acquisitiveness and for creating a public will for an accent on restraint. . . . Sabbath is an arena in which to recognize that we live by gift and not by possession, that we are satisfied by relationships of attentive fidelity and not by amassing commodities."[58] In other words, observing the Sabbath invites us into an economy characterized by divine gifts and creaturely limits.

The practice of resting on the Sabbath can take many different forms.[59] Berry himself is only a "bad-weather churchgoer."[60] Most Sundays he walks through the woods near his house, writes poetry, and "come[s] into the peace of wild things."[61] In the introduction to *This Day*, his collection of

Sabbath poems written between 1979 and 2012, Berry describes the way the Sabbath reminds him of the giftedness of creation and life: "We are to rest on the sabbath also, I have supposed, in order to understand that the providence or the productivity of the living world, the most essential work, continues while we rest. This work is entirely independent of our work, and is far more complex and wonderful than any work we have ever done or will ever do."[62] The belief that our work is necessary, that the world can't go on without us, is the result of hubris, and resting on the Sabbath can be an antidote to this disease.

One way that I (Jeff) practice the Sabbath is to avoid using my computer on Sundays. This can be a challenge during a busy semester when students expect quick responses to their last-minute questions, but establishing this limit allows me to spend time with my family and to redirect my attention away from the many distractions my computer provides: e-mails, sports scores, breaking news stories, social media. Perhaps these things aren't as important as they claim to be; perhaps they don't need my immediate attention. Computers and smart phones are powerful tools, but their design can be detrimental to a grateful orientation because, as Wirzba observes, "they give rise to a manipulative and arrogant disposition within us."[63]

If this seems like an exaggerated claim, consider James Smith's analysis of a recent Michelob Ultra commercial "in which the world obeys the touch commands of an iPhone screen. Don't like that car? *Swipe* for a different one. Wish the scenery was different? *Swipe* for an alternative. . . . A way of relating to a phone has now become a way of relating to the world." In fact, Smith compares this arrogant, ungrateful orientation to the world with the archetypal literary character Berry cites as an example of displaced hubris: "One could suggest that our interface with the iPhone (or any other smartphone) . . . subtly and unconsciously trains us to be more like Milton's Satan . . . and not because of the content communicated via the iPhone but because of how I interact with the device and the subtle pedagogy of the imagination effected by that intimate interface with a tiny machine. . . . To become habituated to an iPhone is to implicitly treat the world as 'available' to *me* and at my disposal—to constitute the world as 'at-hand' for me, to be selected, scaled, scanned, tapped, and enjoyed."[64] Taking a break from these technologies, then, is the least we can do to cultivate a properly grateful posture toward life. If such technologies shape us to believe that our desires should have no limits, limiting our use of these technologies reminds us that such promises are false temptations.[65]

Advising Students to Go Home

What if rather than encouraging our students to go onto graduate school or to seek prestigious jobs in urban centers, professors talked about returning home as a viable option? What if our alumni magazines highlighted graduates living "normal" lives rather than featuring Fortune 500 executives or exciting entrepreneurs? In an effort to reshape our students' narratives of success, we've changed the way we ask them about their life plans and how we advise them.

I (Jack) recently had the opportunity to advise a student on where to attend law school. This student had done so well on his LSAT that he was inundated with options and would likely be attending one of the top law schools in the nation. As we sat and revised his application letter for these programs, we talked at length about the value of studying law at a local state university—both his parents teach at our university, so Spring Arbor was both his hometown and his college town. I could have encouraged him to leave home, to head out of state for graduate studies and "make something of himself." This is, after all, the pattern encouraged by the culture of higher education. Instead, I advised him to consider the local state university as one of his top choices for the opposite reasons: he already was "something," he would not be far from home, he knows the region, and he cares about the people here—in other words, his transition would be minimal. It was a joy to learn that, after being accepted into many prestigious programs, he chose the equally prestigious but local university.

Recognizing the Power of "I Don't Know"

Unfortunately, career ambitions and personal insecurities encourage university professors *not* to admit their own ignorance. Professors are paid to know things, so when we have to acknowledge that we don't know something, it can seem like we're being exposed as academic frauds. Both of us know these temptations all too well. When a colleague nonchalantly mentions the name of a theorist we've never heard of, we're tempted to nod knowingly. When a student asks for our opinion on some issue, it's easier to pontificate some half-baked, impressive-sounding pronouncement than to honestly admit the limits of our understanding. Yet giving into these temptations erodes honest intellectual inquiry and renders university conversations insular and insipid. In other words, arrogance inhibits authentic conversation.

Recognizing our condition as limited human beings, as people who are ignorant of infinitely more than we know, has freed both of us to embrace the dictum, attributed to Confucius, that "a wise man knows what he does not know." So when a colleague mentions an author we've never heard of, we ask her to tell us more about this person. When a student asks a question we can't answer thoroughly or well, we're less afraid to tell him, "I don't know." In fact, this response honors thoughtful questions by acknowledging their true complexity. We then jot these questions down, do some additional research and thinking outside of class, and discuss them in more depth during the next class. This approach to questions demonstrates our own commitment to keep learning, and it models for students a more humble, communal method of education, one that openly acknowledges our dependence on others.

Such vigorous, humble conversations should characterize universities. As Berry writes, "Intellectual engagement among the disciplines, across the lines of the specializations—that is to say *real* conversation—would enlarge the context of work; it would press thought toward a just complexity; it would work as a system of checks and balances, introducing criticism that would reach beyond the professional standards."[66] Part of the problem with Andy's fourth-grade experiments is his isolation; he waits until his parents and siblings are out of the way before attempting to make candles on the stove or testing his ability to rise up the chimney. It's significant that when Edgar tells Gloucester he has survived his "fall" and his life is a miracle, Edgar urges him, "Speak yet again." The proper response to the recognition that life is a miracle is to learn to speak again, to learn to speak in gratitude and wonder so as to learn from others with whom we share this miraculous gift. Honestly voicing our ignorance may not seem very significant, but it can lead to more grateful and responsible conversations.

Conducting Research within Local Limits

Finally, one way to make the sciences and arts practiced at universities more properly grateful is to make them more locally responsible. The problem with Andy's experiments is that they have no standard other than his youthful, irrepressible curiosity. This same standard seems to be operative within too many university laboratories and study carrels. What would it look like if, as Berry repeatedly urges, we changed the standard? What if the health of our community were the standard of our intellectual pursuits? What if researchers experimented only in the presence of those affected by their research? The position of the academic could shift, then, from that of a voracious producer of abstract knowledge to that of a grateful steward of health that belongs to the community. When our pursuit of knowledge remains abstract and theoretical, it can avoid confronting its potential consequences, but when we learn within local contexts, we come face-to-face with the effects of our knowledge.

Academics rely on "theories" because they give us the illusion of control, so the sciences dream up elaborate models of subatomic particles, and the humanities hold conferences on the latest critical lens—postcolonialism, queer studies, posthumanism—rather than the places illuminated by these lenses. All these theories can shed light on the world, but when we clutch them too tightly, we become blind to the ways they misrepresent reality. The problem with these abstract theories is that they devalue particular places: "Finally, [a scientific discovery] is 'brought home' to a specific community of persons and creatures in a specific place. If it is then applied in its abstract or generalized or marketable form, it will obscure the uniquenesses of the subject persons or creatures or places, or of their community, and this sort of application is almost invariably destructive." Thus Berry concludes, "If [science] is to be applied, it should be applied locally by local people on a local scale, using the health of the locality as the standard of application and judgment."[67] While academic professionalism "longs . . . for answers that are uniform and universal," this remains another symptom of our hubristic belief that "the mind is its own place."[68]

The current organization of many universities overvalues theoretical, large-scale investigations because they bring more funding and prestige: "That there has been no effective criticism of science is demonstrated, for instance, by science's failure to attend to the possibility of small-scale or cheap or low-energy or ecologically benign technologies. Most applications of science to our problems result in large payments to large corporations and in damages to ecosystems and communities."[69] What if university professors directed their attention away from the glamorous, large questions and toward local questions? We've already pointed to Paul Quinn College as an example of the exciting interdisciplinary work that can take place when an institution addresses the needs of its community—in this case, the need for fresh, healthy food. Converting the college's football field into the "We over Me Farm" has not only ameliorated the community's food desert status but also provided opportunities for marketing, entrepreneurship, and collaborations with other local schools. Similarly, Messiah College's FlowerPower Oil Program grows sunflowers on campus, harvests the seeds, presses them into oil for use in the dining halls, and then converts the used cooking oil into biodiesel to run campus vehicles.[70] We explore such local, placed thinking in the next chapter, but here it is sufficient to point out that conducting university research on a limited scale fosters rich, interdisciplinary conversations, keeps knowledge accountable, and practices a proper gratitude for the sources of our knowledge.

Local thought is more conducive to proper gratitude because it is more likely to account for the individual value of each creature, of each life. In its relentless quest for general, unifying knowledge, Western science tends to apply abstract theories to particular places in ways that inevitably reduce and impoverish them. Berry's solution to this problem is for university intellectuals to live and think as members of their communities: "The only remedy I can see is for scientists (and artists also) to understand and imagine themselves as members of, and sharers in, the fate of affected communities. Our schools now encourage people to regard as mere privileges the power and influence that they call leadership. But leadership without membership is a terrible thing."[71]

In the next chapter, we explore what such local membership might look like for universities, but it's important to remember that living within our geographic place depends on living within our hierarchical place as well, that practicing faithful membership depends on practicing gratitude for those with whom we share our place. As Berry points out in the following Sabbath poem, nothing erodes community and place more quickly than the caustic belief in human "omniscience."

IX

As if suddenly, little towns
where people once lived all
their lives in the same houses
now fill with strangers who
don't bother to speak or wave.
Life is a lonely business.
Gloss it how you will,
plaster it over with politic
bullshit as you please,
ours has been a brutal
history, punishing without
regret whatever or whomever
belonged or threatened to belong
in place, converting the land
to poverty and money any
way that was quickest. Now

after the long invasion
of alien species, including
our own, in a time of endangered
species, including our own,
we face the hard way: no choice
but to do better. After
the brief cataclysm of "cheap"
oil and coal has long
passed, along with the global
economy, the global village,
the hoards who go everywhere
and live nowhere, after
the long relearning, the long
suffering, the homecoming
that must follow, maybe
there will be a New World
of native communities again:
plants, animals, humans,
soils, stones, stories,
songs, all belonging
to such small, once known
and forgotten, officially unknown
and exploited, beautiful places
such as this, where despite
all we have done wrong
the golden light of October
falls through the turning leaves.
The leaves die and fall,
making wealth in the ground,
making in the ground the only
real material wealth.
Ignoring our paltry dream
of omniscience merely human,
the knowing old land
has lighted the woodland's edges
with the last flowers of the year,
the tiny asters once known
here as farewell-summer.[72]

6

Geography

Reaping the Fruits of Fidelity

In many ways, educating students to dwell faithfully in their geographic place is at the heart of Berry's vision for universities. As institutions, universities have long been wayward, turning their gaze away from the needs and opportunities of their local places to seek recognition and funding from cultural and economic centers. Such institutional waywardness leads to graduates who have been trained to seek better opportunities in better places rather than to settle down and faithfully inhabit a place. Our hope is that if universities reorient themselves toward the particularities of their contexts, their students will be more likely to emulate this committed orientation when they graduate.

Burley Coulter's Reluctant Fidelity

Fidelity to a place does not mean that one's life will be easy or that all one's hopes will be realized. There are no perfect universities or places or jobs because there are no perfect people. But the failure of people and institutions to achieve perfection does not preclude the faithful pursuit of health and wholeness. In other words, committing ourselves to work toward the healing of a place is, perhaps, enough. In his Port William fiction, Berry calls those who are so committed the *membership*. And this membership is particularly developed in the story of the life and death of Burley Coulter, a man who is lovable, confounding, frequently immoral, and a source of much humor—he is, in other words, quite human. But for most of his life Burley has been perceived, especially in the eyes of his distant relation Wheeler Catlett, as *wayward*. As a young man he seemed particularly restless—unlikely to ever become a faithful, rooted inhabitant of his place—but by the end of his life, Burley is one of the presiding elders of the Port William membership. Thus, despite his waywardness, and in his own way, he comes to practice fidelity to Port William—to the place and to the people who need him. Our hope is that as Burley became a faithful member of Port William, in spite of his many flaws, so universities and the individuals invested in these institutions might become faithful members of their places. If Burley Coulter can become faithful, anyone can.

Early in his life, Burley was wayward mostly because he was directionless and didn't want to be bound by a commitment to any one thing: "He wanted to feel that he could leave if he took the notion."[1] Burley didn't want a wife or a farm because he understood that such relationships would constrain his freedom. Yet, owing to circumstances mostly beyond his control, Burley remains faithful to Port William, even as his propensity to wander enables him to understand the wildness of the place. In the story "The Wild Birds," Burley tells his lawyer, Wheeler, how he gradually became someone who is faithful to his place:

> "It was wayward when it come to me," Burley is saying. "Looked like to me I was there, born there and not someplace else, just by accident. I never took to it by nature the way Jarrat did, the way Nathan here, I think, has. I just turned up here, take it or leave it. I might have gone somewhere else when I got mustered out in 1919, but I come back, and looked like I was in the habit of staying, so I stayed. I thought of leaving, but the times was hard and Pap needed me—or needed somebody better, to tell the truth—and I stayed. I stayed to help bring up Tom and Nathan after their mother died. And then Pap died and Mam was old, and I stayed on with her. And when she died I stayed on and done my part with Jarrat; the boys was gone then, and he needed me. And somehow or other along the way, I began to stay because I wanted to. I wanted to be with Jarrat, and Nathan and Hannah here, and Mat and you and the others. And somewhere or other I realized that being here was the life I had because I'd never had another one any place else, and never would have."[2]

Though he has often imagined leaving Port William, Burley remains because he is needed by his family and friends. Burley has been a faithful sticker not by a conscious, deliberate choice but because he has responded to the needs of others. Yet the irregularity of his life has caused irreparable damage to his son Danny and to Danny's mother. This failure is a burden to Burley and a shame, as Hannah Coulter knows: "She knew he grieved that he had not married Kate Helen Branch, Danny's mother, and that he regretted his late acknowledgement of Danny as his son. But she knew, too, how little he had halted in grief and regret, how readily and cheerfully he had gone on, however burdened, to whatever had come next. . . . Though gifted for disappearance, he had never entirely disappeared but had been with them to the end."[3] Though Burley's fidelity is by no means regular or intentional, he is nonetheless faithful.

In the story "Fidelity," Danny Branch steals his dying father away from the hospital to graciously let him die where he would have chosen if he were able: the woods into whose pathless ways Burley often disappeared. Kyle Bode, the detective who attempts to solve Burley's "kidnapping" from the hospital, is at times a foil for Burley. Growing up, Kyle had more reasons than Burley to remain at home and be part of the family business; his father, "under pressure from birth to 'get out of here and make something out of yourself,'" had gone to Louisville to build a life for his family. But Kyle is not much interested in competing with his older brother for a stake in the family business; instead, he is a boomer idealist "with a little bit of an ambition to be a hero."[4]

Unlike Burley, Kyle abandons what he knows and pursues a career as a policeman. And although Kyle does what Burley fails to do—he marries his high school sweetheart—he does not practice fidelity; his marriages are marked by sexual infidelity and immaturity. He divorces his first wife after he becomes "sexually liberated," and he marries his second wife because "he made her pregnant." However, she divorces him because she does not know how to be satisfied with the fidelity required of marriage: "He knew that she had not left him because she was dissatisfied with him but because she was not able to be satisfied for very long with anything. He disliked and feared this in her at the same time that he recognized it in himself. He, too, was dissatisfied; he could not see what he had because he was always looking around for something else that he thought he wanted."[5] Kyle suffers from a deep inability to commit to others, and so he remains uprooted and lonely.

In his loneliness, Kyle clings tightly to the abstract and rigid rules of the law. In this respect, he is rather like Inspector Javert in *Les Misérables*. These rules, handed down from far away, impose a comforting order on his messy, confusing life. So if the rules state that patients should not be taken from the hospital, Kyle will enforce them regardless of the particular, local circumstances of the case. Burley's affection for his place, in all its unruly wildness, stands in stark contrast to Kyle's adherence to abstract rules, and this contrast structures the humorous and poignant story of Burley's death in "Fidelity."

But to understand the ways that Burley and his son Danny practice their extralegal fidelity to each other, we need to return to "The Wild Birds." Burley tries to explain to Wheeler—who, like Kyle, is tasked with upholding the law—that he now wants to acknowledge Danny as his rightful heir: "He was too late, as he thought and said, in acknowledging Danny as his son. But he did acknowledge him, and made him his heir, and brought him and Lyda home with him to live. And so at last he fully honored his marriage in all but name to Kate Helen."[6] Yet this final act of Burely's troubles Wheeler—and it ultimately teaches Wheeler that fidelity sometimes requires painful sacrifices.

"The Wild Birds" tells the story of Burley and Wheeler's argument over who should be Burley's rightful heir. And in some ways, it is the story of the prodigal son and his older brother learning to love each other. Wheeler imagines that he, as Burley's lawyer and friend, knows what is best. Burley's rightful heirs, Wheeler proclaims, ought to be his nephew Nathan Coulter and his wife Hannah. In Wheeler's estimation, Nathan—who was mostly raised by Burley and has been like a son to him—is the obvious choice to carry on Burley's legacy.

Wheeler's ambitions for Burley's farm are good—he is, after all, concerned with the farm's health and sustainability.[7] But Wheeler is offended and upset by Burley's continual desire for the wayward—for the dark country of the night, for the unknown, for the wild. So Wheeler is offended by Burley's desire to leave his farm to Danny because this is contrary to Wheeler's desire for an orderly passing on, one that happens in the daylight, not one marked by illegitimate children. And it is this waywardness "that names the difference that [Wheeler and Burley] are going to have to reckon with" as they sit in Wheeler's office arguing over the farm's rightful heir.[8]

Wheeler has never fully embraced Burley's waywardness because it is not neat or predictable or lawful. It does not follow reason or pattern (or so he thinks), and it is the thing he seeks to safeguard against and correct in his profession as a lawyer. Burley Coulter stands in Wheeler's mind as a man who prefers the wild path, and Wheeler remains unwilling to permit waywardness: "If the things of this world are wayward, then he will say so, and love them as they are. But as his friends all know, it is hard to be a friend of Wheeler's and settle for things as they are. You will be lucky if he will let you settle for the possible, the faults of which he can tell you. The wayward is possible, but there must be a better way than wayward."[9] Wheeler is dealing in dualisms, believing that waywardness cannot lead to fidelity—perhaps because he has little tolerance for the way things are. He is an idealist who sees the potential for order and goodness and strives for these things in his profession and in his community.

But what Wheeler is unable to see until Burley points it out is that even Burley's waywardness follows a pattern and is in fact its own way. Wheeler has known Burley "through all his transformations, from the wildness of his young years, through his years of devotion in kinship and friendship, to his succession as presiding elder of a company of friends that includes Wheeler himself. It has a pattern clear enough, that life, and yet, as Wheeler has long known without exactly admitting, it is a clear pattern that includes the unclear, the wayward. The wayward and the dark."[10] And like the son who imagines himself to be the only one truly faithful to his father, Wheeler fails to see how faithfulness necessarily demands of him a willingness to live with waywardness, to offer even the prodigal son a loving embrace.

Like the son who stayed home, Wheeler is certain that his view is the right one and that Burley's prodigality precludes him from wisely choosing his own heir. He can't imagine that they might both come to fidelity by different paths. Burley attempts to soften Wheeler's implacability with a confession: "I haven't been regular. I've come by a kind of back path—through the woods, you might say, and along the bluffs. Whatever I've come to, I've mostly got there too late, and mostly by surprise. I don't say everybody *has* to be regular. Being out of regular may be all right—I liked it mostly. It may be in your nature. Maybe it's even useful in a way. But it finally gets to be a question of what you can recommend."[11] Up until this point in his life, Burley's waywardness has been a source of humor to those who know him—his stories are legendary for their bawdiness. But he admits that he could not and did not recommend such a path to his nephews Tom and Nathan or to his son Danny. Burley understands what Wheeler will come to know soon enough: the membership of Port William, like the "Kingdom of God," includes both those who follow the straight and narrow and those whose paths are rather circuitous.

In Burley's estimation, the entire world has been tending toward waywardness. Wheeler is correct that there is a better way, but that better way has to make room for even the prodigal sons. Wheeler is a slow student, however, and he attributes Burley's desire to acknowledge Danny to a sudden prick of conscience—a desire to make right what has long been wrong. "You're saying you're sorry for what you've done wrong? And by what you're proposing to do now you hope to make it right?" Wheeler asks.

> "No! God damn it, Wheeler—excuse me, Hannah—no! What is done is done forever. I know that. I'm saying that the ones who have been here have been the way they were, and the ones of us who are here now are the way we are, and to *know* that is the only chance we've got, dead and living, to be here together. I ain't saying we don't have to know what we ought to have been and ought to be, but we oughtn't to let that stand between us. That ain't the way we are. The way we are, we are members of each other. All of us. Everything. The difference ain't in who is a member and who is not, but in who knows it and who don't."[12]

Wheeler struggles to accept the wayward members of Port William, and in this, he is like the prodigal son's elder brother, who has to accept that his father's household includes both of them: him in his ordered, proper way, and his brother in all his embarrassingly foolish prodigality. This truth is clarified when Burley explains that Wheeler too has failed Burley and the Port William membership.

Burley asks Wheeler why he thinks they've been friends all these years, and as Wheeler contemplates the question, Burley tells him it's because "we ain't brothers." A brother, Burley notes, wouldn't have put up with his waywardness (or would have tolerated it only partially). In the past, Wheeler could be amused by Burley's irregularities because his actions were not near enough to deeply affect Wheeler. But now that Wheeler has to confront Burley's waywardness in a way that *does* affect Wheeler, he is offended by it, as a brother would be. At this moment, Wheeler is aware that although he holds himself and others to exacting standards—he requires things to be orderly and proper—he has failed to practice the forgiveness that fidelity requires, thus failing to honor their membership. In other words, Burley has helped Wheeler see that the failure is not Burley's alone; it is suffered by the entire membership. "'Wheeler, if we're going to get this will made out, not to mention all else we've got to do while there's breath in us, I think you've got to forgive me as if I was a brother to you.' He laughs, asserting for the last time the seniority now indisputably his, and casting it aside. 'And I reckon I've got to forgive you for taking so long to do it.'"[13]

Once Wheeler acknowledges his failure to be faithful to Burley, the two men can forgive each other and love each other, in the midst of their differences. And it is this strengthening of fidelity between Burley and Wheeler that allows Wheeler to say of Burley after he has passed out of this world and into mystery, "He learned what he had to, and he changed, and so he made himself exceptional. He was, I will say, a faithful man."[14]

Burley Coulter is a wayward individual who, because he responded to the needs of his community, can say at the end of his life that he was faithful. Perhaps universities, by seeking to meet the needs of their places, can encourage students to settle down after they graduate and work to serve the places where they find themselves. And at the end of their lives, these students, like Burley, may be able to say that they have been faithful. Wheeler Catlett was reluctant to recognize the change in Burley and forgive him for his past waywardness, but he came to practice the forgiveness, communication, and accountability that fidelity requires. So too, individuals and communities that have been damaged by wayward universities may need to forgive these wrongs and work anew to hold their local educational institutions accountable. Even those of us who are committed to our places need to consider how we have enabled unfaithful institutions and have failed to forgive them, and patiently call them to fidelity. Although the remainder of this chapter focuses on how universities can, like Burley, learn to meet the needs of their communities, we want to emphasize that in many cases such a change requires forgiveness and renewed cooperation between institutions and their places.

For educational institutions to be faithful members of their places, faculty and students need to identify and resist the powerful forces within contemporary universities that foster the abstract, displaced knowledge favored by cosmopolitans like Kyle Bode. Berry proposes local or parochial knowledge as a counterweight to the commodifiable, centralized knowledge valued in universities, and although such local knowledge needs to be informed by outside sources, it uniquely enables care for particulars and adaptation to local conditions. Training students to attend faithfully to the needs of their local places does not mean that they should become insular and ignore knowledge and ideas from other places. Rather, faithful care of local places depends on maintaining a robust conversation between parochial communities and the cosmopolitan knowledge favored by universities. We conclude this chapter by offering some specific practices that can foster such a conversation: faculty members can choose to root themselves, students can study abroad and bring home what they learn, teachers can incorporate local knowledge into their curricula, and university administrators can make lower tuition a priority. These practices won't change university cultures overnight, but by patiently and creatively cultivating parochial knowledge, universities can educate students to serve their places more faithfully.

The Wayward Eye of Provincialism and Cosmopolitanism

Berry consistently makes two key distinctions when discussing the dangers of abstract or deracinated knowledge. The first is the distinction between the center and the periphery. As he explains in his essay "Local Knowledge in the Age of Information," "the dichotomy between center and periphery does in fact exist, as does the tendency of the center to be ignorant of the periphery." This division has probably always existed, but it has grown more extreme and more dangerous in the contemporary age of globalized information. As Berry observes, the "center of centers" today "is the global 'free market' economy of the great corporations, the periphery of which is everywhere, and for its periphery this center expresses no concern and acknowledges no responsibility."[15] In many ways, the division between center and periphery parallels the division between internal, subjective standards and external, objective standards discussed in chapter 2. What is needed in both cases is a faithful conversation that maintains these pairs in fruitful harmony. As we argued earlier, the panopticon arrangement of knowledge enables the center to impose its will on the periphery. In the absence of a genuine conversation between the two, the center remains disconnected from the periphery, and this lack of accountability enables the center to exploit and impoverish the periphery. It is this exploitative, colonial relationship that Berry decries.

In defending the need for local knowledge, Berry emphasizes the toxic effect that centralized knowledge and power can have on local cultures and places. He follows Irish poet and critic Patrick Kavanagh in making a further distinction, contrasting a healthy parochial culture with an impoverished provincial one.[16] As Kavanagh explains: "Parochialism and provincialism are opposites. The provincial has no mind of his own; he does not trust what his eyes see until he has heard what the metropolis—toward which his eyes are turned—has to say on any subject. . . . The parochial mentality on the other hand is never in any doubt about the social and artistic validity of his parish. . . . In Ireland we are inclined to be provincial not parochial, for it requires a great deal of courage to be parochial."[17] What Kavanagh describes is how local cultures come to believe in their own inadequacy and thus look toward the center for validation. In many ways, this phenomenon is similar to the Stockholm syndrome, in which the oppressed take on the perspectives and values of the oppressor. Thus the center, and the type of knowledge it values, not only steals material resources from local communities but also steals their self-worth. The provincial person no longer believes in the "social and artistic validity" of his or her local place and looks to the center for entertainment and moral norms.

This fear of being provincial, backward, or out of touch can lead members of universities to disregard their local places and pursue abstract or "universal" knowledge. So whereas Berry claims that "a land grant university is a center with a designated periphery which it is supposed to maintain and improve," universities more often disregard the periphery for which they are nominally responsible.[18] By doing so, universities become provincial places; because they no longer believe in the validity of their local place, they look for approval and status not to their local communities but to other centers.

Such provincialism manifests itself first in the preference for abstract, quantifiable knowledge over local, particular knowledge.[19] Local knowledge resists commodification in the form of external grants and national or international prestige because it can't be easily extracted and applied elsewhere. Thus university faculty and administrators view it as second-rate. In its place, the knowledge industry prefers abstract, quantifiable data that can be divorced from any specific context. For instance, a biology professor cannot merely study water quality in a nearby river to help farmers and local governments make informed decisions about runoff control. Rather, she has to abstract her findings to make them more broadly applicable and thus worthy of publication in a peer-reviewed journal. Similarly, a literature professor is not rewarded for writing an article in the town newspaper about the community's monthly slam poetry evenings. Rather, he has to write about a poet of national stature so that a prestigious journal might publish his essay (where it will likely be read by about five other poetry professors). Thus universities and professors have a vested financial interest in producing knowledge that can be easily applied elsewhere.

Such an obsession with abstract, commodifiable knowledge leads to a dreary sort of blandness. We have a proliferation of "best practices" described in language so vague that they are either painfully obvious or impossible to put into practice. Similarly, the way grants are awarded encourages a stultifying sameness in the conduct of scientific research. As Berry writes, "The agricultural scientists and experts go doggedly on in their 'cutting-edge' rut because they either are employed by agribusiness or because their universities are now helplessly dependent on grants from agribusiness."[20] Between funding bias and the need to publish results in national, peer-reviewed journals, university researchers are under immense pressure to produce more of the bland, abstract knowledge that has contributed to the ecological and economic degradation of local places.[21]

This provincialism, this belief that local knowledge is less valuable or less "true," further manifests itself in the way universities privilege cosmopolitan values.[22] Although cosmopolitans may seem to be the opposite of provincials, both share the belief that the periphery is backward, small-minded, and oppressive. Indeed, in our age of globalization, this belief is nearly ubiquitous. Universities are largely run by cosmopolitans, by well-traveled people who value art, food, and culture from around the globe.[23] While such broad-minded appreciation can contribute to a mosaic of flourishing local cultures, cosmopolitans tend to want the benefits of local places without the obligations required to sustain these gifts. In other words, although cosmopolitans give lip service to the value of local cultures and places, their values contribute to the exploitation of local places and people because they refuse to commit themselves to any one place. In contrast, authentic multiculturalism depends on individuals and communities that practice the difficult virtue of fidelity to place.

Prominent cultural geographer Yi-fu Tuan discusses the tension between cosmopolitan and local values in his book *Cosmos and Hearth: A Cosmopolite's Viewpoint*, and as the subtitle indicates, he sides with the cosmopolitans. He acknowledges that those who try to live in the cosmos can damage particular places; in addition to oppressive political and economic regimes that flatten local cultures, his list of harms caused by cosmopolitan practices includes "the enormous damage to the natural environment in the push toward development; the threat to variety—the earth's natural and cultural plenitudes; the decline of small neighborly communities (intimate hearths) in a cosmopolitan world of strangers;

the arrogance of science—its technological and manipulative ways of thinking and doing." Yet he never explains how these damages might be ameliorated. Tuan's only answer to such criticisms is to claim that the "leading critics of cosmos are themselves cosmopolitans."[24] While this may or may not be true (it's hard to see how Wendell Berry is a cosmopolitan), such a dismissal sidesteps the very real consequences of a cosmopolitan lifestyle.

Tuan clearly has a low opinion of community and fears its constraints or "bondage," so he upholds the cosmos for the unfettered freedom it provides individuals.[25] In fact, Tuan unabashedly links cosmopolitan desires to the human desire to be godlike: "Yearning for the cosmos is rooted in a high sense of human dignity—in the belief that human beings cannot just be creatures of the day, constrained by forces beyond their comprehension or control, and relieved by visceral pleasures that differ little from those of other animals. True, for millennia, only a small elite could aspire to be gods, but once that possibility lay open to more people lower down the social scale—thanks in part to technical inventions that have shifted the balances of power—they too found its allure irresistible."[26] Tuan seems to think it is commendable to succumb to this temptation to be godlike, but Berry would likely point to the biblical story of the Garden of Eden as a warning against giving in to these "irresistible" desires to be superior to our condition. As we argued in the previous chapter, the healthy response to human limits is not to disregard them but to live gratefully within them.

Tuan's awareness of the damage caused by the "hubris of modernism" leads him to conclude his book with a rather contradictory call for a "cosmopolitan hearth":

> Cosmopolitans, viewed positively as I have done in this book, are a people in love with the splendor and plenitude of life. Viewed negatively, they are a people adrift, flitting from one thing to another (language, idea, place, people, custom) with no point of enduring rest and hence no deep knowledge or commitment.... Have I, then, reversed my position...? Not at all. Culture [or the hearth], with its exclusivity and excess burden of taboos, remains problematic. What I would now like to do is to introduce a revised conception of culture, one that has the coziness but not the narrowness and bigotry of the traditional hearth. I shall call it, paradoxically, "cosmopolitan hearth."[27]

Given his definition of these terms, his "paradox" seems more like a linguistic trick than an actual resolution. Indeed, Tuan implicitly acknowledges this when he critiques the Polish philosopher Leszek Kolakowski for describing his ideal dwelling as a place "'deep in the virgin mountain forest on a lake shore at the corner of Madison Avenue in Manhattan and Champs-Elysées, in a small tidy town.'" As Tuan rightly points out, "the place he wants to live in not only does not exist but cannot exist—it is contradictory."[28]

Despite Tuan's recognition of this contradiction, he believes the conflict between the cosmos and the hearth, the center and the periphery, is inevitable: "'Cosmopolitan hearth' is a contradiction in terms and this fact, perhaps, defines our dilemma—a *human* dilemma that has always existed but that becomes more evident as we move from traditional to modern, then high modern. This dilemma is captured by the observation, which George Steiner and others have made, that whereas plants have roots, human beings have feet. Feet make us mobile, but of course we also have minds, a far greater source of instability and uprooting."[29] Tuan is certainly right that we live in a mobile age, one dominated by physical and intellectual travel. What Tuan's use of this contrast between plants and people fails to account for, however, is that geographic rootlessness can make intellectual rootlessness more dangerous. One of the chief causes of irresponsible thought is geographic mobility; mobility enables us to escape the consequences of our thought on particular places, whether those consequences be environmental degradation or other long-term effects. The goal of a placed education is to expand students' minds, enabling them to explore many intellectual paths and yet root this knowledge in a particular place. In this way, knowledge might be made responsible, able to account for and be corrected by its effects.

Tuan's attempted compromise fails to recognize that the "splendor and plenitude of life" depend on individuals and communities that are committed to tending their places faithfully. The cosmopolitan's insistence that the resources of his local hearth are insufficient for his personal fulfillment is a variety of intellectual promiscuity. He aims to maximize his enjoyment by having access to the fruits of a variety of different cultures. But cosmopolitans forget that healthy cultures depend on committed members; they want the benefits of responsible, placed membership without its obligations.

In "The Body and the Earth" Berry compares the infidelity of the cosmopolitan to marital infidelity, arguing that both deny the human limits that make geographic fidelity a necessary condition of responsible love:

> One cannot enact or fulfill one's love for womankind or mankind, or even for all the women or men to whom one is attracted....Similarly, one cannot live in the world; that is, one cannot become, in the easy, generalizing sense with which the phrase is commonly used, a "world citizen." There can be no such thing as a "global village." No matter how much one may love the world as a whole, one can live fully in it only by living responsibly in some small part of it. Where we live and who we live there with define the terms of our relationship to the world and to humanity. We thus come again to the paradox that one can become whole only by the responsible acceptance of one's partiality.[30]

The faithful, patient love Berry advocates makes itself responsible for the consequences of its errors, and it submits to correction from the beloved person or place. The parochial view honors where one is, with all its flaws and insufficiencies, but it doesn't allow these blemishes to turn its gaze elsewhere. Such a wandering eye is true waywardness, the waywardness enacted by the upwardly and laterally mobile who have been trained to look down on out-of-the-way places. Without the limits imposed by fidelity, the cosmopolitan knowledge favored by universities will continue on its wayward and destructive course.

A Courageous and Humble Parochialism

In contrast to the allied attitudes of provincialism and cosmopolitanism, attitudes that perpetuate the center's exploitation of the periphery, universities should cultivate a courageous yet humble parochialism. We derive these terms from Kavanagh, who qualifies his praise for the parochial by warning against the dangers of blindly clinging to one's place: "Advising people not to be ashamed of having the courage of their remote parish, is not free from many dangers. There is always that element of bravado which takes pleasure in the notion that the potato-patch is the ultimate. To be parochial a man needs the right kind of sensitive courage and the right kind of sensitive humility."[31] Berry displays this sensitive courage and humility in his nuanced defense of his own Kentucky community. While he was growing up, his place was largely parochial, confident in its own social and artistic validity. But he acknowledges that in some ways this confidence was misplaced: "the 'social validity' of that place at that time certainly was impaired by racial segregation."[32] As we discussed in chapter 4 on memory, Berry's efforts to draw on other cultural traditions to correct his community's racism demonstrate the sensitive humility required to sustain a healthy parish. Just as maintaining a healthy tradition requires the difficult work of judgment and correction, so maintaining a healthy place requires a humility that recognizes and seeks to restore the deficiencies of that place.

In advocating for a parochial attitude, then, we are *not* defending an insular, ingrown version of place, where no one ever leaves and no outsider is allowed to enter. In fact, at certain times and in certain cultures, an education to leave home may be in order. We, like Berry, are making a contextually contingent argument based on the promiscuous and irresponsible mobility of America's industrialized culture.

A further qualification is that we live in a mobile world, and many people lead displaced lives through no fault of their own.[33] Our universities are full of refugees, military brats, missionary kids, and immigrants. My (Jeff's) mother grew up in a military family and lived throughout the United States. I grew up in Washington State, went to college in Oregon, attended graduate school in Texas, and now teach in Michigan. I'm a typical academic migrant. We do not mean to exclude such people from the opportunities and responsibilities of fidelity to their local places. For as much as fidelity is a virtue that must be practiced, it is also a privilege bequeathed to some by rooted families and healthy local economies. Nevertheless, even wayward or migrant people can settle down and make themselves accountable to the needs and limits of a particular place. Burley Coulter was a wayward person, yet he still practiced fidelity to the place and the community that needed him.

Despite these qualifications, restoring a properly sensitive courage in defending one's place can begin to heal the psychological damage caused by our deracinating educational culture. In his essay "The Work of Local Culture" Berry identifies two consequences of such a provincial education: "Our children are educated . . . to leave home, not to stay home, and the costs of this education have been far too little acknowledged. One of the costs is psychological, and the other is at once cultural and ecological." As Berry elaborates, "apart from the love of a place and a community . . . , education is only the importation into a local community of centrally prescribed 'career preparation' designed to facilitate the export of young careerists."[34] What is needed, then, is an educational culture that values local places and local knowledge and encourages graduates to return home, settle down, and work to meet the needs of their places.

The need to educate students to be faithful members of their places does not preclude travel or time away from home. Indeed, Berry goes on to describe the natural tendency of children to rebel and move away—this is part of growing up. But whereas children once returned home after spending time away, now they often remain "stalled in adolescence," never returning home and never "achieving any kind of reconciliation or friendship with [their] parents."[35] This new pattern of departure and a lifetime of mobility violates the old pattern of departure, struggle, and return represented in stories like *The Odyssey, Sir Gawain and the Green Knight,* and Tolkien's *The Lord of the Rings*. Innocent Smith, the protagonist of G. K. Chesterton's *Manalive*, enacts this pattern of return, claiming, "I have become a pilgrim to cure myself from being an exile."[36] Innocent repeatedly leaves his wife and his home in order to rediscover them in bizarre ways, to allow himself to see them with fresh eyes and love them anew. And it is perhaps telling that one of the essential characteristics of the stories we loved as children—fairy tales—is exodus and homecoming. Such narratives of departure and return root characters to their local places, honoring such places without idolizing them, thus modeling the sensitive courage and humility needed for a responsible and faithful relationship with one's place.[37]

Berry may be drawn to this archetypal narrative in part because he lived it himself. After graduating from the University of Kentucky, he went to graduate school at Stanford, traveled to Italy and France on a Guggenheim Fellowship, and then taught in New York City for two years. Only after spending years away from Kentucky did he and his young family return to their native community. Berry draws on this narrative arc in much of his fiction: as we have already discussed, both Andy Catlett and his father Wheeler spent significant time away from Port William before returning home to commit themselves to their place.

As these examples indicate, parochialism should be both courageous and humble: students can learn to defend the unique goodness of their local places while acknowledging the wisdom and value found elsewhere. This authentically parochial attitude can begin to heal the psychological damage inflicted by an education that teaches one to leave home.

Parochial Care, Local Adaptation, and Authentic Multiculturalism

Ideally, spending four years away from home at a university should prepare students to carry the wisdom they have learned back to their communities. But when universities encourage students to seek better opportunities in better places, they cultivate a cosmopolitan promiscuity that hurts not only their graduates but also the places that lose these knowledgeable, skilled young people. This brings us to the second "cost" incurred by an education that teaches students to leave home, a cost "at once cultural and ecological."[38] Berry explores these costs in many essays, beginning with his seminal book *The Unsettling of America*, in which he outlines the interconnected ways that America's deracinated, boomer way of life damages our character, our agriculture, and our culture. Drawing on Berry's work, we think the irreplaceable benefits of local, parochial knowledge can be understood as serving three related ends: the loving care of particular places, local adaptation to the needs and opportunities of these places, and the flourishing of an authentic multiculturalism.

While faithful care and affection for a local place may seem like fuzzy, sentimental concepts, Berry insists that they have real economic and practical consequences. He admits that our economy, which deals almost exclusively in quantities, doesn't value "such intangible goods as knowledge, memory, familiarity, imagination, affection, sympathy, neighborliness, and so on"; nevertheless, these qualities are "capable of enforcing care in our treatment of persons, places, and things."[39] If universities focus exclusively on abstract, displaced knowledge, they will fail to cultivate these intangible but necessary qualities in their students.

What Berry describes, in effect, is an epistemology of care that contrasts with the epistemology of abstraction that characterizes university knowledge.[40] Thus, Berry claims that "the terms 'love' and 'know'" are "intimately related" and "nearly synonymous."[41] This definition of knowledge lies behind biologist Roger Payne's claim, as cited by Berry, that "'any observant local knows more than any visiting scientist. Always. No exceptions.'"[42] Local affection and care for particular places lead to a kind of attentiveness and insight that out-of-town experts simply cannot compensate for. Students in an average university classroom, however, are unlikely to be taught that they will never fully understand photosynthesis if they don't learn to love particular plants; they won't be taught that they will never fully grasp a mathematical theorem if they don't learn to love the beauty of its instantiation in a well-designed building; they won't be taught that they will never fully know a poem's beauty if they don't learn to love the community that shares this poem; they won't be taught that they will never fully comprehend the law of supply and demand if they don't learn to love people who supply a particular product. In other words, universities don't do a good job of teaching students that loving knowledge exists only in the context of faithful affection for a particular place and community.

We discuss this relation between love and knowledge more fully in the next chapter, but crucial here is to understand that loving knowledge leads to the careful adaptation of information or knowledge to the needs and opportunities of particular places. Care leads to a concern for the myriad particulars of a place, and thus care and local adaptation involve a long "effort of familiarity." Berry most often describes the process by which love is embodied and refined by faithful work in the context of farming, and in chapter 3 we discussed one such description, in which a young farmer begins to work his land "in love." Soon, however, his "thoughts begin to be translated into acts. . . . And daily life, work, and problems gradually alter the visions. . . . One works to better purpose then and makes fewer mistakes, because at last one sees where one is."[43] As Berry's description indicates, local application makes love accountable and leads to a rooted, careful way of knowing. And such a rooted way of life bears fruit in a more healthy place.

Elsewhere, Berry offers another example of such local adaptation motivated by particularizing affection. Berry points to George Sturt's study of the way traditional farm carts "evolved in a long, only partly conscious give and take between the people and the landscape." As Sturt asks, "'Was it to suit the horses or the ruts, the loading or the turning, that the front wheels had to have a diameter of about four feet? Or was there something in the average height of a carter, or in the skill of wheel-makers, that fixed these dimensions?'" Sturt can't identify a precise causal chain, and this reciprocity, Berry claims, is definitive of a healthy local culture: "This is the way a locally adapted culture works. Over a long time it learns to conform its artifacts to the local landscape, local circumstances, and local needs. This is exactly opposite to the way of industrialism, which forces the locality to conform to industrial artifacts, always with the most dreadful consequences to the locality."[44] These examples of a healthy farm community and a well-designed tool illustrate the kind of local, complex adaptation that faithful care can accomplish.[45]

Such elegant, complex adaptations, however, require faithful, loving effort over a long period of time. So a university culture that rewards innovation, originality, and abstractable knowledge fails to nurture this local, affectionate way of knowing. Perhaps universities can begin to properly value such loving knowledge by cultivating the neglected faculty of imagination. We began this book by discussing the importance of imagination, so its foundational role should come as no surprise. The reason imagination is so crucial to the cultivation of placed knowledge is that its "particularizing power" enables local adaptation and an authentic multiculturalism.

Berry acknowledges that the generalizations made by historians, scientists, and other academics are necessary. But he warns that they must be balanced by the "countervailing, particularizing power of imagination," which combats the "dehumanizing and destructive" effect of unchecked abstraction.[46] Imagination, by allowing us to see our places in their particularity, enables adaptation and multiculturalism: "If imagination is to have a real worth to us, it needs to have a practical, an *economic* effect. It needs to establish us in our places with a practical respect for what is there besides ourselves. I think the highest earthly result of imagination is probably local adaptation. If we could learn to belong fully and truly where we live, then we would all finally be native Americans, and we would have an authentic multiculturalism."[47] Berry warns, however, that such a hope depends on a difficult, uphill struggle: the "movement toward local adaptation necessarily is being led from the bottom. And it confronts a leadership from the top—in government, in the corporate economy, in the universities—that is utterly lacking in imagination, local loyalty, and local knowledge."[48] Our aim throughout this chapter, and indeed this book, has been to restore imagination, fidelity, and local knowledge to the university, knowing that this restoration must begin at the bottom with individual students and faculty members making the effort to imagine their place, recognize its needs, and faithfully work to find knowledge adequate to those needs.

While the odds of achieving such a vision are admittedly unfavorable, this goal of an "authentic multiculturalism," of healthy communities adapted to their places, is one worth fighting for. As Berry puts it, "The authentic multiculturalism of adapting our ways of life to the nature of the places where we live . . . would [bring about] a healthier, prettier, more diverse and interesting world, a world less toxic and explosive, than we have now."[49] Such a multiculturalism would sustain a mosaic of local cultures lovingly adapted to their particular places.[50] Berry articulates the interconnections between these features of parochial knowledge:

> [A local culture] continues, and conveys to succeeding generations, the history of the use of the place and the knowledge of how the place may be lived in and used. . . . [T]he pattern of reminding implies affection for the place and respect for it, and so, finally, the local culture will carry the knowledge of how the place may be well and lovingly used, and also the implicit command to use it only well and lovingly. The only true and

effective "operator's manual for spaceship earth" is not a book that any human will ever write; it is hundreds of thousands of local cultures.[51]

Shortly after this passage, Berry expresses his belief that, because "universities are more and more the servants of government and the corporations," they will not contribute to the flourishing of such local cultures.[52] Given Berry's persuasive critique of the abstract, commodifiable knowledge produced at most universities, we find his grim verdict all too reasonable. Like the young Burley Coulter, universities have been wayward, yet Burley became faithful through his loving response to the needs of his community. Similarly, based on our experience within institutions of higher education, we are hopeful that even in these diseased centers of knowledge there are good people seeking to respond faithfully to the needs of their local cultures and places. In the work of these faithful people we find inspiration for the following practices that might foster a more sustaining conversation between university centers and their peripheries.

A Conversation in School

Near the end of *Life Is a Miracle,* Berry describes his lifelong friendship with agricultural scientist Wes Jackson as "a conversation out of school."[53] Their wide-ranging, interdisciplinary conversation about how to make agriculture more sustainable violates the structures and priorities of most conversations sponsored by universities. Here, we consider how university members might host such rooted, faithful conversations about "particular places and people, intimately known and cared about."[54] Such conversations would make the center and the periphery "properly knowledgeable" about each other and would teach them "what they *owe* to each other."[55] But for this to occur, universities have to stop merely communicating their abstract knowledge to the periphery and start listening to local knowledge. As Berry notes, "Communication . . . goes one way, from the center outward to the periphery, but a conversation goes two ways."[56] A genuine conversation would facilitate the internal and external accounting needed for responsible, faithful membership. And by doing so, it might contribute to healing the psychological, ecological, and cultural damage perpetuated by abstract knowledge.

Rooted Faculty and Administrators

One simple, albeit difficult, step that faculty, administrators, and staff can take to foster a conversation with their university's local place is to stick around.

University administrators and faculty are notoriously mobile; administrators climb the management ladder by moving from institution to institution, and successful faculty look for positions at more prestigious schools where they can teach fewer courses and have access to more funds. Although these motivations are understandable, such geographic promiscuity prevents individuals from developing relationships with community members and from learning what kinds of questions a local place might ask of its university. Berry describes the result in rather acerbic terms: "We have . . . a system of institutions which more and more resemble one another, like airports and motels, made increasingly uniform by the transience or rootlessness of their career-oriented faculties and the consequent inability to respond to local conditions. The professor lives in his career, in a ghetto of career-oriented fellow professors. Where he may be geographically is of little interest to him. One's career is a vehicle, not a dwelling; one is concerned less for where it is than for where it will go."[57] Even if Berry's grim indictment does not apply to all professors and administrators, it strikes a bit too close to home.

Yet professional members of universities who commit themselves to remaining in one place can change the standard of their work and their teaching. Rather than seeking to impress their professional colleagues at other institutions, they might begin to realize how their work affects the local community. As Berry argues in an interview, "The teacher, the person of learning, the researcher, the intellectual, the artist, the scientist . . . must commit themselves to a community in such a way that they share the fate of that community—participate in its losses and trials and griefs and hardships and pleasures and joys and satisfactions—so that they don't have this ridiculous immunity that they now have in their specializations and careers."[58] Such a commitment, Berry explains, would transform the way teachers think of their work: "If you supposed to yourself, 'Well, when these kids graduate, that's probably the last I'm going to see of them,' you're going to teach differently than you would teach if you assume that you're going to spend the rest of your life with these people. These kids are going to grow up. They're going to take their place in the community you live in. They're going to be your fellow citizens, your fellow members."[59] So the simple act of stepping out of a *career* and into a *place* changes a teacher's priorities and standards in ways that have far-reaching implications. And choosing to commit oneself to a particular place doesn't require any institutional change; it just requires the difficult work of fidelity.

We certainly recognize that in today's job market, not all teachers can choose to remain faithful to one place. Indeed, perhaps the greatest threat to rooted faculty and local curricula is not online education but the increasing reliance on adjunct instructors. According to a 2009 report by the American Federation of Teachers, tenure-track faculty account for just over one-quarter of "instructional staff" at US universities and colleges.[60] Institutions are increasingly relying on underpaid adjuncts and other instructors with little incentive—or even opportunity—to develop lasting institutional and local relationships (an impossible task, given that many adjuncts are forced to travel throughout a region, teaching at several schools just to barely scrape together a living). Fidelity is a two-way street: if administrators want teachers to commit to their institution, they must offer long-term employment and adequate pay.

Local Curricula

Faculty members who remain in one place will be better able to incorporate local questions, needs, and ideas into their curricula. This can take many forms, but the goal of a local curriculum should be for students to learn how a faithful conversation can be carried on between the knowledge and resources of the center and the particular needs and opportunities of the periphery. Berry describes this conversation in terms of agricultural college extension services, and he emphasizes the need to make this a two-way conversation:

> I am talking about the need for a two-way communication, a conversation, between a land grant university and the region for and to which it is responsible. The idea of the extensions service should be applied to the whole institution. Not just the agricultural extension agents, but also the graduate teachers, doctors, lawyers, and other community servants should be involved. They should be carrying news from the university out into its region. . . . But this would be extension in two directions: They would also be carrying back into the university news of what is happening that works well, what is succeeding according to the best standards, what works locally. And they should be carrying back criticism also: what is not working, what the university is not doing that it should do, what it is doing that it should do better.[61]

Such a conversation would enact local responsibility, making the university a more faithful member of its place.

Embedding this conversation into university curricula can take many forms, and it can begin with very simple steps. For instance, we took the students in our Agrarian Literature and Theology course on a field trip to the Dahlem Center, a local land conservancy. One of the naturalists led us on a walk, pointing out invasive and native species and discussing the challenges of the center's work. Such a valuation of local problems and local authorities undercuts the narrative of the "expert" that universities tend to promulgate. As Berry explains, relying on experts from far away devalues the good work being done by the ordinary people around us: "The ascendancy of the expert involves a withdrawal or relinquishment of confidence in local intelligence—that is, in the knowledge, experience, and mental competence of ordinary people doing ordinary work. The result, naturally, is that the competence of local intelligence has declined. We are losing the use of local minds at work on local problems."[62] This field trip took minimal planning, but it provided a crucial opportunity for our students to learn from a local mind at work on local problems.

For a real conversation to develop between a university and its community, however, occasional field trips are insufficient. Our own efforts to develop a university garden benefited greatly from collaboration with a local church, high school students interested in sustainable agriculture, and a nearby farmers' market. And we've already mentioned the good work being done by institutions like the Berry Center and Paul Quinn College. The Berry Center, in conjunction with St. Catharine College, saw "the urgent need for bolstering rural communities, small farm production, and local markets" and developed a program in farming and ecological agrarianism to meet that need.[63] And Paul Quinn, located in a "federally-recognized food desert," started its own farm to provide healthy food to urban Dallas residents and to train students in sustainable farming.[64] Such collaborative, locally adapted programs are examples of what can develop from a real conversation between centers and the periphery, as people on both sides ask, "What can we do for each other? What do you need that we can supply you with or do for you? What do you need to know that we can tell you?"[65] Such conversations provide hope that some university centers are beginning to treat their local places as worthy of respect and faithful care. Institutions adapted to the needs and opportunities of their particular places would resist the trend Patrick Deneen identifies as the Walmartization of the university and would instead cultivate a more diverse network of locally adapted schools.[66]

Cross-Cultural Study to Promote Homecoming

It's obvious that we would consider local agricultural collaborations a crucial part of faithful habitation, but studying abroad as a means of fostering homecoming may seem more counterintuitive. However, as discussed earlier, the narrative of exodus and return contains an important psychological truth: we often can't fully appreciate our homes until we've left them for a while. Study-abroad programs are often justified by some vague boilerplate about educating students for global citizenship, but cross-cultural study can, if undertaken from the right perspective, teach students to inhabit their own places more wisely. Such travel, however, needs to be framed in such a way that it encourages students not to become footloose tourists, always eager to consume new cultures and experiences, but rather to become thoughtful patriots, learning to love their own homes more courageously and humbly by seeing how other cultures love theirs.

Berry's extensive travel writings are an exemplary model for what this study might look like. While many people think of Berry as a Kentucky farmer who doesn't get out much, he has written long essays about his travels to places as far-flung as Ireland, Peru, the desert Southwest, the Amish-inhabited Midwest, and the forests of Pennsylvania.[67] Throughout these essays, Berry demonstrates his method of listening attentively to the cultures he encounters, learning other ways of farming, forestry, and land use that can inspire and correct his relation to his native Kentucky.

To encourage this kind of local application, teachers and students should approach opportunities to study abroad not as tourism or as an education in the cosmopolitan values of global citizenship but as an opportunity to learn how other cultures love and inhabit their particular places. While such habitation takes different forms in different places, it enables students to reimagine how they might dwell in their own beloved places. Travel undertaken in this way provides a necessary broadening that can equip students to better meet the needs of their own homes.

One of our colleagues in the Sociology Department provides an example of how study abroad can inspire more faithful work at home. Jeremy Norwood leads groups of students on three-week trips to Cambodia, and one year while they were traveling through a red-light district there, they were approached by traffickers selling young girls. This experience devastated the students, and when they got home they began researching human trafficking in the United States. Rather than seeing sex trafficking as a far-away problem, they turned their attention to its local manifestations in truck stops, massage parlors, and strip clubs. Their efforts to learn more led first to a series of conferences and letter-writing campaigns and then to cooperative efforts with the city and the county to educate members of law enforcement and change local laws. This is precisely the kind of local work that cross-cultural trips can inspire; seeing a new culture opened the students' eyes to problems at home that they had never noticed before, and their new perspective led to local curriculum and a genuine, ongoing conversation between the university and its community.

Lower Tuition

Increasingly, America is becoming segregated along economic and educational lines, as those with the ability to do so move to urban areas or "super zips" to maximize their economic opportunities.[68] At least some of this migration of educated young people away from poorer communities could be stemmed if college graduates based their residency decisions on factors other than maximizing their earning potential. But when students accrue huge amounts of debt, such decisions become much more difficult.

Urban theorist Richard Florida points out that Americans are increasingly sorting themselves into silos of similarly educated people. In effect, we are experiencing "a big talent sort . . . , with the highly educated and highly skilled going some places and the less educated and less skilled going to others."[69] Florida's response to this phenomenon, as suggested by the title of his book *Who's Your City? How the Creative Economy Is Making Where to Live the Most Important Decision of Your Life*, is to suggest that privileged individuals maximize their happiness by moving wherever they will have the most opportunities: we all just need to "find the place that fits us best."[70] This narcissistic decision-making method exacerbates the real economic pressures that lead some young college graduates to move to urban centers, where high housing prices and a higher cost of living cancel out much of the economic benefit of moving there. One step graduates can take when thinking about where to move after college is to base that decision not on what amenities and opportunities they think they want but on where they are needed. Like Burley Coulter, they can practice faithfulness to the places and people that need them and that will benefit from their knowledge, even if such faithfulness costs them economically. Then, after many years of habitation, perhaps these graduates will see that they have reaped the fruits of fidelity in friendship, service, and a thriving parochial place.

If students are actually going to return home and settle there after graduating from college, universities must do their part to ensure that they can afford this choice. When students are saddled by thousands of dollars in debt, they face extreme financial pressures to move wherever they can earn the largest salary—forcing them to live in their careers rather than their places. This is why Berry, in a personal letter, pointed to the cost of a college education as its most fundamental problem: "Maybe the way to get at the problems, maybe all of them, of higher education is to ask why it has become so expensive."[71] Berry develops this line of thinking in a recent essay: "For the sake of cultural continuity and community survival we must reconsider the purpose, the worth, and the cost of education—especially of higher education, which too often leads away from home, and too often graduates its customers into unemployment or debt or both. When young people leave their college or university too much in debt to afford to come home, we need to think again. There can never be too much knowledge, but there certainly can be too much school."[72] Elsewhere, he commends the Amish decision to limit formal schooling (but not learning) as a way of mitigating this brain drain, but a better solution would be to make education more affordable so that rural communities can receive the benefits of university knowledge without losing their young people.[73]

University administrators, however, find it difficult to buck the trends that make higher education more and more expensive. The amenities "arms race" continues apace as schools build lavish dormitories, state-of-the-art recreational facilities, and, occasionally, expensive laboratory space. Unfortunately, student demand for such amenities makes this spending profitable for many colleges.[74] But other schools, such as members of the Work Colleges Consortium, have chosen to limit these bells and whistles and thereby keep costs relatively low.[75] The success of these colleges indicates the potential to attract students who are willing to work hard and live in less lavish accommodations in exchange for graduating with less debt and more practical work experience. Some courageous school administrators may accept Berry's challenge to find creative ways to reduce the cost of education: "When is some smart little school finally going to draw the line and say, 'This is far enough. This is enough. We don't have to make it more expensive to make it as intelligent as it can be'? When are the refusals, the institutional refusals, going to start coming? That would be really radical."[76]

What we are calling for, finally, is a "splendid parochialism," a sensitively humble and courageous pride in our local places that enables us to resist the lure of a wayward cosmopolitanism.[77] Such a parochialism, one informed by a responsible conversation between periphery and center, will care for places in their particularity and foster an authentic multiculturalism. Such faithful care certainly does not guarantee that these places will thrive or that graduates who settle there will have easy, happy lives. Our faith, as Berry writes, "is that by staying, and only by staying, we will learn something of the truth, that the truth is good to know, and that it is always both different and larger than we thought."[78]

Berry describes the devastating consequences of Americans' promiscuous relation to place in his poem "Where." The following excerpt charts the way displaced minds project their own desires on their surroundings, extract what they want, and move on. Nevertheless, local knowledge, with the rooted flourishing it enables, remains a possibility if individuals will see a "good fate" in their place and "willingly pa[y] its cost" in faithful habitation.

> The land bears the scars
> of minds whose history
> was imprinted by no example
> of a forbearing mind, corrected,
> beloved. A mind cast loose
> in whim and greed makes
> nature its mirror, and the garden
> falls with the man.
>
> Such a mind is as much
> a predicament as such
> a place. And yet a knowledge
> is here that tenses the throat
> as for song: the inheritance
> of the ones, alive or once
> alive, who stand behind
> the ones I have imagined,
> who took into their minds
> the troubles of this place,
> blights of love and race,
> but saw a good fate here
> and willingly paid its cost,
> kept it the best they could,
> thought of its good,
> and mourned the good they lost.[79]

7
Community
Learning to Love the Membership

We end this book with a chapter on love. We are aware of the danger in invoking so eviscerated a term. Given that we have labored to be precise throughout this argument, we fear we might lose some readers by arguing for love as the foundational communal virtue in higher education. The word dwells in our language as an abstraction of the worst sort; it is probably not too much to say that *love* has lost nearly any real meaning or usefulness—for it is equally acceptable to proclaim that we love our spouses, our children, our dogs, and our pastrami on ryes. Love has been relegated to the dustbin of temporal emotions and is more often than not a descriptor of a fleeting feeling rather than a habit or virtue.

In arguing for love, however, we do not mean the sort of love that is self-referential or self-satisfying—a hollow word flippantly employed in reference to those people or things we like. When *love* refers to a passing emotion, its orientation is selfish; it becomes a term that indicates how something makes us feel. In contrast, we take love to designate something about the inherent value and worth of the beloved, so that love names our proper orientation toward and commitment to a love-worthy other. This is the virtue St. Paul upholds when he envisions the church as a body with many members, a vision that culminates in his famous ode to charity in 1 Corinthians 13. And this is the virtue that lies behind Wendell Berry's reliance on the metaphor of *membership* to describe the proper form of community.

Paul also links love and knowledge in a way that might instruct universities: he proclaims that knowledge must ultimately serve love, and that knowledge apart from love is nothing. A university without love is similarly vapid: to have love as a university's moral telos would be to hold disciplines accountable to their effects on their fellow members, both within the university and within their geographic communities. Too often, however, university curricula are like a random collection of coins causing a cacophonous din as they jangle about in a tin can. The only viable telos in such a community becomes the hope that, by reaching into the tin can, students might pull out enough change at the end of the day to buy something that makes them feel good, maybe one of those pastrami sandwiches they love so much.

Our goal in this chapter, then, is to argue that education without love lacks a healthy telos and is adrift in a sea of competing moral and amoral ends. In his most recent collection of essays, Berry articulates a truth that he has, "from [his] own experience, begun to know: how intimately related, how nearly synonymous, are the terms 'love' and 'know,' how likely impossible it is to know authentically or well what one does not love, and how certainly impossible it is to love what one does not know."[1] So we acknowledge that love is a risky virtue to define, but we also believe that the work of reclamation and imagination is important, and thus we hope to articulate a love that can lead our knowledge to serve the health of people and places. And Berry's novel *Jayber Crow* is a good place to begin this work of reimagining love.

What our culture calls *love* often refers to how something makes *me* feel: the institutions Jayber attends encourage him to love learning for what it enables him to get, whether approval from God or a good career; likewise, Jayber is tempted to love Mattie because she makes him feel good. In contrast, genuine love consists in seeking the good of another: Jayber learns to cultivate true study, which seeks to understand a subject because it's inherently worthy and because his understanding of it can benefit the subject itself; Jayber learns to love Mattie (and then the rest of the Port William community) as an eternally valuable being. Such an attitude aspires to understand and preserve the connections between members because these connections lead to the health of the whole community. In many ways, these are the contrasts we drew in the introduction between boomers and stickers, so Jayber's narrative provides a fitting summation of our argument.

Our examination of this novel is more extended than our readings of Berry's fiction in previous chapters. Berry's diagnosis of the fragmentation that characterizes most educational institutions is particularly nuanced in *Jayber Crow*, and the novel also develops an alternative mode of communal catechesis, one that provides an education in and for love. After describing *Jayber Crow*'s indictment of formal education and the "way of love" Berry offers in its place, we articulate two contrasting modes of intellectual appetite—the curious and the studious. Whereas the curious desire knowledge in order to gain power for themselves, the studious desire knowledge for the sake of the one known. One of the characteristics of a studious person, then, is an ability to make connections and foster complex health—habits that modern universities are particularly bad at fostering. Finally, we consider two practices that might foster this loving orientation toward others: asking connective questions and developing focused attention.

The Failure of Jayber Crow's Formal Education

The full title of Berry's novel, *Jayber Crow: The Life Story of Jayber Crow, Barber, of the Port William Membership, as Written by Himself*, is itself a summary of the work. In the novel, the narrator—an aging, semiretired barber in a small Kentucky community—looks back on his life and measures its meaning by the standard of his love for the membership of Port William. Early in his life, Jayber belongs to three different institutions of learning, and each one fails to cultivate loving knowledge. While they each falter in different ways, all suffer from divisions that lead them to inculcate a knowledge based on controlling and exploiting others for selfish fulfillment. Yet when Jayber wanders back to Port William, he is gradually catechized in a different kind of knowledge, a knowledge that, because it is based on love, seeks the good of the one known rather than the knower.

Early in Jayber's narrative, he recounts the deaths first of his parents and then of the great-aunt and -uncle who took him in. Orphaned twice over, Jayber is cast on the mercy of institutions. He expresses his attitude toward these institutions by remarking that when he left the care of his relatives and entered a church orphanage called The Good Shepherd, he "went out of the hands of love, which certainly included charity as we know it, into the hands of charity as we know it, which included love only as it might."[2] As Jayber recalls his time at The Good Shepherd, he realizes how it shaped him not for health and membership but for division: "At The Good Shepherd I entered for the first time a divided world—divided both from me and within itself. It was divided from me because it did not seem to be present unless I watched it. Within itself, it was divided between an ideal world of order, as prescribed and demanded by the institution, . . . and a real world of disorder, which we students brought in with us as a sort of infection."[3] By trying "so hard to be a world unto itself," The Good Shepherd denies the embodied lives of its students—their pasts, their narratives, their desires—and so Jayber is unable to imagine himself as a member of any real community there.[4] The institution's effort to seal itself off from the external world manifests in the way each student is stripped of his or her name and is known only by a first initial. Children who have lost their parents now become nameless, losing their identities for the sake of The Good Shepherd's order—an order that institutionalizes charity and makes love for particular children merely accidental.

Jayber is ultimately thankful for his time at The Good Shepherd, despite, not because of, any formal teaching he received there. In fact, the greatest lesson he takes from that place is a learned distrust of institutions: "It is true that I dislike the life of institutions and organizations.... This is not a prejudice, but a considered judgment, one that The Good Shepherd taught me to make."[5] But Jayber is careful to give thanks for the good lessons he learned in that place, dropping his sardonic tone to remember the unofficial means by which he was educated for health and unity: the stories he found in The Good Shepherd's library. Under a generous window in this library, Jayber read stories of orphans like Tom Sawyer and Huckleberry Finn, who found their places in communities. He read *The Swiss Family Robinson* and *Walden,* tales of people on the margins of society who built homes for themselves. While The Good Shepherd failed to educate Jayber for membership, these narratives taught him to imagine how even an orphan like himself might come home.[6] It's not surprising, then, that he pens his memoir while living in a Thoreau-like cabin by the river, not far from where he was born.

When Jayber emerges from The Good Shepherd, he is "confused and hopeful and self-deluded," adrift in a sea of possibilities with no direction and only a dubious calling—given the institution's narrow, sectarian orientation, Jayber can only imagine that he must have been called to be a preacher. So he heads to Pigeonville, a small denominational college where he hopes to have some of his many questions answered and his doubts appeased. Yet because The Good Shepherd not only failed to encourage Jayber's embodied personhood but also failed to teach him the goodness of hierarchy, he arrives at Pigeonville afraid of those in authority: "I didn't want to get crosswise with anybody who had authority to punish me; I had had enough of that at The Good Shepherd. I didn't want ever again to stand in front of the desk of somebody who had more power than I had."[7] And so Jayber learns to obey the rules at Pigeonville not because he understands his role in the order of the place and among its people but because he fears order itself. This damage makes his learning more haphazard and irregular than it otherwise might have been.

Like The Good Shepherd, Pigeonville exists in a cordoned-off world; by removing themselves from their places, these institutions fail to foster a knowledge that loves and serves their communities. As Jayber explains about Pigeonville, "It made me feel excluded from it, even while I was in it." This sense of exclusion stems from a malady not unlike that which afflicted The Good Shepherd; in the people at Pigeonville, Jayber sees "the old division of body and soul [he] had known at The Good Shepherd." At Pigeonville, the body is denigrated in favor of the soul: "Everything bad was laid on the body, and everything good was credited to the soul. It scared me a little when I realized that I saw it the other way around."[8]

Jayber begins to see that this dualistic accounting—one marked by division and oriented toward control—is neither internally nor externally coherent. It fails internally because if those at Pigeonville proclaim the God-Man to be risen, his incarnation ought to be paramount to them and, by extension, so must our bodies; however, "these preachers I'm talking about all thought that the soul could do no wrong, but always had its face washed and its pants on and was in agony over having to associate with the flesh and the world. And yet these same people believed in the resurrection of the body."[9] This theology also fails to account for the real complexities of Jayber's experiences in the world, and so he begins to experience "doctrinal trouble." By dividing itself from the world, Pigeonville fails to make its learning serve the needs and questions of its members. It is around this time that Jayber begins to realize he has far too many questions to be a preacher and that perhaps he has misheard his calling.

Seeking advice for the questions that are rattling around in his head, Jayber turns to one of his professors, Dr. Ardmire. As Jayber confesses, "I was afraid to go to him because I knew he was going to tell me the truth. Dr. Ardmire was a feared man. . . . He was known, behind his back, as Old Grit."[10] In turning to this feared professor, Jayber has taken a step into the unknown, he has placed himself in an uncharacteristic position for a solitary loner—he makes himself vulnerable to another person. After Jayber runs down all the questions and doubts he has, Dr. Ardmire confirms Jayber's fear—he has not been called to be a preacher. But more importantly, he does not mock Jayber for believing he had heard God's call; instead, he affirms Jayber's questions and speaks these profound words: "You have been given questions to which you cannot be *given* answers. You will have to live them out—perhaps a little at a time." To this gnomic statement, Jayber replies: "And how long is that going to take?" "I don't know," Dr. Ardmire says, "as long as you live, perhaps." Jayber, who is still innocent and naïve, adds, "That could be a long time." To which Dr. Ardmire so eloquently responds, "I will tell you a further mystery. It may take longer."[11] Dr. Ardmire's is the first institutional voice Jayber has heard that refuses to offer narrowly authoritative answers. Thus, Dr. Ardmire becomes the one who instructs Jayber in membership; by learning to allow his intellectual questions to turn him toward his embodied life, a life he must live alongside real neighbors, Jayber begins his education in love.

Though Pigeonville has failed Jayber in some ways, it has also taught him a very important truth—one's education is inextricably tied to questioning. For Jayber, such questioning and doubting transcend the classroom and permeate all aspects of his life—his faith, his loves, his work, his friendships. Dr. Ardmire has taught Jayber that questioning is not a malady of the human condition but a virtue of it; by turning us away from our desires and preoccupations, questions can prod us to attend more carefully and charitably to others, teaching us finally how to fulfill our membership alongside them. And even though Dr. Ardmire has told Jayber this, he still has to live it out: his life will become a curriculum of questions as he wanders from place to place, and even after he finally settles in Port William.

As Jayber begins his wandering journey to someplace yet unknown, he lands in Lexington, enrolling at his third institution of learning: the University of Kentucky. He attends UK not because he wants to specialize in anything in particular but because he loves learning. Forced to identify a major, Jayber chooses "schoolteacher," but only to appease the "official forces"; Jayber's desire to learn doesn't fit the official expectation that he is there to improve his career opportunities. The problem for Jayber is not that his professors are not knowledgeable or engaging—it is that they "were pretty aloof, like the university itself, and I was as aloof from them as they were from me."[12] The university community was operating not as a membership but as individuals with competing goals who happened to cross paths in the same place, and such competition can be isolating. In other words, the lack of shared order and purpose at the university divided professors from students.

These internal divisions correlate with the university's division from its place. Whereas The Good Shepherd scorned the corruption of the outside world, the University of Kentucky scorned the backwardness of its surrounding community: "The university was in some ways the opposite of The Good Shepherd. The Good Shepherd looked upon the outside world as a threat to its conventional wisdom. The university looked upon itself as a threat to the conventional wisdom of the outside world. According to it, it not only knew more than ordinary people but was more advanced and had a better idea of the world of the future."[13] These attitudes mirror each other, and each institution was engaged in a sort of competition with its community in a way that prevented it from loving and serving its place.

Given their internal divisions and their separation from their communities, all three institutions failed to teach Jayber to know and love his place. The parallel manner in which each of them failed is significant—they all understood themselves as existing apart from the world, apart from their places:

> Every one of the educational institutions that I had been in had been hard at work trying to be a world unto itself. The Good Shepherd and Pigeonville College were trying to be the world of the past. The university was trying to be the world of the future, and maybe it has had a good deal to do with the world as it has turned out to be, but this has not been as big an improvement as the university expected. The university thought of itself as a place of freedom for thought and study and experimentation, and maybe it was, in a way. But it was an island too, a floating or a flying island. It was preparing people from the world of the past for the world of the future, and what was missing was the world of the present, where every body was living its small, short, surprising, miserable, wonderful, blessed, damaged, only life.[14]

Jayber's desire is to be a living member of the present, and his formal education does not prepare him to belong anywhere. As an orphan, he is already like a "floating or a flying island," and his education merely exacerbates his deracination: "So far as I could see, I was going nowhere. And now, more and more, I seemed also to have come from nowhere. Without a loved life to live, I was becoming more and more a theoretical person, as if I might have been a figment of institutional self-justification: a theoretical ignorant person from the sticks, who one day would go to a theoretical somewhere and make a theoretical something of himself—the implication being that until he became that something he would be nothing."[15] When his freedom finally becomes loneliness, Jayber drifts away from formal education and wanders back to his boyhood home. It is here, from within a membership, that he begins to live out his questions and finally learn how to unite knowledge with love for a particular place.

Before moving on to examine how Jayber learns to practice love, we should note that Jayber is partly to blame for the failures of his formal education. As the narrator of *A Place on Earth* explains, "He was vastly more inclined to learn than to be taught; that made him the natural enemy of his teachers, and he suffered for it. He came away from The Good Shepherd, he said, bearing more marks of scholarly discipline on his tail, by a considerable margin, than his teachers had ever been able to imprint on his mind." Jayber's disposition is to be contrary to teachers and institutions, to be unwilling to acknowledge his place in the order of things, and this is as much a critique of his own shortcomings as it is of his professors and educational institutions. If a student is unable to see his professor as an authority, as someone who is leading the student on a journey, he will necessarily commodify that relationship. It is no surprise, then, that Jayber finds himself desiring independence and freedom from such impoverished relationships. Yet while Jayber believes his longing for isolation is one of the benefits of his freedom, he gradually discovers that it is a symptom of his lostness: "He became more and more depressed under the burden of his freedom."[16] So while the people and institutions of Jayber's formal education have in many ways failed him, he is complicit in this failure.

How Jayber Learns to Follow the Way of Love

The beauty of Jayber's story is that, despite the failure of institutions to model an education in love, his long membership in the Port William community fills that void. His tutelary spirit in this regard is Mattie Keith Chatham. Many of our students struggle to understand Jayber's secret and one-sided "marriage" to Mattie, a woman he has known since she was a young girl and who is legally married to Troy Chatham, a man Jayber hates for most of the book. Students are bothered first because Jayber is about twenty-five years old and Mattie is fourteen when he initially notices her beauty, and second because she is already married to Troy when Jayber commits himself to her on his long winter walk back from Hargrave.[17] Indeed, Jayber's initial motives for his "marriage" to Mattie are quite mixed, and his vows are inspired, in part, by his hatred for Troy and all he represents and by his rivalry with Troy. Yet despite Jayber's muddled intentions, this "marriage" becomes the source of his deepest experience of divine love; by it, he learns that it is possible to love even those from whom we are most divided. As his love for Mattie matures and grows, he comes to value her for who she is, rather than for anything he can gain from this unusual relationship. In this regard, Jayber models the kind of studious, other-oriented desire that universities should strive to cultivate.

Throughout most of his life, Jayber harbors a hatred for Troy Chatham. He envies Troy's lawful marriage to Mattie; he thinks about the good such a marriage would provide him and the good he would provide Mattie if he were her husband.[18] In this way, he sees Troy as competition for Mattie and considers him an "impudent son of a bitch" for his aggressiveness toward her even before they are married.[19] Jayber is bothered that Troy acts as though he owns Mattie, or at least owns her affection. Yet in this competition for Mattie, and in his hatred of Troy, Jayber destroys himself—he becomes like the man who consumes poison, hoping it will kill his enemy. It is only a matter of time before Jayber realizes that Troy is not the only one who has been arrogantly imposing himself on Mattie, seeing her as an object of his desire rather than as a living being capable of being loved as God would love and, thus, being loved for herself and not for his own selfish desires. It takes Jayber a good while to realize that he is, in fact, more like Troy than he'd like to admit.

The turning point for Jayber comes one evening when he is at a dance with his lover Clydie. While Jayber and Clydie are dancing, he looks up and sees Troy dancing with a strange woman. Troy winks at Jayber and makes a conspiratorial gesture, and Jayber suddenly realizes that for all his hatred of Troy, the two of them may be alike: "I was thinking . . . , as Troy winked at me and raised his sign: 'We're *not* alike!' And that was what sickened me, because I wasn't sure."[20] Jayber slips away from the dance, leaves his car as a parting gift to Clydie, and makes his secret marriage vow on the long walk home. This vow signifies his determination not to mirror his rival; if Troy's love for Mattie is selfish, then Jayber will cultivate the kind of selfless love she deserves. The novel's epigraph, taken from Andrew Marvell's "The Definition of Love," indicates the character of Jayber's love: "Love is of a birth as rare / As 'tis, for object, strange and high . . . / begotten by Despair, / Upon Impossibility." Jayber's marriage to Mattie, who is already a married woman, is indeed an impossibility. Yet it is precisely the absurdity of this marriage, a covenant that brings no tangible benefits to

Jayber and in fact incurs great costs in celibacy and silent heartache, that teaches Jayber to practice the virtue of love.

For a good portion of his adult life, Jayber has not loved Troy and has selfishly desired Mattie. But he learns that "love fails here . . . because it cannot be fulfilled here. And then I saw something that a normal life with a normal marriage might never have allowed me to see. I saw Mattie was not merely desirable, but desirable beyond the power of time to show." He knows that even if Mattie were his wife, he could never desire her enough—she would always be beyond him because she "was a living soul and could be loved forever. Like every living creature, she carried in her the presence of eternity."[21] By bringing him into the presence of eternity, Jayber's love for Mattie takes him beyond the solitary competition fostered by his formal education and invites him into an inclusive membership: "I prayed unreasonably, foolishly, hopelessly, that everybody in Port William might be blessed and happy—the ones I loved and the ones I did not."[22] Thus, the way of love that begins with a love for Mattie comes to include everyone—even Troy Chatham.

Because Jayber's love for Mattie is at first selfish and driven by consumption, its fruit is envy—envy of Troy—cultivated and nourished by Jayber's isolated competition with him. But by the end of the book, when Mattie is dying of cancer and Troy has clear-cut the stand of old-growth timber on their land, Jayber achieves clarity: there is beauty and goodness in the world, despite its failings—Troy's and his own—and his love for the world brings him to the edge of time. It has brought him as far as love can bring a person. And he has come to know that if we fail to love even our enemies, all else is lost. The "enemies" in Jayber's life have been several, and their presence reminds him of his failure to love the least of these. He has failed his lover Clydie, his rival Troy, and his bitter neighbor Cecelia Overhold, yet he finally forgives them (and himself) for their wrongs, even though none of them asks him to do so. His forgiveness of Troy marks the great distance this way of love has brought him: "As for Troy Chatham, whose enemy I was for so many years, even against my will, though he never knew it, or cared, if he did know it—I have forgiven him too, even him, even if I cannot say yet that the thought of him gladdens me."[23] Because Mattie is not the source of this love but only one of the refracted beams of its light, when Jayber learns to love her rightly, he also learns to recognize the other members of his community as revealed by this same divine light, a light that radiates through the prism of creation.

Jayber had wondered whether his life story would be "a book about Hell— . . . where we are needy and alone, where things that ought to stay together fall apart, where there is such a groaning travail of selfishness in all its forms, where we love one another and die, where we must lose everything to know what we have had." If Jayber had pursued an illicit, selfish relationship with Mattie and continued his rivalry with Troy, it certainly would have been a book about hellish isolation and destruction. But Jayber concludes that his is a book about heaven and the ways "the earth speaks to us of Heaven" through our participation in the membership of love.[24] Through his love for Mattie, Jayber learns to cherish the order of Port William and its people. He is a man connected by love, holding the threads together by an eternal love that remains beyond him yet includes him.

It is outside the walls of any educational institution that Jayber finally learns how to love and participate in the membership of his place. In fact, his education in love is contrary to the divisive and competitive formal education he received. His tenuous relationships with institutions of learning fail because he cannot imagine the good in pursuing knowledge detached from a community and its place. Yet his education continues in his quest to love each person in the membership to which he belongs. The way of love he follows reshapes his desire for solitude and culminates in his rooted, loving membership of Port William.

Jayber Crow thus offers both a cautionary tale of how institutions of learning can fail their students and a model for how communities, as embodied in Port William, can shape people to be members who practice love. This may not seem very promising for universities, but our hope is that some participants in universities might work toward practicing the kind of loving membership that leads students along the way of love. In what follows, we suggest how to begin this process by fostering loving intellectual appetites and a culture that encourages students to make connections.

Knowledge as Loving Participation Rather than Exploitative Control

Throughout this book, we have considered the motivations that underlie different approaches to education and different organizations of knowledge. In light of Jayber's narrative, we turn once again to this theme and probe the different kinds of love that result in different kinds of learning and knowledge. In the epigraph to *The Unsettling of America*, Berry quotes Montaigne's articulation of a key contrast: "Who so hath his minde on taking, hath it no more on what he hath taken." This concisely identifies the core distinction between someone who desires to learn in order to accrue power and control—and thus has his mind on the act of taking itself—and someone who desires to learn in order to participate more intimately in the life of the beloved subject—and thus has his mind on the subject itself.

One way of understanding this difference between knowledge based on a desire to control and exploit others and knowledge based on love for others is the distinction St. Augustine makes between "curious" and "studious" souls. The English word *studious* derives from the Latin word *studium*, meaning "diligent," "application to," and "zeal or affection." *Curious* derives from *cura*, which carries the sense of "worry," "concern," and "meddling." These English words retain only remnants of the connotations of their Latin roots, connotations that Augustine develops to urge his readers to desire knowledge based on love for the subject being studied. In the following passage from *De Trinitate*, Augustine's dense syntax elucidates the complex relationships between our intellectual desires and the way we relate to the subjects of our knowledge:

> Every love that belongs to a studious soul which wants to know what it does not know is not a love of what it does not know but rather of what it does know. It is because of what it does know that it wants to know what it does not know. But someone so curious as to be carried away by nothing other than a love of knowing the unknown, and not because of something already known, should be distinguished from the studious and called curious. But even the curious do not love the unknown. It is more accurate to say that they hate the unknown because they want everything to become known and thus nothing to remain unknown.[25]

Augustine's point is that people can have two motivations for wanting to learn. Studious souls fall in love with a subject, and because they love the small part they know, they want to learn more. These souls desire knowledge so that they can know their beloved subject more intimately. Curious souls, in contrast, don't want to participate more intimately with the known; rather, they hate the unknown because it is beyond their control.

The curious want to know more in order to expand their power, their ability to exploit and benefit from others.[26]

Interestingly, Berry uses these two words in *Jayber Crow*, describing Troy as "curious" and Mattie as "studious."[27] Whether or not he intentionally uses these terms for their patristic connotations, Troy and Mattie certainly embody these contrasting motivations. Troy values only knowledge from which he can profit. For instance, he disregards his father-in-law's long intimacy with the farm and buys a tractor so he can increase the "power and speed of work."[28] In other words, Troy learns not because he loves the farm and wants to learn how to care for it; instead, he learns techniques to make the farm yield a greater profit, regardless of the long-term costs to the farm's health. Like all curious souls, he is dissatisfied with what he knows and desires new knowledge, new equipment, new techniques.[29] Mattie, however, loves the farm on which she was raised. Because of her affection for it, she prevents Troy from harvesting the "Nest Egg"—the old-growth trees on the farm—and she wanders through these woods regularly, delighting in their beauty and harmony. When Jayber first moves to Port William, he shares Troy's desire for knowledge that brings power. As Jayber admits, he bought a car for the same reason that Troy bought a tractor—a deep impatience and a desire to be free from all impediments.[30] However, after he "marries" Mattie, Jayber gives away his car and commits himself to the patient study of his place and community. So later in his life, Jayber takes pleasure in walking through the Nest Egg, sharing Mattie's delight in understanding the woods' deep order.

Unfortunately, university cultures generally foster curious habits of mind rather than studious ones. Part of the problem, as Berry notes, is that "wonder has been replaced by a research agenda."[31] When knowledge becomes instrumental to good grades, external funding, and an impressive CV, it ceases to be a way of participating more intimately with a beloved subject. Hannah Coulter describes the way her son Caleb changed as he earned a bachelor's degree and then a graduate degree in agricultural science: "After not liking school at all, Caleb had got to liking it too much, more anyhow than I would have wanted him to, if I had had any say. He liked knowing the things he was learning. He was beginning to learn the ways of research, and he liked that. He was, maybe you could say, tempted by it."[32] In other words, like Augustine's curious soul, Caleb got carried away by a love of knowing the unknown, and in the process, he lost his love of farming itself; he loved the act of knowing more than he loved the known subject. He pursued agricultural knowledge not to be a better farmer or to take better care of his farm but to publish papers in the "Unknown Tongue" and get tenure.³³

One of the marks of a curious intellectual culture is its insistence on protecting intellectual "property." Paul Griffiths points out the absurdity of treating ideas, or "intelligibilia," as if they were scarce goods that required property laws: "Some things can be given away without thereby being lost to the giver.... The point of importance here is that intelligibilia belong by definition to a commons: any attempt to expropriate them therefrom, to privatize them, corrupts not the intelligibilia (that is impossible) but rather both the one who attempts it and the intimate relationship he attempts to establish between himself and the intelligibilia in question."³⁴ Thus, as Griffiths goes on to argue, intellectual property is an obsession of an economy based on curiosity. From seed DNA to crop futures, ideas can be claimed, owned, and profited from. Berry critiques this misappropriation in *Life Is a Miracle* by approvingly quoting Ananda Coomaraswamy: "'There can be no property in ideas, because these are gifts of the Spirit.... No matter how many times [it] may already have been "applied" by others, whoever conforms himself to an idea and makes it his own, will be working originally, but not so if he is expressing only his own ideals or opinions.'"³⁵ As Coomaraswamy's language indicates, the studious, loving soul understands knowledge as intimate participation rather than exclusive possession.

This emphasis on ownership leads to the disciplinary fragmentation we've examined elsewhere: academics set out to explore ever narrower fields where they can plant their flags on as yet unclaimed ideas. And as academic fields proliferate, university cultures tend to be overly optimistic about the human ability to know pretty much everything. This is the intellectual hubris Berry critiques in *Life Is a Miracle* and essays such as "The Way of Ignorance." Because Berry thinks knowledge is a form of participation rather than ownership, he warns against the fantasies of scientists like E. O. Wilson, who, in Berry's words, equate the "unknown" with the "to-be-known."³⁶ In many ways, Wilson's approach parallels Griffiths's description of the curious soul's attitude toward knowledge: "Learning to approach the world in this way ... involves the assumption that the world will in fact yield itself to your gaze if only you learn how rightly to look.... There is a magical key to knowledge, a perfectly efficacious pickup line that will bring anyone to your arms and your bed, an ideal joke that will make all hearers laugh whenever it is told. That magical key is method."³⁷ This belief in a magical key, a method that grants us control of knowledge, is embodied in Wilson's dream of an "Encyclopedia of

Life" that would make "all key information about life on Earth accessible to anyone, on demand, anywhere in the world."[38] Wilson's dream has resulted in the creation of such an encyclopedia online, and it is certainly a valuable resource. The problem, however, lies in the belief that any technology can actually make "all key information about life on Earth accessible."

Wilson's dream of total knowledge is not simply a fantasy; it is a dangerous fantasy. As Griffiths argues, the optimism of the curious soul "appears absurdly, dangerously, and utopianly [optimistic] to those who think of knowledge as a kind of intimacy with the other, which is always and inevitably tinged with lament. The curious take themselves to be approaching the goal of getting it finally and completely right—the goal, that is, of knowing everything that's to be known and knowing it perfectly, without blemish or error—ever more closely, and will one day get there."[39] What's more, focusing on accessing and controlling knowledge obscures more important questions about how we participate in and use knowledge. This is why Berry continually seeks to connect knowledge with love, asking how we will use our knowledge to benefit others. As Berry suggests, "To think better, to think like the best humans, we are probably going to have to learn again to judge a person's intelligence, not by the ability to recite facts, but by the good order or harmoniousness of his or her surroundings."[40] So rather than assessing knowledge based on whether the knower can access or recite a set of facts, perhaps universities should judge faculty and students on their ability to apply their knowledge to the healing of their contexts. This would be much harder to quantify on a tenure review or an accreditation report, but this shift in standards might foster a more studious culture, one where students are taught to love what they know and thus use their knowledge to serve the beloved.

Knowledge for Loving Connection Rather than Competition

Studious students who seek knowledge in order to better love and serve the subjects of their knowledge and the places they inhabit have to learn how to make connections. Unfortunately, the disconnected, curious culture encouraged by many universities often educates students to be competitive and divisive. *Jayber Crow* provides insight into how one might follow the way of love and make the connections that situate others in their full contexts. In other words, a studious person seeks to know and tend the relationships between things rather than trying to isolate and control objects of knowledge.

In chapter 1 we considered the implications that Berry's metaphor of knowledge as a rooted tree might have for universities. He develops a related metaphor in chapter 11 of *Jayber Crow*, "The Invisible Web," when Jayber returns to his birthplace and to the graves of his barely remembered family. He is moved by their presence and, in reflecting on his childhood from the perspective of an old man, meditates on the mysterious ways that those who have passed from this world "returned to my dreams. In my comings and goings I crossed their tracks, and my own earlier ones, many times a day, weaving an invisible web that was as real as the ground it was woven over, and as I went about I would feel my losses and my debts."[41] At one time, Jayber imagined himself to be alone, and he is moved by the truth that he is intricately connected to these people and this place by an invisible web marked by joy and loss: "There had been a time before they came, and a time before that. And always, from a time before anybody knew of time, the river had been there."[42] Jayber is connected not only to the people but also to the place, to the river, which has been flowing beyond any living memory. And as one of our students so astutely observed, the river is one of Jayber's teachers, instructing him that he is not alone, that he is caught up in the membership of creation: "I saw how all-of-a-piece it was, how never-ending—always coming, always there, always going."[43]

Jayber's formal education certainly failed to teach him to attend to this invisible web. As we have seen, it suffered from both internal divisions—his professors at the University of Kentucky remained "aloof"—and external divisions—each institution he attended was "a floating or a flying island."[44] It's no surprise, then, that Jayber can articulate the power of this invisible web only after he has learned to love Mattie and the entire Port William membership. Yet his life was caught up in this web of love even before he was aware of it, and his journey along the way of love is also a journey of tracing these connections that bind him to his place and history. So if, as we argued in chapter 2, the liberal arts provide the skills for students to order and unify the different branches of their learning, one of the marks of a studious, loving person is his desire to use these skills to observe and tend the connections in which he finds himself caught up. In other words, universities can prepare and encourage students to care for these connections as they grow into more mature and loving members of their communities.

William Cronon describes the attributes and habits of such a student in his essay "'Only Connect . . .': The Goals of a Liberal Education." Cronon begins by asking, "What does it mean to be a liberally educated person?" Rather than answering this question by defining a specific curriculum, Cronon describes the attributes by which one might "recognize liberally educated people." He concludes that, "more than anything else, being an educated person means being able to see connections that allow one to make sense of the world and act within it in creative ways."[45] The liberally educated person becomes, in Cronon's view, a person with the following habits or qualities:

1. They listen and hear. . . .
2. They read and they understand. . . .
3. They can talk with anyone. . . .
4. They can write clearly and persuasively and movingly. . . .
5. They can solve a wide variety of puzzles and problems. . . .
6. They respect rigor not so much for its own sake but as a way of seeking truth. . . .
7. They practice humility, tolerance, self-criticism. . . .
8. They understand how to get things done in the world. . . .
9. They nurture and empower the people around them. . . .
10. They follow E. M. Forster's injunction from *Howards End*: "Only connect."[46]

These ten qualities, though somewhat broad, are a good starting point to describe a graduate who is prepared for membership in the world beyond higher education. In fact, Cronon's list seems to expand on Berry's observation about "the inescapability of connections and of dependences" in his Centre College commencement address. If humans are inescapably connected, we ought to learn to tend these connections and foster their health. Thus Cronon's list is descriptive, in that it defines the qualities of a student who has been taught to make connections, yet it also carries prescriptive implications for curriculum development.

Cronon offers two important caveats to his injunction to connect, both of which corroborate the critique of formal education in *Jayber Crow*. The first is that no curriculum can guarantee these outcomes. He admits his question—"What does it mean to be a liberally educated person?"—is misleading if it implies that a student "can somehow take a group of courses, or accumulate a certain number of credits, or undergo an obligatory set of learning experiences, and emerge liberally educated at the end of the process." Instead, he notes that a "liberal education is not something any of us ever *achieve*; it is not a *state*. Rather, it is a way of living in the face of our own ignorance, a way of groping toward wisdom in full recognition of our own folly, a way of educating ourselves without any illusion that our educations will ever be complete."[47] The failures in Jayber's formal education cannot be rectified by some curricular quick fix; although these institutions certainly could have taught him in a healthier, more loving way, even the best institutions cannot ensure that their graduates will practice love. Such work may be fostered within educational institutions, but faculty members and graduates must continue this difficult work of love throughout their lives.

Cronon's second caveat is that despite his focus on the attributes of individual graduates, a liberal education is inherently communal; to use Berry's word, it is an education for *membership*. Cronon cautions his readers not to confuse his emphasis on individual freedom and formation for an argument in favor of solipsistic individualism; rather, it is an argument for wisdom, for the value of individual persons properly oriented toward their communities. As Cronon explains:

> Education for human freedom is also education for human community. The two cannot exist without each other. Each of the qualities I have described is a craft or a skill or a way of being in the world [or, in the terms we've been using, a virtue] that frees us to act with greater knowledge or power. But each of these qualities also makes us ever more aware of the connections we have with other people and the rest of creation, and so they remind us of the obligations we have to use our knowledge and power responsibly. If I am right that all these qualities are finally about connecting, then we need to confront one further paradox about liberal education. In the act of making us free, it also binds us to the communities that gave us our freedom in the first place; it makes us responsible to those communities in ways that limit our freedom. In the end, it turns out that liberty is not about thinking or saying or doing whatever we want. It is about exercising our freedom in such a way as to make a difference in the world and make a difference for more than just ourselves.[48]

As we noted in chapter 2, this is the paradoxical nature of the liberal arts—their freeing power lies in their ability to shape us into people who are properly limited by our communities and places. To commit to a people and a place, we must connect, and to make healthy connections, we must work to love all those with whom we share these connections.

The title of Cronon's essay, as well as its theme, is taken from E. M. Forster's novel *Howards End*. Berry takes the title of his Jefferson Lecture, "It All Turns on Affection," from the same work, in which Forster critiques what Berry terms "mechanical thought" that leads to "the withdrawal of affection from places." Berry goes on to quote from Uncle Ernst's indictment of German rationalism: "'Your universities? Oh, yes, you have learned men, who collect more facts than do the learned men of England. They collect facts, and facts, and empires of facts. But which of them will rekindle the light within?'"[49] Berry identifies this light within as affection, and both he and Cronon base their arguments on the need to kindle and stoke the light of affection.

Cronon and Berry clarify that by basing their arguments on love or affection they are not referring to a subjective emotion but rather to a virtue that properly values and serves our communities. As Cronon concludes, "Liberal education nurtures human freedom in the service of human community, which is to say that in the end it celebrates love."[50] Berry echoes this theme when he writes, "The word 'affection' and the terms of value that cluster around it—love, care, sympathy, mercy, forbearance, respect, reverence—have histories and meanings that raise the issue of worth. We should, as our culture has warned us over and over again, give our affection to things that are true, just, and beautiful."[51] As Jayber learns through his strange "marriage" to Mattie, we are always learning about and working with and living among beings who bear "the presence of eternity."[52] In the contemporary drive to make education quantifiable and efficient, it is easy to lose sight of these high stakes. Does our way of teaching and learning honor its subjects and their contexts? Do we love what we study? These questions are not easily answerable. Rather, like all questions involving our affections, they are "questions to which [we] cannot be *given* answers. [We] will have to live them out—perhaps a little at a time."[53]

Institutional Solutions

Universities can encourage two practices that would further a connective education: asking careful questions and fostering studious attention. Both practices orient students toward others, teaching them that what Jayber learns about Mattie's eternal value is true of all life. Universities can bear witness to the inherent value of all creatures, to the truth that they are worthy of study, of questioning, of listening, of attention not because these practices give us control over others or provide personal wealth but because such practices may enable us to be charitable and to honor and care for our neighbors—both human and nonhuman.

A Curriculum of Questions

In recent speeches and essays, Berry has proposed various curricula based on questions rather than demarcated disciplinary fields.[54] These questions generally begin with place: Where are we? What is going on here? What does this place need from us? In his 2009 commencement speech at Northern Kentucky University, Berry provided a list of such questions:

1. What has happened here? By "here" I mean wherever you live and work.
2. What should have happened here?
3. What is here now? What is left of the original natural endowment? What has been lost? What has been added?
4. What is the nature, or genius, of this place?
5. What will nature permit us to do here without permanent damage or loss?
6. What will nature help us to do here?
7. What can we do to mend the damages we have done?
8. What are the limits: Of the nature of this place? Of our intelligence and ability?[55]

Berry explains that such a curriculum would counteract the divisions present in university structures, divisions that isolate academics from their neighbors. He warns, however, that these questions will not lead to any final answers because each place exists uniquely in time and space: "Obviously, these questions cannot be answered—and they are not likely to be asked—by a specialist, or by many specialists working in isolation. They can be asked, and eventually answered to a significant extent, by a conversation with a foreseeable, or even a possible, end. It would be carried on necessarily in the face of forever changing conditions and circumstances, leading to further revelations of ignorance, and thus to necessary refinements or changes in the agenda of questions."[56] The kind of conversations generated by these questions would indeed connect university communities with their places in loving, caring ways.[57]

Organizing knowledge around a set of placed questions changes the center of learning. Instead of focusing on what I want and what I need to know to obtain these things, Berry's questions focus on what our places need and what we need to know to serve these needs. Certainly, because we are members of our places, our personal needs and desires play a role in how we approach these questions, but they are no longer the starting point. While it might be unreasonable to expect eighteen-year-old freshmen to have the maturity to ask such other-oriented questions, the typical university culture reinforces the naturally selfish tendencies of students. When students arrive on campus, they are constantly asked, "What do you want to do with your life?" Students might approach education differently if instead they were asked, "What does your community need, and what do you need to learn to meet those needs?" Such questions invite a richer understanding of love, one that defines love not as a descriptor of how something makes me feel but as a virtue that entails caring for my fellow members.

Even if these outward-oriented questions don't replace curricula organized around disciplinary boundaries, they can reshape the way universities approach learning. Administrators can make strategic decisions based on what their local communities need rather than on what consultants tell them other universities are doing. Admissions staff and student life counselors can encourage students to consider the needs and opportunities of their places when choosing which courses to take. Professors can ask locally derived questions when approaching their subjects, thus modeling for students ways of using their expertise to serve their neighbors. And students can ask these questions throughout their courses, preparing themselves to use the knowledge gained to participate lovingly in the life of their places.

Attentive Study

In a way, claiming that attentive study can foster love seems trivial; all education should involve such study. However, thinking of study as an act during which we forget ourselves and our desires and enter into an external reality reminds students and faculty that studying can shape our affections. We have already explored the connection between studiousness and love, but French philosopher Simone Weil expands on some of the implications of this connection in her brief yet profound essay "Reflections on the Right Use of School Studies in View of the Love of God." Weil argues that studious attention involves getting ourselves out of the way in order to focus on another; thus studying can exercise the virtue of love.

Weil's main thesis is that such attention can train us to pray, which she defines as "the orientation toward God with all the attention of which the soul is capable."⁵⁸ Such prayer may indeed be the highest form of love; as Jayber grows in his love for Mattie, he begins to pray again, having given up prayer many years ago because of his unanswered theological questions. Similarly, as we discussed in chapter 4, a well-ordered memory enables us to offer others sustained attention that can lead to forgiveness and restoration: we can *tend* to others only after we have *attended* to them. We turn to Weil's analysis of attention and study here because of its practicality; she focuses on the mundane tasks of actually learning something, so in spite of its deeply philosophical framing, her essay remains grounded.

Although students often focus on subjects in which they excel, Weil argues that the real benefit of studying is the way it forms attention. Paradoxically, then, the subjects a student struggles with may actually be the most beneficial in cultivating the ability to attend: "One must therefore study without any desire to obtain good grades, to succeed in exams, to obtain a scholarly result, without any regard for taste or natural aptitude, applying oneself equally to all the exercises with the idea that they all serve to form this attention that is the substance of prayer."⁵⁹ Weil's claim here aligns with our argument concerning the need to study not to better one's self or to compete with others but to understand, to connect, to love. This is precisely how Jayber learns to attend to Mattie—not to win her for himself or to get anything from her but to know her and love her for who she is.

In addition to focusing on the form of their study, Weil urges students to "rigorously consider" their failures. While students may be tempted to glance over a corrected test or paper and move on, Weil argues that "nothing is more necessary for academic success" than a careful examination of "one's own stupidity."⁶⁰ This self-examination helps students practice the humility necessary for learning.

Weil clarifies the shape of genuine attention in a way that parallels Augustine's distinction between studiousness and curiosity:

> Most often, we confuse attention with a kind of muscular effort. If we say to the students, "you must pay attention," we can see them frown with their eyebrows, hold their breath and contract their muscles. If after two minutes we ask them what they're paying attention to, they cannot respond. They are paying attention to nothing. They are not paying attention. They are contracting their muscles. . . . Contrary to what we ordinarily believe, [willpower] hardly ever has a place in studies. The intelligence can only be led by desire. . . . Attention is

an effort, perhaps the greatest of all efforts, but it is a negative effort. ... Attention consists in suspending our thought; letting it become available, empty and able to be penetrated by the object.[61]

As she notes, if students focus on the act of attention itself, on the act of knowing or learning as its own end, they will fail to attend fully to the subject. As we discussed earlier, Montaigne makes a similar distinction in the epigraph of Berry's *The Unsettling of America*: "Who so hath his minde on taking, hath it no more on what he hath taken." Weil applies this insight to the way students should approach their studies: "There is a specific way to wait for the truth with desire for each academic exercise, without allowing yourself to search for it—a way to pay attention to the data of a geometric problem without seeking a solution. For a Latin or Greek text, the words just come on their own and place themselves under the pen, while we reject only the inadequate words."[62] True attention involves a self-forgetting and a rapt participation in the subject itself. And this method of attention exercises the virtue of love.

Weil ends her essay by connecting this form of attention with an increased ability to love one's neighbor: "The fullness of love for neighbor is simply the capacity to ask the question, 'What is your agony?'"[63] This is quite similar to the question Berry challenges stickers to ask: "What do you need?"[64] Both questions value the other enough to put their needs first, and Weil's point about study is that it can train students to habitually attend to the needs of our neighbors: "Thus it is true, however paradoxical, that Latin translation or a geometric problem, even if we get it wrong—provided only that we have granted an appropriate kind of effort—can make us better able to give an afflicted person . . . exactly the help required to save them."[65] Students who study in the manner Weil suggests are exercising and strengthening their ability to love their fellow members.

The mysterious connections between knowledge and love cannot be easily articulated. As we noted at the beginning of this chapter, even in his eighty-first year, Berry acknowledges that he is only beginning to understand this relationship: "I have, from my own experience, begun to know . . . how intimately related, how nearly synonymous, are the terms 'love' and 'know,' how likely impossible it is to know authentically or well what one does not love, and how certainly impossible it is to love what one does not know."[66] But by living out our questions and studiously attending to our places and to the needs of our neighbors, we can hope to participate more fully in the membership of our community.

In one of his most well-known "Mad Farmer" poems, Berry expresses some of the paradoxes that those who pursue love have to endure. In order to love, we may have to do things that "won't compute," to "ask the questions that have no answers," to "plant sequoias," to "be joyful though [we] have considered all the facts," to "practice resurrection."

Manifesto: The Mad Farmer Liberation Front

Love the quick profit, the annual raise,
vacation with pay. Want more
of everything ready-made. Be afraid
to know your neighbors and to die.
And you will have a window in your head.
Not even your future will be a mystery
any more. Your mind will be punched in a card
and shut away in a little drawer.
When they want you to buy something
they will call you. When they want you
to die for profit they will let you know.
So, friends, every day do something
that won't compute. Love the Lord.
Love the world. Work for nothing.
Take all that you have and be poor.
Love someone who does not deserve it.
Denounce the government and embrace
the flag. Hope to live in that free
republic for which it stands.
Give your approval to all you cannot
understand. Praise ignorance, for what man
has not encountered he has not destroyed.
Ask the questions that have no answers.
Invest in the millennium. Plant sequoias.
Say that your main crop is the forest
that you did not plant,
that you will not live to harvest.
Say that the leaves are harvested
when they have rotted into the mold.
Call that profit. Prophesy such returns.
Put your faith in the two inches of humus

that will build under the trees
every thousand years.
Listen to carrion—put your ear
close, and hear the faint chattering
of the songs that are to come.
Expect the end of the world. Laugh.
Laughter is immeasurable. Be joyful
though you have considered all the facts.
So long as women do not go cheap
for power, please women more than men.
Ask yourself: Will this satisfy
a woman satisfied to bear a child?
Will this disturb the sleep
of a woman near to giving birth?
Go with your love to the fields.
Lie down in the shade. Rest your head
in her lap. Swear allegiance
to what is nighest your thoughts.
As soon as the generals and the politicos
can predict the motions of your mind,
lose it. Leave it as a sign
to mark the false trail, the way
you didn't go. Be like the fox
who makes more tracks than necessary,
some in the wrong direction.
Practice resurrection.[67]

Conclusion

Doing Work that Sustains Hope

The Mad Farmer's injunction to plant sequoias may not make much sense to a culture that measures success based on quarterly profit statements. But these expectations for immediate, easily measurable results contribute to a diseased, displaced culture in which we treat symptoms with quick fixes and then sell out and move on rather than doing the hard work of cultivating long-term, rooted health. Jayber likewise struggles with the apparent insufficiency of his love for Mattie and the Port William membership in the face of the ongoing disintegration and destruction of his community: Mattie dies of cancer, Troy clear-cuts the Nest Egg, children are killed in wars or move away, never to return. As Jayber asks, "What did love have to say to its own repeated failure to transform the world that it might yet redeem? What did it say to our failures to love one another and our enemies? What did it say to hate? What did it say to time? Why doesn't love succeed?" Yet Jayber concludes that despite these seeming failures, the love he comes to share nonetheless changes him and his relationships, and maybe that is sufficient: "A life cannot limit [love]. Maybe to have it in your heart all your life in this world, even when it fails here, is to succeed. Maybe that is enough."[1]

Our aim in this book, then, is quite humble. The hope Berry offers for universities is not a grand new program or some big solution: we're not calling for a fund-raising campaign to establish Wendell Berry University. Rather, Berry's vision offers us a small, humble, practice-able hope. Higher education is under immense economic and cultural pressure to prepare graduates for upward and lateral mobility, regardless of the costs to our ecosystem, communities, and souls. But change can take place if we tell students different stories—stories about rooted, contented lives; about the grateful, loving pursuit of wisdom; about people who sacrificed their private ambitions to serve the health of their local places. Such stories cultivate the virtues needed to shape the knowledge students currently learn in universities. Graduates who practice the virtues of memory, gratitude, fidelity, and love will be prepared to inhabit the membership of their places. An agrarian hope for higher education, then, begins with the simple act of telling better stories, stories that might lead to renewed imaginations, a more responsible language, and faithful work that serves the health of our communities.

We recognize the sober reality that, as Berry writes, "universities are more and more the servants of government and the corporations," yet we continue to hope that some universities might become servants of their places.[2] Even Berry, who has a fraught relationship with universities, can't seem to give up on them entirely. Just a few years after withdrawing his papers from the University of Kentucky due to its continued "alliance" with the coal industry, Berry supported a new agricultural program at St. Catharine College.[3] And after he quit teaching at the University of Kentucky for the first time, he wrote in a letter to Gary Snyder: "It's a relief. I get disillusioned at a pace just short of geological, but I finally saw undeniably that, aside from my 'reputation,' the university had no use for me, and that, aside from the library and two or three people, I had no use for it. It and I are going in perfectly opposite directions—which means we're bound to meet again, doesn't it?"[4] Indeed, after a brief hiatus, Berry was once again teaching at the University of Kentucky, and as we've argued throughout this book, despite his strident critiques of universities, Berry's vision has much to offer these wayward institutions. We hope his writings will continue to inspire and guide readers to renew higher education, shaping institutions and communities that can put knowledge in the service of their places.

We locate this hope in the good work people are doing at universities across the country, whether they are students planting campus gardens and weaning themselves from excessive reliance on their computers or professors inviting students over to share a meal and conversation and finding ways to incorporate local problems into their curricula. Such work sustains hope. As Berry explained in an interview, "Hope is a virtue and that means you're supposed to have it. You've got to go hunt for the reasons, and I know that within limits, people can change. I've seen the proof. I know that people can do good work, and I've seen the proof of that. I know that people can cooperate and help each other, and I've seen the proof of that."[5] We don't have the luxury of waiting for some big solution; rather, we have the obligation to work now, where we are, to sustain genuine hope.

Berry models this approach in an exchange of letters with education professor Madhu Suri Prakash. Prakash urged Berry to write an open letter to President Obama requesting $5 billion to fund small farmers. Given Berry's stature, such a letter would at least generate attention on behalf of family farmers. Yet Berry declined to write to the president, noting that he has already spoken his mind in his many essays, and he dislikes public life and its temptations to oversimplification. However, he offered a word of hope:

> What we both want to happen—a counter movement to greed and waste and the dominance of corporations—is already happening. It is happening simply because a lot of people have seen things needing to be done and are doing them. They are at work without grants, without official instruction or permission, and mostly unnoticed by the politicians and the news industry. Eventually this movement will have political powers which will be in some ways regrettable. I hope it will have the sense and strength to remain locally oriented, and to resist the simplification and corruption that will come with power.[6]

Berry remains convinced that genuine change begins locally rather than in the halls of centralized power. Furthermore, there is no way that universities on their own can heal our deracinated culture. Rather, our hope lies in the good work being done by students and teachers and administrators across the country who are living as members of their communities. These people are asking of their place, "What do you need?" and then they are setting about doing it. These particular actions, each adapted to their place, are the grounds of our hope.

By celebrating such efforts, we are trying to tell the stories right, to tell them in a way that will retie the threads that have been unraveled by American universities. These threads of imagination, language, and work might foster practices that can connect graduates to their places in healthy, sustainable ways. We can start doing good work where we are even without a better system or better policies or more money. Our contention is that a university that invites its students to memorize poems, observe the Sabbath, work in gardens, and ask studious questions will be more effectively educating placed inhabitants—people habituated to care for their place—than a university that pays lip service to the importance of local food or sustainability but fails to educate students in these virtues of place. And such virtues will sustain hope.

Afterword

The Authors and Their Stories

There aren't many English Departments in which two-fifths of the professors study Wendell Berry. So when Jeff took a job as an Americanist at Spring Arbor University and joined Jack, a medievalist by training, we immediately began to talk about collaborating on a project. Our many long, wide-ranging conversations culminated in this book.

As newly minted PhDs, both rather jaded by the egoism and careerism our profession too often rewards, we hoped our work as teachers and scholars would have a greater purpose than promotions, research leave, and more prestigious job offers. Thus the healthier vision for the university laid out in Berry's agrarian writings provided a balm to our overpedigreed souls. So as much as we, like Jayber Crow, are "ignorant pilgrims," Berry's understanding of education and place has profoundly guided us, and we "have been unable to shake off the feeling that [we] have been led—make of that what you will."[1]

In our own lives, we have faced the very real vocational challenges of serving our places while working within the modern university industry. Our different stories in this regard may be instructive, since they illustrate that seeking the health of one's place is a process that can take many different forms. I (Jeff) grew up in Washington State, near Seattle. When I was eleven years old, my family moved to a small community with about ninety year-round residents in the eastern part of the state. Stehekin is a remote place accessible only by boat, by plane, or by foot, and its inhabitants practice the neighborly virtues Berry describes in his fiction. After a year, my family returned to a more "normal" life in suburbia, but living in this unique place allowed us to experience the joys of a rooted community. Our year in Stehekin changed our family culture and left me with a desire for such an intergenerational, placed lifestyle. Thus, when my wife and I left for graduate school in Texas, we told ourselves this would be a five- or six-year adventure, after which we would return home. But the academic job market being what it is, my interviews with schools in the Northwest did not result in any job offers, and we had to choose between jobs in Tennessee and Michigan. So while our entire extended family lives in the Northwest, we now reside half a country away.

The economic reasons that led us to Michigan are well respected in our culture. But I know from my parents' story that staying away from home for the sake of a job isn't the only option. My parents moved to Connecticut so my dad could go to graduate school, and after he earned his master's degree, they turned down a job in the East in order to return to Seattle with their infant daughter, despite having no home and no job prospects there. The economics of their situation were different, I know, and my dad was able to find a good job within a few weeks (although in a field unrelated to his master's degree), but I'm still impressed by the courage they demonstrated by moving home without the assurance of a job to support their young family.

Yet even though my wife and I didn't return home, we are working to make a home in this place. We attend church, subscribe to the local paper, shop at the farmers' market, pick and preserve local fruit, and visit local cultural venues. We bought a neglected house, worked hard to repair and restore it, and planted a garden. We built a shared mailbox with several neighbors and distributed Christmas cookies around the neighborhood. We've learned the history of the neighborhood over coffee in others' homes, and we exchange greetings when we work in our yard or take walks. This isn't an intergenerational, economically interdependent community. This isn't the rich community I witnessed in Stehekin or the membership Berry describes in his fiction, but we're trying to deepen the forms of neighborliness and community that are available to us in our suburban location. We're trying to knit ourselves into the fabric of this place.

I (Jack) grew up in Shelby, a small town in western Michigan. With a population of just over 2,000, it's easy to miss it when tourists travel US 31 along the shoreline toward the golden beaches and crystal blue waters of Silver Lake or Charles Mears State Park in Pentwater. Like many small towns in America, Shelby used to be a thriving community—surviving on tourism, robust fruit farms, and local processing and canning factories. I love my hometown. I miss it dearly. But most of all, I mourn for it. My parents still reside in my childhood home—a craftsman foursquare built in 1907 by the original owner of the Rankin Hardware store in town. The town is dying. Jobs have disappeared, homes have lost considerable value, and culture has quickly petrified. Perhaps there is still hope. There are many good people (stickers like my father, who serves on the township board) working for its revitalization.

Before I left home for college, I could already sense what was happening to my hometown, which only encouraged my determination to leave home for good. I saw college as the opportunity to make something of myself, to go somewhere that was alive and not dying; Shelby stood for everything stagnant—for lost health and wholeness. Of course, my thinking was in many ways misguided. Wasn't this the same mind-set—that leaving Shelby was good for me—that led so many others, young and old alike, to turn away from their homes in the hope of finding a better life elsewhere? And how many of them actually found that life? How many began their journey as itinerants and never settled down long enough in any one place to really become a part of it? Well, I was one of those itinerants throughout the years of my higher education, and it wasn't until I left Michigan for graduate studies in Indiana that I began to feel a deep connection to my home state and hometown.

When my family and I would drive back to Shelby to visit my parents during this period, I was struck by my deep longing to be a part of the geography I knew so well. On these weekend visits, I waxed poetic about how much I desired to return to my home state. Until I lived elsewhere, I never knew how spiritually connected to Michigan I was. It was what I knew, where I had lived all but a few years of my life, and I couldn't shake the overwhelming sense of loss I had at the prospect of not returning there to work and live. In humility, we rejoice that we were able to return to Michigan. We now live in the south-central part of the state—directly between both sets of parents—and we are working to make Spring Arbor our home, to fit our lives to this place. And it is here that I am continuing the process of reshaping my affections for a different place, thinking often about how I ought to live in order to care for the health of Spring Arbor, as well as the health of my students—to be committed to a sticker mentality in a boomer profession. To echo Jayber Crow once again, we simply cannot have any hope of this place being home if we have no prospect of staying here. And so, in some ways, Spring Arbor has become my Shelby—my new hometown—and I will work to cultivate the right affections in my own heart, in the hearts of my children, and in the hearts of my students.

As our stories indicate, we are trying to narrate our lives in ways that counter the prevailing academic norms, to live stories not typically celebrated at academic conferences and in graduate student lounges. By orienting our lives within this narrative of homemaking, we desire to cultivate a different set of virtues than those measured by tenure committees. Yet as our meandering lives testify, we're certainly not deeply rooted people in the way that Wendell Berry is. We don't live where our grandparents grew up; we don't go out to milk the cows each morning before heading off to class. Rather, we're just two young academics who are trying to learn how to serve our places rather than our careers. By doing so—and by articulating the kinds of imagination, language, and practices that might lead to an education in the service of place—we also hope to educate our students to be virtuous members of their communities rather than technically proficient migratory servants of the industrial economy.

Acknowledgments

One of our joys while working on this project was to experience the great affection of friends, colleagues, and family who encouraged us to write what we believe. And as Proverbs 27:17 proclaims: "Iron sharpeneth iron; so a man sharpeneth the countenance of his friend." This work is the result of such a sharpening of our thoughts and a strengthening of our friendships.

We would like to express our gratitude to Wendell and Tanya Berry for their lives, their example, and their hospitality. Though they both embody a deep humility, they deserve a great deal of praise for their example of fidelity to their place and to each other.

We're thankful for our colleagues and friends who supported this project since its inception: Kimberly Moore-Jumonville, our department chair, for her tireless advocacy and encouragement of our scholarship and teaching; our colleagues and students at Spring Arbor University, who put up with our incessant references to Wendell Berry and asked thoughtful questions; Jason Peters for his direction and rapscallion humor; Millard Kimmery for his thoughtful comments on a draft of the manuscript; Steven Petersheim for his honest, tough questions that helped develop our ideas; Alison Westra for her help in compiling the index; Tom Pohrt for donating his talents to create the beautiful cover art; Steve Wrinn for believing in this project at an early stage; Allison Webster and Norman Wirzba for ably shepherding us through the publication process.

We likewise owe a debt of gratitude to several librarians who tracked down sources and facilitated our research. We are glad to call Robbie Bolton—the director of White Library at Spring Arbor and an incomparable sports podcaster—our friend. His work and encouragement mean a great deal to us. Thank you to Kami Moyer, who is an interlibrary loan wizard; Susan Panak, who is an archivist extraordinaire; and Stan Campbell, who graciously came to work on a holiday to let us read Berry's 1978 Centre College commencement address, which is this book's foreword.

Several organizations encouraged and supported us during the course of our work: the Front Porch Republic gave us an opportunity to present an early form of our ideas at its conference, *Christian Scholar's Review* published an essay in which we worked out earlier versions of these ideas, Spring Arbor University granted us course release time, and the McKenna Fellowship provided invaluable financial support.

I (Jack) give thanks for Kelly Baker and her endless encouragement, her hopefulness, and her blessed companionship. She is a deep inspiration and joy to me. May we reside in our "room of love" and "live a little while entirely in a gift" and be free. "What could be more heavenly than to have desire and satisfaction in the same room?" I give thanks for my beloved children, Owen, Silvia, and Griffin, and for the imagination they call out of me. Owen, your inquisitiveness is astounding, and your encouragement and creativity abound: you are strong. Silvia, your thoughtfulness and curiosity stir in me a love of beauty and innocence: you are wise like an ancient forest. Griffin, your playfulness and humor convince me that there is hope yet for the world: you are radiant in your cheerfulness. I give thanks for my parents, who never asked me what I was going to do with a degree in medieval studies, and for their support at every stage of my career. I give thanks for my sister Megan and her family—for her enthusiasm, encouragement, and love. And finally, I give thanks for Brent, Matt, and Robbie and their abiding friendship: "The way we are, we are members of each other."

I (Jeff) give thanks for my parents, Tom and Sharon; they taught me and my siblings to live against the grain of our restless, consumerist culture by fostering a rich family economy. I give thanks for my wife Melissa and daughter Hannah, who draw me out of my intellectual obsessions and invite me into an abiding community.

Notes

Foreword

1. John Milton, *The Riverside Milton,* ed. Roy Flannagan (Boston: Houghton Mifflin, 1998), 170–71.

2. The text of Berry's address was transcribed from a typed copy that contains minor edits made in pen. The copy is housed in the Centre College archives. When Berry gave us permission to print this address as the foreword to our book, he reread it before writing to us, "It seems all right to me as it stands." We have reproduced it exactly, including the revisions made in pen.

Introduction

1. Wendell Berry, "Bellarmine Commencement Address," 2007, http://christianstudycenter.org/wp-content/uploads/2009/10/WendellBerry-BellarmineCommencement.pdf.

2. Wendell Berry, *Hannah Coulter* (Berkeley, CA: Counterpoint, 2005), 5.

3. Ibid., 120.

4. Ibid., 83.

5. Ibid., 112.

6. Ibid., 113.

7. University communities are difficult to describe because, for all students and for some faculty and staff, they are temporary waypoints; for others, the university can form a stable, rooted community. One of our hopes is that faculty members can cultivate contentment and resist an academic climate that encourages them to look for the next best job that offers more research funds and reduced class loads. We explore these questions at greater length in Jack R. Baker and Jeffrey Bilbro, "Putting Down Roots: Why Universities Need Gardens," *Christian Scholar's Review* 45, no. 2 (2016): 125–42.

8. Berry, *Hannah Coulter,* 113.

9. Ibid., 114. Richard Gamble also draws on Hannah's emphasis on telling the right stories in "An Education for Membership," in *The Humane Vision of Wendell Berry,* ed. Mark T. Mitchell and Nathan W. Schlueter (Wilmington, DE: ISI Books, 2011), 28–39.

10. See his citation of MacIntyre and others in James K. A. Smith, *Imagining the Kingdom: How Worship Works* (Grand Rapids, MI: Baker Books, 2013), 108–9.

11. Ibid., 7.

12. Ibid., 14.

13. Berry, "Bellarmine Commencement Address."

14. "Unambitious Loser with Happy, Fulfilling Life Still Lives in Hometown," *The Onion*, July 24, 2013, http://www.theonion.com/articles/unambitious-loser-with-happy-fulfilling-life-still,33233/.

15. William T. Cavanaugh, *Being Consumed: Economics and Christian Desire* (Grand Rapids, MI: Eerdmans, 2008), 47.

16. Wendell Berry, "Major in Homecoming: For Commencement, Northern Kentucky University," in *What Matters? Economics for a Renewed Commonwealth* (Washington, DC: Counterpoint, 2010), 33.

17. Wendell Berry, "The Conservation of Nature and the Preservation of Humanity," in *Another Turn of the Crank: Essays* (Washington, DC: Counterpoint, 1995), 68–69.

18. Wendell Berry, *The Unsettling of America: Culture & Agriculture* (San Francisco: Sierra Club Books, 1996), 7.

19. Wendell Berry, *It All Turns on Affection: The Jefferson Lecture and Other Essays* (Berkeley, CA: Counterpoint, 2012), 11.

20. Our argument here has been clarified by conversations with some of Berry's sympathetic critics. For the context of this online discussion, see Jeffrey Bilbro's post "Place Isn't Just Geographical," Front Porch Republic, May 2013, http://www.frontporchrepublic.com/2013/05/place-isnt-just-geographical/.

21. Berry, "Conservation of Nature," 69.

22. Ibid., 70.

23. Wes Jackson, *Becoming Native to This Place* (Washington, DC: Counterpoint, 1996), 3.

24. Steven Bouma-Prediger and Brian Walsh, "Education for Homelessness or Homemaking? The Christian College in a Postmodern Culture," *Christian Scholar's Review* 32, no. 3 (2003): 281–82. Mitchell describes the problem in similar terms: "Liberal education too often amounts to little more than an overpriced means of creating cosmopolitans of the worst sort: people who have little interest in or concern for local communities, customs, stories, or places." Mark T. Mitchell, *The Politics of Gratitude: Scale, Place & Community in a Global Age* (Dulles, VA: Potomac Books, 2012), 173.

25. Wendell Berry, "Higher Education and Home Defense," in *Home Economics: Fourteen Essays* (Berkeley, CA: Counterpoint, 1987), 52.

26. Berry, *Unsettling of America*, 7. Berry also expands on this line of questioning in two recent commencement addresses, urging graduates to ask questions about where they are and how they can serve these places. See "Bellarmine Commencement Address"; "Major in Homecoming," 34–35.

27. Wendell Berry, "Wendell Berry on His Hopes for Humanity," interview by Bill Moyers, November 29, 2013, http://billmoyers.com/segment/wendell-berry-on-his-hopes-for-humanity/.

28. Wendell Berry, "Two Economies," in *Home Economics* (New York: North Point Press, 1987), 54–55.

29. C. S. Lewis, *The Abolition of Man* (San Francisco: Harper, 2001), 83. See also Wirzba, who compares education to an apprenticeship: "The apprentice has learned a more fitting and responsible (responsive to his or her context) focus, has become more attentive to the surrounding context, and has given up ambition to take the world by force. . . . The apprentice becomes a master not by bending the world to his or her own will but by submitting to, learning to work within, and developing an affection for the rich possibilities latent within the craft." Norman Wirzba, *Living the Sabbath: Discovering the Rhythms of Rest and Delight*, The Christian Practice of Everyday Life (Grand Rapids, MI: Brazos Press, 2006), 133.

30. Berry, "Conservation of Nature," 83–84.

31. Berry, *Hannah Coulter*, 132.

32. Wendell Berry, *Life Is a Miracle: An Essay against Modern Superstition* (Washington, DC: Counterpoint, 2000), 137.

33. William Major does a fine job of putting agrarianism in conversation with academic theorists. For a further consideration of agrarianism's critique of current critical theory, see William H. Major, *Grounded Vision: New Agrarianism and the Academy* (Tuscaloosa: University of Alabama Press, 2011).

34. Wendell Berry, "Nature as an Ally: An Interview with Wendell Berry," interview by Sarah Leonard, *Dissent Magazine*, 2012, http://www.dissentmagazine.org/article/nature-as-an-ally-an-interview-with-wendell-berry.

35. Wendell Berry, "Thoughts in the Presence of Fear," in *Citizenship Papers* (Washington, DC: Shoemaker & Hoard, 2003), 21.

36. Wendell Berry, "Local Knowledge in the Age of Information," in *The Way of Ignorance: And Other Essays* (Berkeley, CA: Counterpoint, 2006), 120–21.

37. Wendell Berry, "Discipline and Hope," in *A Continuous Harmony: Essays Cultural and Agricultural* (San Diego: Harcourt Brace, 1972), 164.

38. Aldo Leopold, *A Sand County Almanac: And Sketches Here and There* (New York: Oxford University Press, 1989), 224–25.

39. Berry, *Unsettling of America*, 103.

40. See, for example, Timothy Morton's critique of "health" and "nature" in *Ecology without Nature: Rethinking Environmental Aesthetics* (Cambridge, MA: Harvard University Press, 2009) and *The Ecological Thought* (Cambridge, MA: Harvard University Press, 2010). He finds health too oppressive and seeks an ecological ethic that does not depend on any concept of "nature" or "hierarchy." For a criticism of this approach, see Jeffrey Bilbro, "Review of *The Ecological Thought*," *Christianity and Literature* 61, no. 4 (2012): 693–97. For a comparison of Morton and Berry, see Jeffrey Bilbro, "Sublime Failure: Why We'd Better Start Seeing Our World as Beautiful," *South Atlantic Review* 80, no. 1–2 (2015): 133–58.

41. See Jackson, *Becoming Native to This Place;* Michael Pollan, *The Omnivore's Dilemma: A Natural History of Four Meals* (New York: Penguin, 2007); Vandana Shiva, *The Vandana Shiva Reader,* Culture of the Land: A Series in the New Agrarianism (Lexington: University Press of Kentucky, 2014).

42. Wendell Berry, "The Futility of Global Thinking," *Harper's Magazine,* September 1989, 22.

43. Wendell Berry, "Caught in the Middle on Abortion and Homosexuality," *Christian Century,* March 20, 2013, http://www.christiancentury.org/article/2013-03/caught-middle.

44. Wendell Berry, "The Gift of Good Land," in *The Gift of Good Land: Further Essays Cultural and Agricultural* (Berkeley, CA: Counterpoint, 2009), 267.

45. Patrick J. Deneen, "We're All to Blame for MOOCs," *Chronicle of Higher Education,* June 3, 2013, http://chronicle.com/article/Were-All-to-Blame-for-MOOCs/139519/.

46. Clayton M. Christensen and Henry J. Eyring, *The Innovative University: Changing the DNA of Higher Education from the Inside Out* (San Francisco: Jossey-Bass, 2011).

47. Wayne Drehs, "School Turns Football Field into Farm," ESPN, November 26, 2014, http://espn.go.com/nfl/story/_/id/11942279/texas-football-field-turned-farm-provides-local-produce-dallas-cowboys-stadium.

48. Wendell Berry, "Why I Am Not Going to Buy a Computer," in *What Are People For? Essays* (New York: North Point Press, 1990), 177.

49. Berry, *Life Is a Miracle,* 134.

50. In a similar vein, Henderson and Hursh critique the way that neoliberalism takes decision making out of the hands of local agents and gives it to government agencies and large philanthropic organizations. Joseph A. Henderson and David W. Hursh, "Economics and Education for Human Flourishing: Wendell Berry and the Oikonomic Alternative to Neoliberalism," *Educational Studies* 50, no. 2 (March 1, 2014): 170–71.

51. Wendell Berry, "The Work of Local Culture," in *What Are People For? Essays* (New York: North Point Press, 1990), 168–69.

52. Wendell Berry, "Preface: The Joy of Sales Resistance," in *Sex, Economy, Freedom & Community: Eight Essays* (New York: Pantheon, 1993), xix.

53. See "BA in Farming and Ecological Agrarianism," St. Catharine College Kentucky, http://www.sccky.edu/academics/arts-sciences/earth-studies/sustainablefarming_ba.php (accessed March 20, 2014).

54. Wendell Berry, "Poetry and Place," in *Standing by Words: Essays* (Washington, DC: Shoemaker & Hoard, 2005), 192.

55. For more on MacIntyre's understanding of "practice," see the introduction to part 2.

56. Wendell Berry, "The Chubb Fellowship—Wendell Berry," December 7, 2013, http://chubbfellowship.org/speakers/current/wendell_berry.

57. Wendell Berry, *This Day: New and Collected Sabbath Poems 1979–2012* (Berkeley, CA: Counterpoint, 2013), 355.

1. Imagining the Tree of Wisdom

1. Wendell Berry, *Remembering: A Novel* (Berkeley, CA: Counterpoint, 2008), 59.

2. Ibid., 63.

3. Ibid., 75–76.

4. Ibid., 56.

5. Ibid., 57.

6. Gamble, "Education for Membership," 28–39, offers a complementary reading of *Remembering*, emphasizing different features of Andy's journey home.

7. Wendell Berry, "The Loss of the University," in *Home Economics: Fourteen Essays* (Berkeley, CA: Counterpoint, 1987), 82.

8. Clark Kerr, *The Uses of the University*, 5th ed. (Cambridge, MA: Harvard University Press, 2001), 103.

9. Wellmon makes a similar observation: "Although universities had always been devoted in different ways to the life of the mind and the pursuit of knowledge, historically their ethical resources, the basis of their underlying norms and authority, had been tied either to the church or to the state." Chad Wellmon, *Organizing Enlightenment: Information Overload and the Invention of the Modern Research University* (Baltimore: Johns Hopkins University Press, 2015), 154. Wellmon goes on to argue that eighteenth-century German universities managed to organize themselves around the pursuit of science itself, but he also admits that they remained vulnerable to being conscripted to mercantilist or national ends. Given that knowledge is always shaped according to its ends, this failure to sustain a university devoted to knowledge in the abstract is to be expected.

10. Berry mourns this failure in several places, but his most extended treatment of the problems with land-grant universities is in chapter 8 of *Unsettling of America*, 143–69.

11. Andrew Delbanco, *College: What It Was, Is, and Should Be* (Princeton, NJ: Princeton University Press, 2012), 148.

12. Kerr, *Uses of the University*, 214.

13. Wendell Berry, "In Defense of Literacy," in *A Continuous Harmony: Essays Cultural and Agricultural* (San Diego: Harcourt Brace, 1972), 169–70.

14. "Innovating for the Future," State Council of Higher Education for Virginia, 2011, http://www.schev.edu/innovation.asp.

15. "Florida Blue Ribbon Task Force on State Higher Education Reform," November 6, 2012, 22, http://www.fgcu.edu/FacultySenate/files/2-22-2013_Resolution_Supplement_3.pdf.

16. Neil Postman, *Technopoly: The Surrender of Culture to Technology* (New York: Knopf, 1992), 186.

17. See Delbanco, *College;* Anthony T. Kronman, *Education's End: Why Our Colleges and Universities Have Given up on the Meaning of Life* (New Haven, CT: Yale University Press, 2008); Harry Lewis, *Excellence without a Soul: Does Liberal Education Have a Future?* (New York: Public Affairs, 2007); C. John Sommerville, *The Decline of the Secular University* (Oxford: Oxford University Press, 2006).

18. See David Lyle Jeffrey, "The Pearl of Great Wisdom: The Deep and Abiding Biblical Roots of Western Liberal Education," *Touchstone Magazine,* October 2007, http://www.touchstonemag.com/archives/article.php?id=20-08-025-f; Alasdair MacIntyre, *God, Philosophy, Universities: A Selective History of the Catholic Philosophical Tradition* (Lanham, MD: Rowman & Littlefield, 2011); Stanley Hauerwas, *The State of the University: Academic Knowledges and the Knowledge of God* (Malden, MA: Blackwell, 2007).

19. Madhu Suri Prakash, "What Are People For? Wendell Berry on Education, Ecology, and Culture," *Educational Theory* 44, no. 2 (1994): 154.

20. Key works that incorporate Berry into this conversation include Madhu Suri Prakash and Gustavo Esteva, *Escaping Education: Living as Learning within Grassroots Cultures* (New York: P. Lang, 2008); David W. Orr, *Earth in Mind: On Education, Environment, and the Human Prospect* (Washington, DC: Island Press, 2004); C. A. Bowers, *Educating for Eco-Justice and Community* (Athens: University of Georgia Press, 2001); James J. Farrell, *The Nature of College: How a New Understanding of Campus Life Can Change the World* (Minneapolis: Milkweed Editions, 2010); Kathryn Blanchard and Kevin O'Brien, *An Introduction to Christian Environmentalism: Ecology, Virtue, and Ethics* (Waco, TX: Baylor University Press, 2014); Henderson and Hursh, "Economics and Education," 167–86; Rebecca A. Martusewicz, Jeff Edmundson, and John Lupinacci, *Ecojustice Education: Toward Diverse, Democratic, and Sustainable Communities,* Sociocultural, Political, and Historical Studies in Education (New York: Routledge, 2011). For a continuation of the conversation about how Berry might teach us "what education should mean in the face of the devastating effects of 'boomer' culture," see Rebecca A. Martusewicz, Jeff Edmundson, and Richard Kahn, "On Membership, Humility, and Pedagogical Responsibilities: A Correspondence on the Work of Wendell Berry," *Mid-Western Educational Researcher* 25, no. 3 (2013): 46. See also Rebecca Martusewicz, "Eros, Education, and Eco-Ethical Consciousness: Re-Membering the 'Room of Love' in Wendell Berry's Hannah Coulter," *Educational Studies* 49, no. 5 (2013): 443–50; Walter G. Moss, "Professors and Politics a la Wendell Berry," *LA Progressive,* March 14, 2014, http://www.laprogressive.com/left-wing-professors/.

21. Bouma-Prediger and Walsh, "Education for Homelessness or Homemaking?" 281–96.

22. Gamble, "Education for Membership," 37.

23. J. Matthew Bonzo and Michael R. Stevens, *Wendell Berry and*

the Cultivation of Life: A Reader's Guide (Grand Rapids, MI: Brazos Press, 2008). See also J. Matthew Bonzo and Michael R. Stevens, "Seed Will Sprout in the Scar: Wendell Berry on Higher Education," *The Other Journal*, August 13, 2008, http://theotherjournal.com/2008/08/13/seed-will-sprout-in-the-scar-wendell-berry-on-higher-education/.

24. Schreck's dissertation on the educational principles inherent in Berry's Port William fiction is perhaps the lone exception. Although it is an excellent resource, Schreck's work is, by her own admission, a "survey" of Berry's thinking on education (6). As a result, much of the dissertation is a digest of Berry's essays and fiction; only in the last chapter does Schreck consider the implications of Berry's ideas. See Jane Margaret Hedahl Schreck, "Wendell Berry's Philosophy of Education: Lessons from Port William" (PhD diss., University of North Dakota, 2013), http://gradworks.umi.com/35/87/3587458.html.

25. Sommerville, *Decline of the Secular University*, 48.

26. Hauerwas, *State of the University*, 104.

27. Berry, "Higher Education and Home Defense," 52.

28. We derive this contrast between a pilgrimage and a map from Peter M. Candler Jr., *Theology, Rhetoric, Manuduction, or Reading Scripture Together on the Path to God* (Grand Rapids, MI: Eerdmans, 2006).

29. Paul Griffiths, *Intellectual Appetite: A Theological Grammar* (Washington, DC: Catholic University of America Press, 2009), 16.

30. On the seventeenth-century efforts to map all knowledge and the subsequent birth of the modern research university organized around disciplinary specialization, see Wellmon, *Organizing Enlightenment*.

31. Schreck also notes the broader cultural divisions that Berry sees contributing to divisions within universities: "[Berry] argues that higher education represents disconnection itself: institutions disconnected from their communities, disciplines disconnected from each other, research disconnected from its consequences, teaching disconnected from emotions or values, and curricula disconnected from possibility. Often the result is that higher education works to disconnect students from home." Schreck, "Wendell Berry's Philosophy of Education," 350.

32. Michel Foucault, *Discipline and Punish: The Birth of the Prison*, trans. Alan Sheridan (New York: Pantheon Books, 1977), 195–228.

33. Eric O. Jacobsen, *The Space Between: A Christian Engagement with the Built Environment* (Grand Rapids, MI: Baker Academic, 2012), 33–54.

34. Berry, *Unsettling of America*, 11. Berry expands on his diagnosis throughout that work, and his critique centers on these divisions and the unhealthy level of specialization they lead to. As he states, "The disease of the modern character is specialization" (ibid., 19). See also Alasdair MacIntyre, "Politics, Philosophy, and the Common Good," in *The MacIntyre Reader*, ed. Kelvin Knight (Notre Dame, IN: University of Notre Dame Press, 1998), 248—

wherein he claims that "the forms of compartmentalization characteristic of advanced modernity are inimical to the flourishing of local community." And Wirzba notes that ecological science can offer an alternative method of thinking because of its focus on relationships and context. See Norman Wirzba, *The Paradise of God: Renewing Religion in an Ecological Age* (Oxford: Oxford University Press, 2007), 99.

35. See Lewis, *Abolition of Man*, 83.
36. Berry, "Loss of the University," 77.
37. Ibid., 82–83.
38. Ibid., 83.
39. Ibid., 86.
40. Ibid., 82.
41. Berry, "Discipline and Hope," 164.
42. Berry, "Two Economies," 54–56. Herman Daly compares these two contrasting economies to Aristotle's *oikonomia* and *chrematistics* in his foreword to *What Matters? Economics for a Renewed Commonwealth*, by Wendell Berry (Berkeley, CA: Counterpoint, 2010), x. See also Henderson and Hursh, "Economics and Education," 180–82.
43. Berry, "Loss of the University," 96.
44. Ibid., 81.
45. Ibid. Berry returns to this dual standard in a more recent essay: "Can we imagine a way of education that would turn passive consumers into active and informed critics, capable of using their own minds in their own defense? It will not be the purely technical education-for-employment now advocated by the most influential 'educators' and 'leaders.' We have good technical or specialized criticism: A given thing is either a good specimen of its kind or it is not. A valid general criticism would measure work against its context. The health of the context—the body, the community, the ecosystem—would reveal the health of the work." Wendell Berry, "Paragraphs from a Notebook," in *Our Only World: Ten Essays* (Berkeley, CA: Counterpoint, 2015), 14.
46. C. S. Lewis, *A Preface to Paradise Lost* (London: Oxford University Press, 1961), 11. Chesterton makes a similar point in one of his essays regarding the need to understand the standard by which we judge a successful education: "The word success can of course be used in two senses. It may be used with reference to a thing serving its immediate and peculiar purpose, as of a wheel going round; or it can be used with reference to a thing adding to the general welfare, as of a wheel being a useful discovery." G. K. Chesterton, *What's Wrong with the World* (Peru, IL: Sherwood Sugden, 1910), 169.
47. Berry, "Loss of the University," 96.
48. Berry asserts that universities have generally failed to cultivate such imaginative judgment in *Life Is a Miracle*: "This is the 'objectivity' of the schools and the professions, which allows a university or a corporation to look at the community—its *own* community—as one looks at a distant landscape

through fog. This sort of objectivity functions in art much the same as in science; it obstructs compassion; it obscures the particularity of creatures and places. In both, it is a failure of imagination" (86).

49. Berry offers an extended reading of the conclusion of *Huckleberry Finn* in "Writer and Region," in *What Are People For? Essays* (New York: North Point Press, 1990), 71–79.

50. Peter Jackson, *The Lord of the Rings: The Return of the King* (New Line Home Video, 2004).

51. Berry, "Work of Local Culture," 161–63.

52. bell hooks, *Belonging: A Culture of Place* (New York: Routledge, 2008).

53. Rod Dreher, *The Little Way of Ruthie Leming: A Southern Girl, a Small Town, and the Secret of a Good Life* (New York: Grand Central Publishing, 2013).

54. Rod Dreher, "Wendell Berry: A Latter-Day St. Benedict," in *The Humane Vision of Wendell Berry*, ed. Mark Mitchell and Nathan Schlueter (Wilmington, DE: ISI Books, 2011), 275–87.

55. Wendell Berry, *Jayber Crow: A Novel* (Washington, DC: Counterpoint, 2000), 30.

2. Standing by Our Words

1. Berry, *Hannah Coulter*, 132.
2. Berry, *Remembering*, 8.
3. Ibid., 10.
4. Ibid., 14.
5. Ibid., 18.
6. Ibid., 19.
7. Ibid., 20. This story has its roots in Berry's family history; he describes the autobiographical version in *It All Turns on Affection*, 9–10.
8. Berry, *Remembering*, 12.
9. Ibid., 15.
10. Wendell Berry, "Standing by Words," in *Standing by Words: Essays* (Washington, DC: Shoemaker & Hoard, 2005), 24–25.
11. Ibid., 31.
12. Ibid., 29–30.
13. Ibid., 37.
14. Ibid., 38.
15. Ibid., 38–39.
16. Wendell Berry, "The Way of Ignorance," in *The Way of Ignorance: And Other Essays* (Berkeley, CA: Counterpoint, 2006), 65.
17. Berry, "Standing by Words," 60.
18. Mitchell, *Politics of Gratitude*, 173.
19. Ibid., 174.
20. Ibid., 175.

21. C. S. Lewis traces this development in the meaning of the words "free" and "liberty" in *Studies in Words* (Cambridge: Cambridge University Press, 1960), 111–32.

22. William Cronon makes a similar argument in his excellent essay "'Only Connect . . .': The Goals of a Liberal Education," *American Scholar* 67, no. 4 (1998): 79. See also Henderson and Hursh, "Economics and Education," 178–79.

23. Berry, "Thoughts in the Presence of Fear," 21.

24. For other examples of educators translating the classical liberal arts into contemporary contexts, see Dorothy Sayers, "The Lost Tools of Learning," Great Books Tutorial,1947, http://www.gbt.org/text/sayers.html; Stratford Caldecott, *Beauty in the Word: Rethinking the Foundations of Education* (Kettering, OH: Angelico Press, 2012) and *Beauty for Truth's Sake: On the Re-enchantment of Education* (Grand Rapids, MI: Brazos Press, 2009); Jeffry C. Davis, Philip Graham Ryken, and Leland Ryken, eds., *Liberal Arts for the Christian Life* (Wheaton, IL: Crossway, 2012).

25. Berry, "Standing by Words," 53.

26. Berry, *Unsettling of America*, 157.

27. For a thorough introduction to the trivium, see Sister Miriam Joseph, *The Trivium: The Liberal Arts of Logic, Grammar, and Rhetoric; Understanding the Nature and Function of Language* (Philadelphia: Paul Dry Books, 2002).

28. For the development of the liberal arts in twelfth-century Europe, see John of Salisbury, *The Metalogicon: A Twelfth-Century Defense of the Verbal and Logical Arts of the Trivium*, trans. Daniel McGarry (Philadelphia: Paul Dry Books, 2009); Hugh of St. Victor, *The Didascalicon of Hugh of St. Victor: A Medieval Guide to the Arts,* trans. Jerome Taylor (New York: Columbia University Press, 1991).

29. Scott F. Crider, *Office of Assertion: An Art of Rhetoric for Academic Essay* (Wilmington, DE: ISI Books, 2005), 12. Crider's text works very well in college writing courses, and Berry's influence on him is clear from the book's epigraph and its concluding sentence.

30. Ibid., 7.

31. Ibid., 12.

32. Wendell Berry, *Conversations with Wendell Berry,* ed. Morris A. Grubbs, Literary Conversations Series (Jackson: University Press of Mississippi, 2007), 11.

33. Morris A. Grubbs, "A Practical Education: Wendell Berry the Professor," in *Wendell Berry Life and Work,* ed. Jason Peters, Culture of the Land: A Series in the New Agrarianism (Lexington: University Press of Kentucky, 2010), 140.

34. Berry, "In Defense of Literacy," 165–66.

35. Ibid., 170.

36. Ibid., 171; emphasis in original.

37. Berry, "Preface: The Joy of Sales Resistance," xiii.

38. Berry, "Loss of the University," 91.

39. Ibid., 92. Oehlschlaeger observes that Berry's careful treatment of people and places, especially in his created world of Port William, is not unlike the biblical writers who were "trying to write the truth." Fritz Oehlschlaeger, *The Achievement of Wendell Berry: The Hard History of Love*, Culture of the Land: A Series in the New Agrarianism (Lexington: University Press of Kentucky, 2011), 3.

40. Berry, "Loss of the University," 91.

41. Ibid., 92.

42. Ibid., 93.

43. George Orwell, "Politics and the English Language," in *Essays on Language and Usage*, ed. Leonard F. Dean and Kenneth G. Wilson (New York: Oxford University Press, 1963), 327; emphasis in original.

44. Ibid., 325.

45. Ibid., 332.

46. J. R. R. Tolkien, "Mythopoeia," in *Tree and Leaf* (London: HarperCollins, 2001), 88.

47. Grubbs, "Practical Education," 137–38.

48. *The Bible: Authorized King James Version*, ed. Robert Carroll and Stephen Prickett (New York: Oxford University Press, 2008), 2 Sam. 12:1–7.

49. David Jeffrey and Gregory Maillet, *Christianity and Literature: Philosophical Foundations and Critical Practice* (Downers Grove, IL: IVP Academic, 2011), 126. Illich, describing the medieval understanding of reading taught by Hugh of St. Victor, articulates a similar process: "The readers' order is not imposed on the story, but the story puts the reader into its order." Ivan Illich, *In the Vineyard of the Text: A Commentary to Hugh's Didascalicon* (Chicago: University of Chicago Press, 1993), 31.

50. Rainer Maria Rilke, *Selected Poems of Rainer Maria Rilke*, trans. Robert Bly (New York: Harper & Row, 1981), 147. Berry articulates a similar experience in his poem about Pierodella Francesca's fresco *The Resurrection*. After describing the unspeakable power of Christ's face, Berry compares himself with the dazed soldiers lying on the ground: "And we who were sleeping, seeking the dead / among the dead, dare to be awake. We who see / see we are forever seen, by sight have been / forever changed." Berry, *This Day*, 329. Jason Peters offers a parallel analysis of the demands literature makes on us in "Whoring in Shittim," Front Porch Republic, January 2012, http://www.frontporchrepublic.com/2012/01/whoring-in-shittim/.

51. Berry, *This Day*, 287–88.

3. Doing Good Work

1. Berry, *Remembering*, 137.

2. Wendell Berry, *The Memory of Old Jack* (Berkeley, CA: Counterpoint, 1999), 30.

3. Ibid., 44.
4. Ibid., 50.
5. Ibid., 60.
6. Ibid., 64.
7. Ibid., 61.
8. Ibid., 125.
9. Ibid., 102–3.

10. For an expanded reading of *The Memory of Old Jack* and the vision of good work this novel imagines, see Jeffrey Bilbro, *Loving God's Wildness: The Christian Roots of Ecological Ethics in American Literature* (Tuscaloosa: University of Alabama Press, 2015), 168–77.

11. In his brief, incisive essay "What Are People For?" Berry questions this cultural assumption, arguing that doing good, healing work is at least one of the ends humans should pursue. See Wendell Berry, "What Are People For?" in *What Are People For? Essays* (New York: North Point Press, 1990), 123–25.

12. Berry's diagnosis of our culture's debased view of work is expanded on by Kimberly K. Smith, *Wendell Berry and the Agrarian Tradition: A Common Grace* (Lawrence: University Press of Kansas, 2003), 155–77, and Major, *Grounded Vision*, 86–124. For a popular treatment of the value of work, see Matthew B. Crawford, *Shop Class as Soulcraft: An Inquiry into the Value of Work* (New York: Penguin, 2010).

13. Wendell Berry, "A Defense of the Family Farm," in *Home Economics: Fourteen Essays* (Berkeley, CA: Counterpoint, 1987), 166.

14. Eric Gill, *A Holy Tradition of Working: Passages from the Writings of Eric Gill* (West Stockbridge, MA: Lindisfarne Press, 1983), 61–62.

15. Berry, "Defense of the Family Farm," 166.

16. Ibid.

17. Berry, "Nature as an Ally."

18. Wendell Berry, "Christianity and the Survival of Creation," in *Sex, Economy, Freedom & Community: Eight Essays* (New York: Pantheon, 1993), 105. The best essay on Berry's critique of dualism is Jason Peters, "Wendell Berry's Vindication of the Flesh," *Christianity and Literature* 56, no. 2 (2007): 317–32.

19. Wendell Berry, *The Hidden Wound* (Berkeley, CA: Counterpoint, 2010), 105.

20. Berry, "Local Knowledge," 118.

21. Berry, "Chubb Fellowship."

22. Jim Halverson, "Restored through Learning: Hugh of St. Victor's Vision for Higher Education," *Christian Scholar's Review* 41, no. 1 (2011): 36.

23. Hugh of St. Victor, *On the Sacraments of the Christian Faith (De Sacramentis) of Hugh of Saint Victor*, trans. Roy J. Deferrari (Cambridge, MA: Medieval Academy of America, 1951), 98.

24. Halverson, "Restored through Learning," 43.

25. For more on the history of the mechanical arts, see Elspeth Whitney, *Paradise Restored: The Mechanical Arts from Antiquity through the Thirteenth Century* (Philadelphia: American Philosophical Society, 1990).

26. Berry, *Unsettling of America*, 144–45.

27. Ibid., 156.

28. Ibid., 158.

29. Ibid.

30. Berry, *It All Turns on Affection*, 37.

31. Berry, *Unsettling of America*, 148.

32. Marta Zaraska, "Is Lab-Grown Meat Good for Us?" *The Atlantic*, August 19, 2013, http://www.theatlantic.com/health/archive/2013/08/is-lab-grown-meat-good-for-us/278778/.

33. Berry, "Standing by Words," 42–46.

34. Berry, *Unsettling of America*, 149.

35. Wendell Berry, "People, Land, and Community," in *Standing by Words: Essays* (Washington, DC: Shoemaker & Hoard, 2005), 69.

36. Ibid., 70.

37. Berry expresses this relationship in slightly different terms in *Life Is a Miracle*: "Both imagination and a competent sense of reality are necessary to our life, and they necessarily discipline one another. Only imagination, for example, can give our home landscape and community a presence in our minds that is a sort of vision at once geographical and historical, practical and protective, affectionate and hopeful. But if that vision is not repeatedly corrected by a fairly accurate sense of reality, if the vision becomes fantastical or merely wishful, then both we and the landscape fall into danger; we may destroy the landscape, or the landscape (especially if damaged by us in our illusion) may destroy us" (85).

38. Berry, *Memory of Old Jack*, 75.

39. Wendell Berry, "Hunting for Reasons to Hope: A Conversation with Wendell Berry," interview by Harold K. Bush, *Christianity and Literature* 56, no. 2 (2007): 223.

40. Berry, "Chubb Fellowship."

41. Smith, *Imagining the Kingdom*, 4. Although Smith's argument is explicitly about Christian universities, it applies equally to all educational institutions.

42. Berry, "Local Knowledge," 118.

43. Wendell Berry, *New Collected Poems* (Berkeley, CA: Counterpoint, 2013), 169.

44. Wendell Berry, "Feminism, the Body, and the Machine," in *The Art of the Commonplace* (Washington, DC: Shoemaker & Hoard, 2002), 76.

45. "About—The Labor Program at Berea College," http://www.berea.edu/labor-program/ (accessed July 23, 2014); "Work Education," College of the Ozarks, http://www.cofo.edu/Page/Students/Work-Education.96.html (accessed July 23, 2014); "Warren Wilson College," http://www.warren-wilson.edu/work/ (accessed July 23, 2014).

46. "Welcome to the Work Colleges Consortium!" http://www.workcolleges.org/ (accessed July 23, 2014).

47. Schreck, "Wendell Berry's Philosophy of Education," 411.

48. Ibid., 414.

49. "BA in Farming and Ecological Agrarianism."

50. We discuss our campus garden in Baker and Bilbro, "Putting Down Roots." See also Wirzba's discussion of how the practice of gardening forms us spiritually and ecologically in *Paradise of God*, 113–19, 194–95.

51. For more on the history of the Foxfire project, see "The Foxfire Fund, Inc.," http://www.foxfire.org/ (accessed July 24, 2014).

52. Wendell Berry, "Think Little," in *A Continuous Harmony: Essays Cultural and Agricultural* (San Diego: Harcourt Brace, 1972), 84. See also Wendell Berry, "The Reactor and the Garden," in *The Gift of Good Land: Further Essays Cultural and Agricultural* (Berkeley, CA: Counterpoint, 2009), 161–70.

53. Berry, *New Collected Poems*, 377–78.

Introduction to Part 2

1. Berry, "Bellarmine Commencement Address."

2. Alasdair MacIntyre, *After Virtue: A Study in Moral Theory* (Notre Dame, IN: University of Notre Dame Press, 1984), 191; emphasis in original.

3. MacIntyre defines practice carefully: "By a 'practice' I am going to mean any coherent and complex form of socially established cooperative human activity through which goods internal to that form of activity are realized in the course of trying to achieve those standards of excellence which are appropriate to, and partially definitive of, that form of activity, with the result that human powers to achieve excellence, and human conceptions of the ends and goods involved, are systematically extended." Ibid., 187.

4. Ibid.

5. Ibid., 216.

6. Smith, *Imagining the Kingdom*, 108.

7. MacIntyre, *After Virtue*, 226–27. Neil Postman, while not explicitly discussing virtues, also emphasizes the role that narratives play in shaping education in *Technopoly*, 171–80.

8. Berry, *Unsettling of America*, 121. Kimberly Smith also cites this passage in supporting her claim that Berry's understanding of "discipline" is akin to MacIntyre's "practice"; see *Wendell Berry and the Agrarian Tradition*, 161. For further analysis of the links between Berry and MacIntyre, see Oehlschlaeger, *Achievement of Wendell Berry*, 12–14.

9. MacIntyre, *After Virtue*, 219.

10. Ibid., 187–88.

11. In later works, MacIntyre further develops the connections between virtues and local communities, even referencing Berry's work. See in particular his essay "Politics, Philosophy, and the Common Good," in *MacIntyre Reader*.

12. Pope Francis makes a similar claim regarding the necessity of habits or virtues in environmental education: "education, aimed at creating an 'ecological citizenship,' is at times limited to providing information, and fails to instill good habits.... Only by cultivating sound virtues will people be able to make a selfless ecological commitment." Francis, "Laudato Si," May 2015, http://w2.vatican.va/content/francesco/en/encyclicals/documents/papa-francesco_20150524_enciclica-laudato-si.html.

4. Tradition

1. Berry, "Loss of the University," 88–89.
2. Berry, *Conversations*, 196.
3. Berry, *It All Turns on Affection*, 205.
4. Wendell Berry, "Pray without Ceasing," in *That Distant Land: The Collected Stories* (Washington, DC: Shoemaker & Hoard, 2004), 38.
5. Ibid., 41.
6. Ibid., 43.
7. Ibid., 44.
8. Ibid., 68.
9. Ibid., 69.
10. Ibid., 70.
11. Ibid., 75.
12. Berry, "Work of Local Culture," 154.
13. Berry, *Conversations*, 107.
14. Berry, *Life Is a Miracle*, 3.
15. Berry, "Pray without Ceasing," 44.
16. Portions of the following paragraphs borrow material from Bilbro, *Loving God's Wildness*, 143–44.
17. Berry's understanding of tradition is similar to that of Hans-Georg Gadamer. Gadamer articulates how our inevitable involvement in tradition does not fatally impinge on human agency: "The fact is that in tradition there is always an element of freedom and of history itself.... [Tradition] needs to be affirmed, embraced, cultivated" for it to be handed down. The limits tradition imposes on human agency are simply the limitations of human contingency—when and where one is born and by whom one is raised—and by claiming that all understanding is a communal act of tradition, Gadamer foregrounds each interpreter's role in reforming tradition: "Understanding is to be thought of less as a subjective act than as participating in an event of tradition, a process of transmission in which past and present are constantly mediated." Hans-Georg Gadamer, *Truth and Method*, 2nd rev. ed., trans. Joel Weinsheimer and Donald G. Marshall (London: Sheed & Ward, 1999), 281, 290.
18. Berry, "Conservation of Nature," 73–74.
19. For an example of how Berry draws on the Buddhist understanding of "right livelihood," see his essay "The Gift of Good Land."

20. Berry, "Christianity and the Survival of Creation," 96.
21. Ibid.
22. Berry, *Life Is a Miracle*, 47.
23. Ibid., 48.
24. Wendell Berry, "Poetry and Marriage," in *Standing by Words: Essays* (Washington, DC: Shoemaker & Hoard, 2005), 101–2.
25. Smith, *Wendell Berry and the Agrarian Tradition*, 6.
26. Wendell Berry, "The Making of a Marginal Farm," in *Recollected Essays: 1965-1980* (New York: North Point Press, 1993), 335. Berry's description of his farm matches comments he made in an interview with Katherine Dalton in which he uneasily defines himself as "a marginal Christian," one troubled by much of this religion's history. See Berry, *Conversations*, 192.
27. Berry, *Hidden Wound*, 92–102.
28. Augustine, *Confessions*, trans. Henry Chadwick (Oxford: Oxford University Press, 1998), 10:12.
29. St. Augustine's image surely draws on the mnemonic technique described in classical rhetorical texts whereby spatial memory is harnessed to remember various facts or parts of a speech. This technique, in fact, is featured in the BBC's *Sherlock*; in this television series, Sherlock retreats to his "mind palace" at key junctures to recall specific information. In St. Augustine's hands, however, the memory palace is not merely a mnemonic device but a metaphor for the value of a large, well-ordered memory.
30. Augustine, *Confessions*, 10:18. This quote comes from a section in which St. Augustine makes the case for a Platonic view of learning as essentially the remembering of eternal truths forgotten by the soul. However, one doesn't have to fully agree with the concept of Platonic and Augustinian memory to recognize that learning depends on reorganizing knowledge—perhaps in response to newly received knowledge—within memory.
31. Berry, "Local Knowledge," 121. Berry makes a similar point in an interview: "We're assuming in this society that we can 'access' the necessary information. But 'accessing' the information takes time. And then determining which information is pertinent is an impossible task if you're overloaded with information that you don't know how to apply. So there's a difference between so-called information and the knowledge that is shapely in the mind of a good worker. That knowledge is immediately available because it lives not just in the mind and the memory, but in the body and hands of the person doing the work." Berry, *Conversations*, 110. See also Berry, "Paragraphs from a Notebook," 11–12.
32. T. S. Eliot, *Collected Poems, 1909–1962* (New York: Harcourt Brace Jovanovich, 1991), 147. Berry's cites the first three lines in his introduction to *This Day*. He comments, "This quantitative endlessness, including also the idea of endless economic 'growth,' is clearly different from the inexhaustibility of Nature on her terms, and of goodness, beauty, and truth on ours" (xxiii).
33. For an examination of Eliot's influence on Berry's understanding of

memory, see Jeffrey Bilbro, "The Ecology of Memory: Augustine, Eliot, and the Form of Wendell Berry's Fiction," *Christianity and Literature* 65, no. 3 (2016): 327–42.

34. Plato, *Phaedrus,* trans. Robin Waterfield (Oxford: Oxford University Press, 2002), 68–69.

35. Halverson, "Restored through Learning," 36–37.

36. Hugh used various exercises to train his students' memories, and all of them emphasized not only the spatial features of memory but also the action required to navigate its rooms: "The child's mind was trained to build the memory mazes, and to establish the habit to dart and retrieve in them. Remembrance was not conceived as an act of mapping but of psychomotor, morally charged activity." Illich, *In the Vineyard,* 37.

37. Ibid., 45. Berry quoted Illich's claims regarding the physicality of reading in his remarks upon being inducted into the Kentucky Writers Hall of Fame. Wendell Berry, "Kentucky Writers Hall of Fame: Wendell Berry's Remarks," Carnegie Center for Literacy and Learning, January 28, 2015, http://carnegiecenterlex.org/2015/02/kentucky-writers-hall-fame-wendell-berrys-remarks/.

38. Berry, *Jayber Crow,* 54.

39. Nicholas Carr, *The Shallows: What the Internet Is Doing to Our Brains* (New York: W. W. Norton, 2011); Nicholas Carr, *The Glass Cage: Automation and Us* (New York: W. W. Norton, 2014).

40. Berry, "Why I Am Not Going to Buy a Computer," 170–77.

41. Pam A. Mueller and Daniel M. Oppenheimer, "The Pen Is Mightier than the Keyboard: Advantages of Longhand over Laptop Note Taking," *Psychological Science* 25, no. 6 (June 1, 2014): 1159–68.

42. Clay Shirky, "Why I Just Asked My Students to Put Their Laptops Away. . . ," *Medium,* September 9, 2014, https://medium.com/@cshirky/why-i-just-asked-my-students-to-put-their-laptops-away-7f5f7c50f368.

43. Alfred Corn, *The Poem's Heartbeat: A Manual of Prosody* (Port Townsend, WA: Copper Canyon Press, 2008), xv.

44. Ibid., xvi.

45. For further reflection on the power of memorizing poetry, see Dana Gioia, "Poetry as Enchantment," *Poetry Daily,* 2015, http://poems.com/special_features/prose/essay_gioia_enchantment.php.

46. Berry, *Conversations,* 87.

47. Caldecott, *Beauty in the Word,* 59.

48. John Lukacs, *Last Rites* (New Haven, CT: Yale University Press, 2009), 31.

49. Berry approvingly cites Lukacs's view of human knowledge in *It All Turns on Affection,* 26.

50. Kuhn supports this view of human inquiry—even scientific inquiry—as embedded within historical consciousness. See Thomas S. Kuhn, *The Structure of Scientific Revolutions,* 4th ed. (Chicago: University of Chicago Press, 2012).

51. See, for example, Emiliano Salvucci, "Selfishness, Warfare, and Econom-

ics; or Integration, Cooperation, and Biology," *Frontiers in Cellular and Infection Microbiology* 2, no. 54 (May 1, 2012): 1–12.

52. Burdette Andrews, ed., *The Echo of Spring Arbor University Seminary* 5 (1926): 77–78.

53. Merlin G. Smith, "The Farm," *The Echo of Spring Arbor University Seminary* 6 (1927): 83.

54. Berry, *New Collected Poems*, 217–18.

5. Hierarchy

1. Martin Heidegger and J. Glenn Gray, *What Is Called Thinking?* (New York: Harper & Row, 1972), 138–46.

2. Peter J. Leithart, *Gratitude: An Intellectual History* (Waco, TX: Baylor University Press, 2014), 190.

3. Roger Lundin, *From Nature to Experience: The American Search for Cultural Authority*, American Intellectual Culture (Lanham, MD: Rowman & Littlefield, 2005), 132.

4. Wendell Berry, "Andy Catlett: An Early Education," in *A Place in Time: Twenty Stories of the Port William Membership* (Berkeley, CA: Counterpoint, 2012), 82. During a personal conversation, Berry told us that this story is largely autobiographical.

5. Ibid., 83.
6. Ibid., 84.
7. Ibid.
8. Ibid., 85.
9. Ibid.
10. Ibid., 86.
11. Ibid., 87.
12. Ibid., 86.
13. Ibid., 87. There may be a link in Berry's imagination between this image of Andy's mother enforcing strict consequences and the medieval figure of Dame Nature, who is likewise uncompromising toward those who overstep proper limits.

14. Berry, "Standing by Words," 60.

15. Berry, *Life Is a Miracle*, 3, 4.

16. William Shakespeare, *King Lear*, in *The Riverside Shakespeare*, ed. G. Blakemore Evans and J. J. M. Tobin (Boston: Houghton Mifflin, 1997), 4.6.50–55. References are to act, scene, and line.

17. Berry, *Life Is a Miracle*, 5.

18. *King Lear*, 4.6.75–77.

19. Berry, *Life Is a Miracle*, 5, 6–7.

20. Nathaniel Hawthorne provides a similar warning in his short story "The Birthmark," in which the scientist Aylmer succeeds in eliminating the mark on his bride's cheek only by eliminating her life. As Lake argues, Aylmer destroys his

wife because he loves his "own idealistic vision" of her more than who she actually is; by reducing his wife to the terms of his ideal of beauty, he destroys her. Christina Bieber Lake, *Prophets of the Posthuman: American Fiction, Biotechnology, and the Ethics of Personhood* (Notre Dame, IN: University of Notre Dame Press, 2013), 48.

21. George Steiner, *Martin Heidegger* (Chicago: University of Chicago Press, 1991), 131. This is why Heidegger is critical of modern forms of technology that, rather than letting being be, work to control and manipulate being (ibid., 136–41). See also Martin Heidegger, *The Question Concerning Technology, and Other Essays*, trans. William Levitt (New York: Harper Torchbooks, 1982).

22. Heidegger and Gray, *What Is Called Thinking?* 143.

23. Ibid., 146.

24. Berry, "Standing by Words," 56. See also Berry, "Poetry and Place," 185.

25. Berry, "Poetry and Place," 180.

26. Ibid., 182–83.

27. Wirzba, *Living the Sabbath*, 38.

28. Ibid., 36. Wirzba develops this same line of thinking in his essay "An Economy of Gratitude," in *Wendell Berry Life and Work*, ed. Jason Peters, Culture of the Land: A Series in the New Agrarianism (Lexington: University Press of Kentucky, 2010), 142–55.

29. See, for example, Yi-fu Tuan's critique of reciprocity in ancient, communal contexts in *Cosmos and Hearth: A Cosmopolite's Viewpoint* (Minneapolis: University of Minnesota Press, 1996), 147–48.

30. Leithart, *Gratitude*, 192–93.

31. Ibid., 225–26.

32. Heidegger and Gray, *What Is Called Thinking?* 143.

33. Leithart, *Gratitude*, 7.

34. For an extended discussion of stewardship in the Christian tradition—and a response to Lynn White's famous essay critiquing Christian stewardship—see Wirzba, *Paradise of God*, 123–48.

35. Berry, "Poetry and Marriage," 101–2.

36. Wilfred M. McClay, "Introduction: Why Place Matters," in *Why Place Matters: Geography, Identity, and Civic Life in Modern America*, ed. Wilfred M. McClay and Ted V. McAllister (New York: New Atlantis Books, 2014), 6.

37. Berry, *Life Is a Miracle*, 133.

38. Ibid., 132.

39. Berry, *Hidden Wound*, 112.

40. Berry, *Life Is a Miracle*, 62.

41. Ibid., 58.

42. Wirzba makes a similar critique of the careerism that education encourages: "Educational institutions are perceived to be valuable insofar as they equip our students with the tools for increased financial gain. To this end, the emphasis is on careerism, which includes not only the training for a particular job but also

the training to move up the ranks within a job. Success is measured less by the quality of one's life—notice the desperate, frenetic pace of our day-to-day lives—and more by the quantity of things one accrues." Wirzba, *Paradise of God*, 97–98.

43. David Brooks, "Transcript of David Brooks, The Gathering 2014," *The Gathering*, http://thegathering.com/e-updates/transcript-david-brooks-gathering-2014/ (accessed October 21, 2014).

44. Berry, "Gift of Good Land," 270.

45. Ibid., 272, 273.

46. Ibid., 274.

47. Ibid., 277–78.

48. Berry, *Life Is a Miracle*, 55–56.

49. Milton, *Riverside Milton*, 362.

50. Berry, "Gift of Good Land," 278.

51. Berry, "Standing by Words," 57.

52. Berry, "Gift of Good Land," 280.

53. Berry develops his thinking on ignorance and limits in several works, most notably "Standing by Words," "Way of Ignorance," "Local Knowledge," and *Life Is a Miracle*.

54. Berry, *Life Is a Miracle*, 135, 149.

55. Berry, "Standing by Words," 49.

56. Alan Jacobs, "The Two Cultures, Then and Now," *Books and Culture*, February 2014, http://www.booksandculture.com/site/utilities/print.html?type=article&id=116715 (accessed March 1, 2014).

57. Leithart, *Gratitude*, 15.

58. Walter Brueggemann, *Sabbath as Resistance: Saying No to the Culture of Now* (Louisville, KY: Westminster John Knox Press, 2014), 84–85.

59. For further reading on the Sabbath, see Wirzba's excellent book *Living the Sabbath*.

60. Berry, *This Day*, xxi.

61. Berry, *New Collected Poems*, 79.

62. Berry, *This Day*, xxii.

63. Wirzba, *Living the Sabbath*, 138. See also Crouch, who reflects on a Lenten fast from screens, noting that this Sabbatarian break made him realize anew the narcissism that digital technologies encourage: "Our screens, increasingly, pay a great deal of attention to us. They assure us that someone, or at least something, cares. The mediated world constantly falls over itself to tell us, often in entirely automated ways, that we matter every bit as much as we secretly hope we do. They tell us we are liked, retweeted, favorited—that we are significant, useful, and urgently needed." Andy Crouch, "Small Screens, Big World: Easter in Florence; The Fiction of Mark Helprin, and a Lent without Glowing Rectangles," April 8, 2015, http://andy-crouch.com/articles/small_screens_big_world. Obviously, such a narcissistic formation fosters ingratitude and arrogance, vices the Sabbath directly combats.

64. Smith, *Imagining the Kingdom*, 143.

65. For a more in-depth exploration of these issues, see Matthew B. Crawford, *The World beyond Your Head: On Becoming an Individual in an Age of Distraction* (New York: Farrar, Straus & Giroux, 2015).

66. Berry, *Life Is a Miracle*, 94.

67. Ibid., 147, 148. Berry makes a similar argument in "Going to Work," in *Citizenship Papers* (Washington, DC: Shoemaker & Hoard, 2003), 38–39. Wallis argues that for Berry, his local, familiar place changes the way he sees. Rather than "settling" on a theory and forcing all the particulars to fit this framework, dwelling in a place makes Berry open to the unpredictable wonders of particular creatures: "this shift occurs on the scale of the local because it is the intimacy with the local, one's immediate surrounding that one has come to know well, that tends to reveal its saturation and mystery." Bryan Wallis, "More Real than Real: The Weird Localism of Ralph Eugene Meatyard and Wendell Berry," *Australasian Journal of Ecocriticism and Cultural Ecology* 2 (August 4, 2013): 75–95.

68. Berry, *Life Is a Miracle*, 15.

69. Ibid., 21.

70. Sunflower Project, 2011, https://www.youtube.com/watch?v=Ok4OwF-f5Hc&feature=youtube_gdata_player.

71. Berry, *Life Is a Miracle*, 148.

72. Berry, *This Day*, 232–34.

6. Geography

1. Wendell Berry, *Nathan Coulter: A Novel* (Berkeley, CA: Counterpoint, 2008), 6.

2. Wendell Berry, "The Wild Birds," in *That Distant Land: The Collected Stories* (Washington, DC: Shoemaker & Hoard, 2004), 350.

3. Wendell Berry, "Fidelity," in *That Distant Land: The Collected Stories* (Washington, DC: Shoemaker & Hoard, 2004), 405.

4. Ibid., 398.

5. Ibid.

6. Ibid., 424.

7. Berry, "Wild Birds," 339.

8. Ibid., 345.

9. Ibid.

10. Ibid.

11. Ibid., 354.

12. Ibid., 356.

13. Ibid., 362–63.

14. Berry, "Fidelity," 425.

15. Berry, "Local Knowledge," 113.

16. Wendell Berry, "American Imagination and the Civil War," in *Imagination in Place: Essays* (Berkeley, CA: Counterpoint, 2010), 17.

17. Patrick Kavanagh, *Collected Pruse* (Worcester, MA: MacGibbon & Kee, 1967), 282.

18. Berry, "Local Knowledge," 113.

19. Chad Wellmon approves of this outward orientation, contrasting it with the local focus of older universities: "Unlike the modern research university, where success in national and international disciplinary communities determines prestige and thus tenure and promotion, allegiances in the medieval and early modern university were primarily to a local body." Wellmon, *Organizing Enlightenment*, 155. While hiring professors based on their prestige within specialized, scholarly communities certainly has its merits, standards that are internal to a discipline should be combined with local standards, such as how a particular candidate can serve the needs of the particular institution and community. Many smaller schools already consider these qualifications under the rubric of "fit," and this category could be expanded to consider local investment more broadly, as we suggest at the end of this chapter.

20. Wendell Berry, "Our Deserted Country," in *Our Only World: Ten Essays* (Berkeley, CA: Counterpoint, 2015), 122–23.

21. Two recent scandals in the sciences have caused scholars to consider accountability and academe's seemingly unhealthy and inordinate emphasis on "publish or perish" for tenure-track faculty. Diederik Stapel, whose fraud went on for years before coming to light in 2011, recently spoke with the *Chronicle of Higher Education* about his misdeeds. While taking full responsibility for his actions, he also notes that the environment of higher education places undue pressure on researchers to produce scholarship at any cost: "There's something about the environment. The publication pressure. The need for simple answers instead of allowing for complexity. The focus on egos and individual researchers, first authors, and grants to individuals versus groups or universities." Stapel likewise describes the importance of local accountability: "It could have been avoided by more group relationships, more social control, and also real interest in each other's work. If I look back now, I say we were counting each other's journal articles. 'Hey, Tom or Jim has another paper. Oh, well, wonderful!' Nobody said, 'What was the paper about?' or 'What did he prove?'" Tom Bartlett, "Can a Longtime Fraud Help Fix Science?" *Chronicle of Higher Education*, June 22, 2015, http://chronicle.com/article/Can-a-Longtime-Fraud-Help-Fix/231061/; Tom Bartlett, "The Unraveling of Michael LaCour," *Chronicle of Higher Education*, June 2, 2015, http://chronicle.com/article/The-Unraveling-of-Michael/230587/.

22. Although we focus on Yi-fu Tuan as a representative spokesperson for this view, much has been written about the virtues of cosmopolitanism as an alternative to nationalism and tribalism. Ursula K. Heise's *Sense of Place and Sense of Planet: The Environmental Imagination of the Global* (Oxford: Oxford University Press, 2008), offers one analysis of how cosmopolitan values can lead to environmental preservation. For a critique of Heise, see Bilbro, "Sublime Failure." Ronald Osborn draws on Berry's ideas to provide a related critique of cos-

mopolitan notions of citizenship and migrant rights in "Seyla Benhabib, Wendell Berry, and the Question of Migrant and Refugee Rights," *Humanitas* 23, no. 1-2 (2010): 118-38. See also G. K. Chesterton's critique of Rudyard Kipling's cosmopolitan poetic in *Heretics* (Stilwell, KS: Digireads.com, 2006), 13-19.

23. For an excellent introduction to the way graduate schools and the job market train professors to be cosmopolitans, see Eric Zencey, "Rootless Professors," in *Rooted in the Land: Essays on Community and Place*, ed. William Vitek and Wes Jackson (New Haven, CT: Yale University Press, 1996), 15-19. See also Major, *Grounded Vision*, 35-37, 193.

24. Tuan, *Cosmos and Hearth*, 137.

25. Ibid., 147.

26. Ibid., 150.

27. Ibid., 180-81.

28. Ibid., 181.

29. Ibid., 187.

30. Berry, *Unsettling of America*, 122.

31. Kavanagh, *Collected Pruse*, 283.

32. Berry, "American Imagination," 18.

33. Smith poignantly describes the situation of such people through the protagonist of his No. 1 Ladies' Detective Agency. Mma Ramotswe has led a deeply placed life, but she knows that in her case this was a privilege more than a virtue: "It was all very well for her, she thought; she knew exactly where she came from and where she belonged, but there were many people who did not, who had been uprooted, forced out by need or victimization, by being simply the wrong people in the wrong place. There were many such people in Africa, and they ate a very bitter fruit; they were extra, unwanted persons, like children who are not loved." Alexander McCall Smith, *The Good Husband of Zebra Drive* (New York: Anchor Books, 2008), 124.

34. Berry, "Work of Local Culture," 164.

35. Ibid., 165.

36. G. K. Chesterton, *Manalive* (New York: John Lane, 1912), 265.

37. Katherine Dalton, a Kentucky native and a senior editor at the Front Porch Republic, recounts her experience of leaving home to attend college in Connecticut in similar terms: "I went shaking the dust of Kentucky off my feet. None of my plans included Kentucky, and in my mind the place I was going was like a garden in March: all potential and no weeds. But if travel is broadening to the mind, what broadened for me was my affection for what I had left. Living up north, I came to realize as I never had at home what was valuable back in Kentucky, and what was unreproducible elsewhere, and just where it was I was from." Katherine Dalton, "Birthright," in *Front Porch Manifesto*, ed. Jason Peters and Mark Mitchell (Eugene, OR: Front Porch Republic Books, forthcoming).

38. Berry, "Work of Local Culture," 164.

39. Berry, "Our Deserted Country," 126.

40. In this regard, there is much overlap between Berry and some proponents of indigenous epistemologies, who argue that local ways of knowing are significantly different from the Enlightenment pursuit of universal knowledge. See, for example, Marie Battiste and James Youngblood Henderson, *Protecting Indigenous Knowledge and Heritage: A Global Challenge* (Saskatoon, SK: Purich, 2000); Margaret Elizabeth Kovach, *Indigenous Methodologies: Characteristics, Conversations, and Contexts,* reprint ed. (Toronto: University of Toronto Press, 2010).

41. Berry, "Our Deserted Country," 116.

42. Berry, "Local Knowledge," 120.

43. Berry, "People, Land, and Community," 69–70.

44. Berry, *Life Is a Miracle,* 141.

45. Berry discusses the formal or patterned nature of such adaptation in many other essays, perhaps most explicitly in "Solving for Pattern," in *The Gift of Good Land: Further Essays Cultural and Agricultural* (Berkeley, CA: Counterpoint, 2009), 134–47.

46. Berry, "American Imagination," 33.

47. Ibid., 33–34.

48. Ibid., 34.

49. Berry, *Life Is a Miracle,* 134. Berry's observation is echoed by many proponents of localism. As Wilfred McClay notes in his introduction to *Why Place Matters,* "Could it be the case that the variety and spontaneous diversity of the world as we have known it for all the prior centuries of human history is being gradually leveled and effaced, and insensibly transformed into something standardized, artificial, rootless, pastless, and bland—a world of interchangeable airport terminals and franchise hotels and restaurants, a world of smooth surfaces designed to facilitate perpetual movement rather than rooted flourishing?" (7).

50. Tuan, *Cosmos and Hearth,* 177, claims that such a vision is part of cosmopolitanism: "A diversity of hearths is itself a cosmopolitan ideal." But as we have seen, Tuan thinks hearths can be sustained without the fidelity that Berry believes is required for their health.

51. Berry, "Work of Local Culture," 166.

52. Ibid., 168.

53. Berry, *Life Is a Miracle,* 121.

54. Ibid., 126.

55. Berry, "Local Knowledge," 121.

56. Ibid., 122.

57. Berry, *Unsettling of America,* 147–48.

58. Berry, *Conversations,* 101.

59. Ibid., 111. Berry develops a similar line of reasoning in "Discipline and Hope," 135–38.

60. American Federation of Teachers, "American Academic: The State of the Higher Education Workforce 1997–2007," 2009, 10, http://www.aftface.org/storage/face/documents/ameracad_report_97-07for_web.pdf.

61. Berry, "Local Knowledge," 123–24.
62. Ibid., 118.
63. "BA in Farming and Ecological Agrarianism."
64. "We over Me Farm," Paul Quinn College, http://www.weovermefarm.com/ (accessed March 17, 2015).
65. Berry, "Local Knowledge," 124.
66. Deneen, "We're All to Blame for MOOCs."
67. See the following works by Wendell Berry: "Irish Journal," in *Home Economics* (New York: North Point Press, 1987), 21–48; "An Agricultural Journey in Peru," in *The Gift of Good Land: Further Essays Cultural and Agricultural* (Berkeley, CA: Counterpoint, 2009), 3–46; "Three Ways of Farming in the Southwest," ibid., 47–76; "Seven Amish Farms," ibid., 249–63; "A Forest Conversation," in *Our Only World: Ten Essays* (Berkeley, CA: Counterpoint, 2015), 21–52. In addition, Berry has mentioned his debt to the sustainable farming practices he observed in Tuscany during the year he and his family lived in Italy. See "A Gentle Man Speaks: A Conversation with Wendell Berry," interview by Glenn Thompson, *Iron Blade*, September 28, 2010, http://www2.ferrum.edu/ironblade/archives/2010-11/extra.pdf.
68. Charles A. Murray, *Coming Apart: The State of White America, 1960–2010* (New York: Crown Forum, 2013), 75–103.
69. Richard Florida, "High-School Dropouts and College Grads Are Moving to Very Different Places," *CityLab*, June 16, 2014, http://www.citylab.com/work/2014/06/high-school-dropouts-and-college-grads-are-moving-to-very-different-places/372065/.
70. Richard Florida, *Who's Your City? How the Creative Economy Is Making Where to Live the Most Important Decision of Your Life* (New York: Basic Books, 2008), 7.
71. Wendell Berry, personal communication, August 16, 2014.
72. Wendell Berry, "Local Economies to Save the Land and the People," in *Our Only World: Ten Essays* (Berkeley, CA: Counterpoint, 2015), 64–65.
73. Berry, "Our Deserted Country," 128.
74. Brian Jacob, Brian McCall, and Kevin M. Stange, "College as Country Club: Do Colleges Cater to Students' Preferences for Consumption?" working paper, National Bureau of Economic Research, January 2013, http://www.nber.org/papers/w18745. One of the allures of many for-profit institutions is the amenity-laden campus hub, such as Grand Canyon University's Thunder Alley, which "opened in 2011 and features a variety of dining options including some popular national restaurants and a convenience store. The lower level of Thunder Alley includes a 6-lane bowling alley as well as a club-like music venue known as Thunderground, which holds concerts performed by nationally-recognized Christian artists" (http://www.gcu.edu/About-Us/University-Development.php). But facilities like Thunder Alley cost students a lot of money in the long run. In fact, national studies have demonstrated that for-profit universities are more expensive than

private and public four-year institutions, that for-profit graduates struggle to find employment, and that for-profit borrowers default at higher rates. It isn't too hard to understand why such universities cost students so much—they are, after all, *for profit*. See also Susannah Snider, "3 Must-Know Facts about For-Profit Colleges, Student Debt," *US News & World Report,* October 1, 2014, http://www.usnews.com/education/best-colleges/paying-for-college/articles/2014/10/01/3-facts-for-students-to-know-about-for-profit-colleges-and-student-debt (accessed August 25, 2015); "Digest of Education Statistics, 2013," http://nces.ed.gov/programs/digest/d13/tables/dt13_330.10.asp?current=yes (accessed June 29, 2015); John Lauerman, "For-Profit College Costs Surpass Nonprofit Peers in U.S. Study," *Bloomberg.com,* May 25, 2011, http://www.bloomberg.com/news/articles/2011-05-26/for-profit-college-costs-surpass-nonprofit-peers-in-u-s-study.

75. "Welcome to the Work Colleges Consortium!"
76. Schreck, "Wendell Berry's Philosophy of Education," 405.
77. Chesterton, *Heretics,* 19.
78. Berry, "Poetry and Marriage," 98.
79. Berry, *New Collected Poems,* 206–8.

7. Community

1. Berry, "Our Deserted Country," 116.
2. Berry, *Jayber Crow,* 30.
3. Ibid., 32.
4. Ibid., 41.
5. Ibid., 33.
6. Ibid., 35–36.
7. Ibid., 47.
8. Ibid., 49.
9. Ibid.
10. Ibid., 53.
11. Ibid., 54.
12. Ibid., 69.
13. Ibid., 70.
14. Ibid., 70–71.
15. Ibid., 72–73.
16. Wendell Berry, *A Place on Earth: A Novel* (Washington, DC: Counterpoint, 2001), 63–64.
17. One way of understanding the relationship between Jayber and Mattie is through the subtle but clear connections Berry makes to the relationship between Dante and Beatrice. For a consideration of these parallels and the way they illuminate the spiritual dimension of Jayber's strange marriage, see Anthony Esolen, "If Dante Were a Kentucky Barber," in *The Humane Vision of Wendell Berry,* ed. Mark T. Mitchell and Nathan Schlueter (Wilmington, DE: ISI Books, 2011), 255–74; Bilbro, *Loving God's Wildness,* 160–68.

18. For a brief treatment of the virtue of spiritual joy over spiritual envy, see Anthony Esolen, "Secular Grendel," *Touchstone: A Journal of Mere Christianity*, January/February 2011, http://www.touchstonemag.com/archives/article.php?id=24-01-020-f.

19. Berry, *Jayber Crow*, 138.

20. Ibid., 238.

21. Ibid., 249.

22. Ibid., 252.

23. Ibid., 355.

24. Ibid., 354.

25. Quoted in Griffiths, *Intellectual Appetite*, 19.

26. Our understanding of Augustine's distinction here is indebted to Paul Griffiths's argument in *Intellectual Appetite*.

27. Berry, *Jayber Crow*, 195, 199.

28. Ibid., 184.

29. Another character in *Jayber Crow*, Cecelia Overhold, shares Troy's desire for newness at the expense of the good she already has: "Cecelia thought that whatever she already had was no good, by virtue of the fact that she already had it. The things she desired all were things she didn't have." Ibid., 209.

30. Ibid., 187.

31. Berry, "Way of Ignorance," 55.

32. Berry, *Hannah Coulter*, 128.

33. Ibid., 132. Berry expands on these two contrasting ways of knowing in his essay "Two Minds," where he argues that universities foster the "Rational Mind," which "is motivated by the fear of being misled, of being wrong. Its purpose is to exclude everything that cannot empirically or experimentally be proven to be a fact." In opposition to this mind, Berry defends the "Sympathetic Mind," which "is motivated by fear of error of a very different kind: the error of carelessness, of being unloving. Its purpose is to be considerate of whatever is present, to leave nothing out." Wendell Berry, "Two Minds," in *Citizenship Papers* (Washington, DC: Shoemaker & Hoard, 2003), 88.

34. Griffiths, *Intellectual Appetite*, 161.

35. Berry, *Life Is a Miracle*, 72.

36. Ibid., 27.

37. Griffiths, *Intellectual Appetite*, 148.

38. E. O. Wilson, "My Wish: Build the Encyclopedia of Life," Ted, March 2007, http://www.ted.com/talks/e_o_wilson_on_saving_life_on_earth/transcript?language=en#t-1215000.

39. Griffiths, *Intellectual Appetite*, 153.

40. Berry, "People, Land, and Community," 77.

41. Berry, *Jayber Crow*, 130–31.

42. Ibid., 131.

43. Ibid., 132.

44. Ibid., 71.
45. Cronon, "'Only Connect,'" 73, 76, 78.
46. Ibid., 76–78.
47. Ibid., 79.
48. Ibid.
49. E. M. Forster, *Howards End*, ed. David A. Lodge (New York: Penguin, 2000), 25.
50. Cronon, "'Only Connect,'" 80.
51. Berry, *It All Turns on Affection*, 15.
52. Berry, *Jayber Crow*, 249.
53. Ibid., 54.
54. See, for instance, Berry, *Life Is a Miracle*, 14; Berry, "Going to Work," 33–41; Berry, "Bellarmine Commencement Address"; Graduate Fellows Conference 2014—Part 2, Carrollton, KY, http://www.youtube.com/watch?v=XWhgU3qECJc&feature=youtube_gdata_player. Such an approach apparently characterized Berry's teaching. In describing a class he took with Berry, Grubbs writes, "A set of critical and practical questions emerged from our conversations with the text and with each other: . . . These questions became our mantra." Grubbs, "Practical Education," 137.
55. Berry, "Major in Homecoming," 34–35.
56. Ibid., 35.
57. Schreck considers the benefits of Berry's proposed curriculum of questions in "Wendell Berry's Philosophy of Education," 416.
58. Simone Weil, *Awaiting God: A New Translation of* Attente de Dieu *and* Lettre à un Religieux, trans. Brad Jersak (Abbotsford, BC: Fresh Wind Press, 2013), 21.
59. Ibid., 23.
60. Ibid., 23–24.
61. Ibid., 24–26.
62. Ibid., 26–27.
63. Ibid., 28.
64. Berry, "Wendell Berry on His Hopes for Humanity."
65. Weil, *Awaiting God*, 28–29.
66. Berry, "Our Deserted Country," 116.
67. Berry, *New Collected Poems*, 173–74.

Conclusion

1. Berry, *Jayber Crow*, 249.
2. Berry, "Work of Local Culture," 168–69.
3. Cheryl Truman, "Wendell Berry Pulling His Personal Papers from UK," June 2010, http://www.kentucky.com/2010/06/23/1319383/wendell-berry-pulling-his-personal.html (accessed July 7, 2015).
4. Wendell Berry and Gary Snyder, *Distant Neighbors: The Selected Let-*

ters of Wendell Berry & Gary Snyder, ed. Chad Wriglesworth (Washington, DC: Counterpoint, 2014).

5. Berry, "Hunting for Reasons to Hope," 222.

6. Wendell Berry and Madhu Suri Prakash, "A Quieter Life Now," *YES! Magazine,* June 29, 2011, http://www.yesmagazine.org/issues/beyond-prisons/a-quieter-life-now.

Afterword

1. Berry, *Jayber Crow,* 133.

Bibliography

"About—The Labor Program at Berea College." http://www.berea.edu/labor-program/. Accessed July 23, 2014.

American Federation of Teachers. "American Academic: The State of the Higher Education Workforce 1997–2007." 2009. http://www.aftface.org/storage/face/documents/ameracad_report_97-07for_web.pdf.

Andrews, Burdette, ed. *The Echo of Spring Arbor University Seminary* 5 (1926): 77–78.

Augustine. *Confessions*. Translated by Henry Chadwick. Oxford: Oxford University Press, 1998.

"BA in Farming and Ecological Agrarianism." St. Catharine College Kentucky. http://www.sccky.edu/academics/arts-sciences/earth-studies/sustainablefarming_ba.php. Accessed March 20, 2014.

Baker, Jack R., and Jeffrey Bilbro. "Putting Down Roots: Why Universities Need Gardens." *Christian Scholar's Review* 45, no. 2 (2016): 125–42.

Bartlett, Tom. "Can a Longtime Fraud Help Fix Science?" *Chronicle of Higher Education*, June 22, 2015. http://chronicle.com/article/Can-a-Longtime-Fraud-Help-Fix/231061/.

———. "The Unraveling of Michael LaCour." *Chronicle of Higher Education*, June 2, 2015. http://chronicle.com/article/The-Unraveling-of-Michael/2305?87/.

Battiste, Marie, and James Youngblood Henderson. *Protecting Indigenous Knowledge and Heritage: A Global Challenge*. Saskatoon, SK: Purich, 2000.

Berry, Wendell. "An Agricultural Journey in Peru." In *The Gift of Good Land: Further Essays Cultural and Agricultural*, 3–46. Berkeley, CA: Counterpoint, 2009.

———. "American Imagination and the Civil War." In *Imagination in Place: Essays*, 17–38. Berkeley, CA: Counterpoint, 2010.

———. "Andy Catlett: An Early Education." In *A Place in Time: Twenty Stories of the Port William Membership*, 81–87. Berkeley, CA: Counterpoint, 2012.

———. "Bellarmine Commencement Address." 2007. http://christianstudycenter.org/wp-content/uploads/2009/10/WendellBerry-BellarmineCommencement.pdf.

———. "Caught in the Middle on Abortion and Homosexuality." *Christian Cen-*

tury, March 20, 2013. http://www.christiancentury.org/article/2013-03/caught-middle.

———. "Christianity and the Survival of Creation." In *Sex, Economy, Freedom & Community: Eight Essays*, 93–116. New York: Pantheon, 1993.

———. "The Chubb Fellowship—Wendell Berry." December 7, 2013. http://chubbfellowship.org/speakers/current/wendell_berry.

———. "The Conservation of Nature and the Preservation of Humanity." In *Another Turn of the Crank: Essays*, 64–85. Washington, DC: Counterpoint, 1995.

———. *Conversations with Wendell Berry*. Edited by Morris A. Grubbs. Literary Conversations Series. Jackson: University Press of Mississippi, 2007.

———. "A Defense of the Family Farm." In *Home Economics: Fourteen Essays*, 162–78. Berkeley, CA: Counterpoint, 1987.

———. "Discipline and Hope." In *A Continuous Harmony: Essays Cultural and Agricultural*, 86–168. San Diego: Harcourt Brace, 1972.

———. "Feminism, the Body, and the Machine." In *The Art of the Commonplace*, 65–80. Washington, DC: Shoemaker & Hoard, 2002.

———. "Fidelity." In *That Distant Land: The Collected Stories*, 372–427. Washington, DC: Shoemaker & Hoard, 2004.

———. "A Forest Conversation." In *Our Only World: Ten Essays*, 21–52. Berkeley, CA: Counterpoint, 2015.

———. "The Futility of Global Thinking." *Harper's Magazine*, September 1989.

———. "A Gentle Man Speaks: A Conversation with Wendell Berry." Interview by Glenn Thompson. *Iron Blade*, September 28, 2010. http://www2.ferrum.edu/ironblade/archives/2010-11/extra.pdf.

———. "The Gift of Good Land." In *The Gift of Good Land: Further Essays Cultural and Agricultural*, 267–81. Berkeley, CA: Counterpoint, 2009.

———. "God and Country." In *What Are People For? Essays*, 95–102. New York: North Point Press, 1990.

———. "Going to Work." In *Citizenship Papers*, 33–41. Washington, DC: Shoemaker & Hoard, 2003.

———. *Hannah Coulter*. Berkeley, CA: Counterpoint, 2005.

———. *The Hidden Wound*. Berkeley, CA: Counterpoint, 2010.

———. "Higher Education and Home Defense." In *Home Economics: Fourteen Essays*, 49–53. Berkeley, CA: Counterpoint, 1987.

———. "Hunting for Reasons to Hope: A Conversation with Wendell Berry." Interview by Harold K. Bush. *Christianity and Literature* 56, no. 2 (2007): 215–34.

———. "In Defense of Literacy." In *A Continuous Harmony: Essays Cultural and Agricultural*, 169–73. San Diego: Harcourt Brace, 1972.

———. "Irish Journal." In *Home Economics*, 21–48. New York: North Point Press, 1987.

———. *It All Turns on Affection: The Jefferson Lecture and Other Essays*. Berkeley, CA: Counterpoint, 2012.

———. *Jayber Crow: A Novel*. Washington, DC: Counterpoint, 2000.
———. "Kentucky Writers Hall of Fame: Wendell Berry's Remarks." Carnegie Center for Literacy and Learning, January 28, 2015. http://carnegiecenterlex.org/2015/02/kentucky-writers-hall-of-fame-wendell-berrys-remarks/.
———. *Life Is a Miracle: An Essay against Modern Superstition*. Washington, DC: Counterpoint, 2001.
———. "Local Economies to Save the Land and the People." In *Our Only World: Ten Essays*, 53–67. Berkeley, CA: Counterpoint, 2015.
———. "Local Knowledge in the Age of Information." In *The Way of Ignorance: And Other Essays*, 113–25. Berkeley, CA: Counterpoint, 2006.
———. "The Loss of the University." In *Home Economics: Fourteen Essays*, 76–97. Berkeley, CA: Counterpoint, 1987.
———. "Major in Homecoming: For Commencement, Northern Kentucky University." In *What Matters? Economics for a Renewed Commonwealth*, 31–36. Washington, DC: Counterpoint, 2010.
———. "The Making of a Marginal Farm." In *Recollected Essays: 1965–1980*, 329–40. New York: North Point Press, 1993.
———. *The Memory of Old Jack*. Berkeley, CA: Counterpoint, 1999.
———. *Nathan Coulter: A Novel*. Berkeley, CA: Counterpoint, 2008.
———. "Nature as an Ally: An Interview with Wendell Berry." Interview by Sarah Leonard. *Dissent Magazine*, 2012. http://www.dissentmagazine.org/article/nature-as-an-ally-an-interview-with-wendell-berry.
———. *New Collected Poems*. Berkeley, CA: Counterpoint, 2013.
———. "Our Deserted Country." In *Our Only World: Ten Essays*, 105–57. Berkeley, CA: Counterpoint, 2015.
———. "Paragraphs from a Notebook." In *Our Only World: Ten Essays*, 3–14. Berkeley, CA: Counterpoint, 2015.
———. "People, Land, and Community." In *Standing by Words: Essays*, 64–79. Washington, DC: Shoemaker & Hoard, 2005.
———. *A Place on Earth: A Novel*. Washington, DC: Counterpoint, 2001.
———. "Poetry and Marriage." In *Standing by Words: Essays*, 92–105. Washington, DC: Shoemaker & Hoard, 2005.
———. "Poetry and Place." In *Standing by Words: Essays*, 106–213. Washington, DC: Shoemaker & Hoard, 2005.
———. "Pray without Ceasing." In *That Distant Land: The Collected Stories*, 38–76. Washington, DC: Shoemaker & Hoard, 2004.
———. "Preface: The Joy of Sales Resistance." In *Sex, Economy, Freedom & Community: Eight Essays*, xi–xxii. New York: Pantheon, 1993.
———. "The Reactor and the Garden." In *The Gift of Good Land: Further Essays Cultural and Agricultural*, 161–70. Berkeley, CA: Counterpoint, 2009.
———. *Remembering: A Novel*. Berkeley, CA: Counterpoint, 2008.
———. "Seven Amish Farms." In *The Gift of Good Land: Further Essays Cultural and Agricultural*, 249–63. Berkeley, CA: Counterpoint, 2009.

———. "Solving for Pattern." In *The Gift of Good Land: Further Essays Cultural and Agricultural*, 134–47. Berkeley, CA: Counterpoint, 2009.

———. "Standing by Words." In *Standing by Words: Essays*, 24–63. Washington, DC: Shoemaker & Hoard, 2005.

———. "Think Little." In *A Continuous Harmony: Essays Cultural and Agricultural*, 71–85. San Diego: Harcourt Brace, 1972.

———. *This Day: New and Collected Sabbath Poems 1979–2012*. Berkeley, CA: Counterpoint, 2013.

———. "Thoughts in the Presence of Fear." In *Citizenship Papers*, 17–22. Washington, DC: Shoemaker & Hoard, 2003.

———. "Three Ways of Farming in the Southwest." In *The Gift of Good Land: Further Essays Cultural and Agricultural*, 47–76. Berkeley, CA: Counterpoint, 2009.

———. "Two Economies." In *Home Economics*, 54–75. New York: North Point Press, 1987.

———. "Two Minds." In *Citizenship Papers*, 85–105. Washington, DC: Shoemaker & Hoard, 2003.

———. *The Unsettling of America: Culture & Agriculture*. San Francisco: Sierra Club Books, 1996.

———. "The Way of Ignorance." In *The Way of Ignorance: And Other Essays*, 53–67. Berkeley, CA: Counterpoint, 2006.

———. "Wendell Berry on His Hopes for Humanity." Interview by Bill Moyers, November 29, 2013. http://billmoyers.com/segment/wendell-berry-on-his-hopes-for-humanity/.

———. "What Are People For?" In *What Are People For? Essays*, 123–25. New York: North Point Press, 1990.

———. "Why I Am Not Going to Buy a Computer." In *What Are People For? Essays*, 170–77. New York: North Point Press, 1990.

———. "The Wild Birds." In *That Distant Land: The Collected Stories*, 337–64. Washington, DC: Shoemaker & Hoard, 2004.

———. "The Work of Local Culture." In *What Are People For? Essays*, 153–69. New York: North Point Press, 1990.

———. "Writer and Region." In *What Are People For? Essays*, 71–87. New York: North Point Press, 1990.

Berry, Wendell, and Madhu Suri Prakash. "A Quieter Life Now." *YES! Magazine*, June 29, 2011. http://www.yesmagazine.org/issues/beyond-prisons/a-quieter-life-now.

Berry, Wendell, and Gary Snyder. *Distant Neighbors: The Selected Letters of Wendell Berry & Gary Snyder*. Edited by Chad Wriglesworth. Washington, DC: Counterpoint, 2014.

The Bible: Authorized King James Version. Edited by Robert Carroll and Stephen Prickett. New York: Oxford University Press, 2008.

Bilbro, Jeffrey. "The Ecology of Memory: Augustine, Eliot, and the Form of

Wendell Berry's Fiction." *Christianity and Literature* 65, no. 3 (2016): 327–42.

———. *Loving God's Wildness: The Christian Roots of Ecological Ethics in American Literature*. Tuscaloosa: University of Alabama Press, 2015.

———. "Place Isn't Just Geographical." Front Porch Republic, May 2013. http://www.frontporchrepublic.com/2013/05/place-isnt-just-geographical/.

———. "Review of *The Ecological Thought*." *Christianity and Literature* 61, no. 4 (2012): 693–97.

———. "Sublime Failure: Why We'd Better Start Seeing Our World as Beautiful." *South Atlantic Review* 80, no. 1–2 (2015): 133–58.

Blanchard, Kathryn, and Kevin O'Brien. *An Introduction to Christian Environmentalism: Ecology, Virtue, and Ethics*. Waco, TX: Baylor University Press, 2014.

Bonzo, J. Matthew, and Michael R. Stevens. "Seed Will Sprout in the Scar: Wendell Berry on Higher Education." *The Other Journal*, August 13, 2008. http://theotherjournal.com/2008/08/13/seed-will-sprout-in-the-scar-wendell-berry-on-higher-education/.

———. *Wendell Berry and the Cultivation of Life: A Reader's Guide*. Grand Rapids, MI: Brazos Press, 2008.

Bouma-Prediger, Steven, and Brian Walsh. "Education for Homelessness or Homemaking? The Christian College in a Postmodern Culture." *Christian Scholar's Review* 32, no. 3 (2003): 281–96.

Bowers, C. A. *Educating for Eco-Justice and Community*. Athens: University of Georgia Press, 2001.

Brooks, David. "Transcript of David Brooks, The Gathering 2014." *The Gathering*.http://thegathering.com/e-updates/transcript-david-brooks-gathering-2014/. Accessed October 21, 2014.

Brueggemann, Walter. *Sabbath as Resistance: Saying No to the Culture of Now*. Louisville, KY: Westminster John Knox Press, 2014.

Caldecott, Stratford. *Beauty for Truth's Sake: On the Re-enchantment of Education*. Grand Rapids, MI: Brazos Press, 2009.

———. *Beauty in the Word: Rethinking the Foundations of Education*. Kettering, OH: Angelico Press, 2012.

Candler, Peter M., Jr. *Theology, Rhetoric, Manuduction, or Reading Scripture Together on the Path to God*. Grand Rapids, MI: Eerdmans, 2006.

Carr, Nicholas. *The Glass Cage: Automation and Us*. New York: W. W. Norton, 2014.

———. *The Shallows: What the Internet Is Doing to Our Brains*. New York: W. W. Norton, 2011.

Cavanaugh, William T. *Being Consumed: Economics and Christian Desire*. Grand Rapids, MI: Eerdmans, 2008.

Chesterton, G. K. *Heretics*. Stilwell, KS: Digireads.com, 2006.

———. *Manalive*. New York: John Lane, 1912.

———. *What's Wrong with the World*. Peru, IL: Sherwood Sugden, 1910.
Christensen, Clayton M., and Henry J. Eyring. *The Innovative University: Changing the DNA of Higher Education from the Inside Out*. San Francisco: Jossey-Bass, 2011.
Corn, Alfred. *The Poem's Heartbeat: A Manual of Prosody*. Port Townsend, WA: Copper Canyon Press, 2008.
Crawford, Matthew B. *Shop Class as Soulcraft: An Inquiry into the Value of Work*. New York: Penguin, 2010.
———. *The World beyond Your Head: On Becoming an Individual in an Age of Distraction*. New York: Farrar, Straus & Giroux, 2015.
Crider, Scott F. *Office of Assertion: An Art of Rhetoric for Academic Essay*. Wilmington, DE: ISI Books, 2005.
Cronon, William. "'Only Connect . . .': The Goals of a Liberal Education." *American Scholar* 67, no. 4 (1998): 73–80.
Crouch, Andy. "Small Screens, Big World: Easter in Florence, The Fiction of Mark Helprin, and a Lent without Glowing Rectangles." April 8, 2015. http://andy-crouch.com/articles/small_screens_big_world.
Dalton, Katherine. "Birthright." In *Front Porch Manifesto*, edited by Jason Peters and Mark Mitchell. Eugene, OR: Front Porch Republic Books, forthcoming.
Daly, Herman. Foreword to *What Matters? Economics for a Renewed Commonwealth*, by Wendell Berry, ix–xiv. Berkeley, CA: Counterpoint, 2010.
Davis, Jeffry C., Philip Graham Ryken, and Leland Ryken, eds. *Liberal Arts for the Christian Life*. Wheaton, IL: Crossway, 2012.
Delbanco, Andrew. *College: What It Was, Is, and Should Be*. Princeton, NJ: Princeton University Press, 2012.
Deneen, Patrick J. "We're All to Blame for MOOCs." *Chronicle of Higher Education*, June 3, 2013. http://chronicle.com/article/Were-All-to-Blame-for-MOOCs/139519/.
"Digest of Education Statistics, 2013." http://nces.ed.gov/programs/digest/d13/tables/dt13_330.10.asp?current=yes. Accessed June 29, 2015.
Dreher, Rod. *The Little Way of Ruthie Leming: A Southern Girl, a Small Town, and the Secret of a Good Life*. New York: Grand Central Publishing, 2013.
———. "Wendell Berry: A Latter-Day St. Benedict." In *The Humane Vision of Wendell Berry*, edited by Mark Mitchell and Nathan Schlueter, 275–87. Wilmington, DE: ISI Books, 2011.
Drehs, Wayne. "School Turns Football Field into Farm." ESPN, November 26, 2014. http://espn.go.com/nfl/story/_/id/11942279/texas-football-field-turned-farm-provides-local-produce-dallas-cowboys-stadium.
Eliot, T. S. *Collected Poems, 1909–1962*. New York: Harcourt Brace Jovanovich, 1991.
Esolen, Anthony. "If Dante Were a Kentucky Barber." In *The Humane Vision of Wendell Berry*, edited by Mark T. Mitchell and Nathan Schlueter, 255–74. Wilmington, DE: ISI Books, 2011.

———. "Secular Grendel." *Touchstone: A Journal of Mere Christianity*, January/February 2011. http://www.touchstonemag.com/archives/article.php?id=24-01-020-f.

Farrell, James J. *The Nature of College: How a New Understanding of Campus Life Can Change the World*. Minneapolis: Milkweed Editions, 2010.

"Florida Blue Ribbon Task Force on State Higher Education Reform." November 6, 2012. http://www.fgcu.edu/FacultySenate/files/2-22-2013_Resolution_Supplement_3.pdf.

Florida, Richard. "High-School Dropouts and College Grads Are Moving to Very Different Places." *CityLab*, June 16, 2014. http://www.citylab.com/work/2014/06/high-school-dropouts-and-college-grads-are-moving-to-very-different-places/372065/.

———. *Who's Your City? How the Creative Economy Is Making Where to Live the Most Important Decision of Your Life*. New York: Basic Books, 2008.

Forster, E. M. *Howards End*. Edited by David A. Lodge. New York: Penguin, 2000.

Foucault, Michel. *Discipline and Punish: The Birth of the Prison*. Translated by Alan Sheridan. New York: Pantheon Books, 1977.

"The Foxfire Fund, Inc." http://www.foxfire.org/. Accessed July 24, 2014.

Francis. "Laudato Si." May 2015. http://w2.vatican.va/content/francesco/en/encyclicals/documents/papa-francesco_20150524_enciclica-laudato-si.html.

Gadamer, Hans-Georg. *Truth and Method*. 2nd rev. ed. Translated by Joel Weinsheimer and Donald G. Marshall. London: Sheed & Ward, 1999.

Gamble, Richard. "An Education for Membership." In *The Humane Vision of Wendell Berry*, edited by Mark T. Mitchell and Nathan W. Schlueter, 28–39. Wilmington, DE: ISI Books, 2011.

Gill, Eric. *A Holy Tradition of Working: Passages from the Writings of Eric Gill*. West Stockbridge, MA: Lindisfarne Press, 1983.

Gioia, Dana. "Poetry as Enchantment." *Poetry Daily*, 2015. http://poems.com/special_features/prose/essay_gioia_enchantment.php.

Graduate Fellows Conference 2014—Part 2. Carrollton, KY. http://www.youtube.com/watch?v=XWhgU3qECJc&feature=youtube_gdata_player.

Griffiths, Paul J. *Intellectual Appetite: A Theological Grammar*. Washington, DC: Catholic University of America Press, 2009.

Grubbs, Morris A. "A Practical Education: Wendell Berry the Professor." In *Wendell Berry Life and Work*, edited by Jason Peters, 137–41. Culture of the Land: A Series in the New Agrarianism. Lexington: University Press of Kentucky, 2010.

Halverson, Jim. "Restored through Learning: Hugh of St. Victor's Vision for Higher Education." *Christian Scholar's Review* 41, no. 1 (2011): 35–50.

Hauerwas, Stanley. *The State of the University: Academic Knowledges and the Knowledge of God*. Malden, MA: Blackwell, 2007.

Heidegger, Martin. *The Question Concerning Technology, and Other Essays.* Translated by William Levitt. New York: Harper Torchbooks, 1982.

Heidegger, Martin, and J. Glenn Gray. *What Is Called Thinking?* New York: Harper & Row, 1972.

Heise, Ursula K. *Sense of Place and Sense of Planet: The Environmental Imagination of the Global.* Oxford: Oxford University Press, 2008.

Henderson, Joseph A., and David W. Hursh. "Economics and Education for Human Flourishing: Wendell Berry and the Oikonomic Alternative to Neoliberalism." *Educational Studies* 50, no. 2 (March 1, 2014): 167–86.

hooks, bell. *Belonging: A Culture of Place.* New York: Routledge, 2008.

Hugh of St. Victor. *The Didascalicon of Hugh of St. Victor: A Medieval Guide to the Arts.* Translated by Jerome Taylor. New York: Columbia University Press, 1991.

———. *On the Sacraments of the Christian Faith (De Sacramentis) of Hugh of Saint Victor.* Translated by Roy J. Deferrari. Cambridge, MA: Medieval Academy of America, 1951.

Illich, Ivan. *In the Vineyard of the Text: A Commentary to Hugh's Didascalicon.* Chicago: University of Chicago Press, 1993.

"Innovating for the Future." State Council of Higher Education for Virginia, 2011. http://www.schev.edu/innovation.asp.

Jackson, Peter. *The Lord of the Rings: The Return of the King.* New Line Home Video, 2004.

Jackson, Wes. *Becoming Native to This Place.* Washington, DC: Counterpoint, 1996.

Jacob, Brian, Brian McCall, and Kevin M. Stange. "College as Country Club: Do Colleges Cater to Students' Preferences for Consumption?" Working paper, National Bureau of Economic Research, January 2013. http://www.nber.org/papers/w18745.

Jacobs, Alan. "The Two Cultures, Then and Now." *Books and Culture,* February 2014. http://www.booksandculture.com/site/utilities/print.html?type=article&id=116715. Accessed March 1, 2014.

Jacobsen, Eric O. *The Space Between: A Christian Engagement with the Built Environment.* Grand Rapids, MI: Baker Academic, 2012.

Jeffrey, David Lyle. "The Pearl of Great Wisdom: The Deep and Abiding Biblical Roots of Western Liberal Education." *Touchstone Magazine,* October 2007. http://www.touchstonemag.com/archives/article.php?id=20-08-025-f.

Jeffrey, David Lyle, and Gregory Maillet. *Christianity and Literature: Philosophical Foundations and Critical Practice.* Downers Grove, IL: IVP Academic, 2011.

Joseph, Sister Miriam. *The Trivium: The Liberal Arts of Logic, Grammar, and Rhetoric; Understanding the Nature and Function of Language.* Philadelphia: Paul Dry Books, 2002.

Kavanagh, Patrick. *Collected Pruse.* Worcester, MA: MacGibbon & Kee, 1967.
Kerr, Clark. *The Uses of the University.* 5th ed. Cambridge, MA: Harvard University Press, 2001.
Kovach, Margaret Elizabeth. *Indigenous Methodologies: Characteristics, Conversations, and Contexts.* Reprint ed. Toronto: University of Toronto Press, 2010.
Kronman, Anthony T. *Education's End: Why Our Colleges and Universities Have Given up on the Meaning of Life.* New Haven, CT: Yale University Press, 2008.
Kuhn, Thomas S. *The Structure of Scientific Revolutions.* 4th ed. Chicago: University of Chicago Press, 2012.
Lake, Christina Bieber. *Prophets of the Posthuman: American Fiction, Biotechnology, and the Ethics of Personhood.* Notre Dame, IN: University of Notre Dame Press, 2013.
Lauerman, John. "For-Profit College Costs Surpass Nonprofit Peers in U.S. Study." *Bloomberg.com,* May 25, 2011. http://www.bloomberg.com/news/articles/2011-05-26/for-profit-college-costs-surpass-nonprofit-peers-in-u-s-study.
Leithart, Peter J. *Gratitude: An Intellectual History.* Waco, TX: Baylor University Press, 2014.
Leopold, Aldo. *A Sand County Almanac: And Sketches Here and There.* New York: Oxford University Press, 1989.
Lewis, C. S. *The Abolition of Man.* San Francisco: Harper, 2001.
———. *A Preface to* Paradise Lost. London: Oxford University Press, 1961.
———. *Studies in Words.* Cambridge: Cambridge University Press, 1960.
Lewis, Harry. *Excellence without a Soul: Does Liberal Education Have a Future?* New York: Public Affairs, 2007.
Lukacs, John. *Last Rites.* New Haven, CT: Yale University Press, 2009.
Lundin, Roger. *From Nature to Experience: The American Search for Cultural Authority.* American Intellectual Culture. Lanham, MD: Rowman & Littlefield, 2005.
MacIntyre, Alasdair. *After Virtue: A Study in Moral Theory.* Notre Dame, IN: University of Notre Dame Press, 1984.
———. *God, Philosophy, Universities: A Selective History of the Catholic Philosophical Tradition.* Lanham, MD: Rowman & Littlefield, 2011.
———. *The MacIntyre Reader.* Edited by Kelvin Knight. Notre Dame, IN: University of Notre Dame Press, 1998.
Major, William H. *Grounded Vision: New Agrarianism and the Academy.* Tuscaloosa: University of Alabama Press, 2011.
Martusewicz, Rebecca. "Eros, Education, and Eco-Ethical Consciousness: Re-Membering the 'Room of Love' in Wendell Berry's Hannah Coulter." *Educational Studies* 49, no. 5 (2013): 443–50.
Martusewicz, Rebecca A., Jeff Edmundson, and Richard Kahn. "On Member-

ship, Humility, and Pedagogical Responsibilities: A Correspondence on the Work of Wendell Berry." *Mid-Western Educational Researcher* 25, no. 3 (2013): 44–68.

Martusewicz, Rebecca A., Jeff Edmundson, and John Lupinacci. *Ecojustice Education: Toward Diverse, Democratic, and Sustainable Communities.* Sociocultural, Political, and Historical Studies in Education. New York: Routledge, 2011.

McClay, Wilfred M. "Introduction: Why Place Matters." In *Why Place Matters: Geography, Identity, and Civic Life in Modern America,* edited by Wilfred M. McClay and Ted V. McAllister, 1–9. New York: New Atlantis Books, 2014.

Milton, John. *The Riverside Milton.* Edited by Roy Flannagan. Boston: Houghton Mifflin, 1998.

Mitchell, Mark T. *The Politics of Gratitude: Scale, Place & Community in a Global Age.* Dulles, VA: Potomac Books, 2012.

Morton, Timothy. *The Ecological Thought.* Cambridge, MA: Harvard University Press, 2010.

———. *Ecology without Nature: Rethinking Environmental Aesthetics.* Cambridge, MA: Harvard University Press, 2009.

Moss, Walter G. "Professors and Politics a la Wendell Berry." *LA Progressive,* March 14, 2014. http://www.laprogressive.com/left-wing-professors/.

Mueller, Pam A., and Daniel M. Oppenheimer. "The Pen Is Mightier than the Keyboard: Advantages of Longhand over Laptop Note Taking." *Psychological Science* 25, no. 6 (June 1, 2014): 1159–68.

Murray, Charles A. *Coming Apart: The State of White America, 1960–2010.* New York: Crown Forum, 2013.

Oehlschlaeger, Fritz. *The Achievement of Wendell Berry: The Hard History of Love.* Culture of the Land: A Series in the New Agrarianism. Lexington: University Press of Kentucky, 2011.

Orr, David W. *Earth in Mind: On Education, Environment, and the Human Prospect.* Washington, DC: Island Press, 2004.

Orwell, George. "Politics and the English Language." In *Essays on Language and Usage,* edited by Leonard F. Dean and Kenneth G. Wilson, 325–36. New York: Oxford University Press, 1963.

Osborn, Ronald. "Seyla Benhabib, Wendell Berry, and the Question of Migrant and Refugee Rights." *Humanitas* 23, no. 1–2 (2010): 118–38.

Peters, Jason. "Wendell Berry's Vindication of the Flesh." *Christianity and Literature* 56, no. 2 (2007): 317–32.

———. "Whoring in Shittim." Front Porch Republic, January 2012. http://www.frontporchrepublic.com/2012/01/whoring-in-shittim/.

Plato. *Phaedrus.* Translated by Robin Waterfield. Oxford: Oxford University Press, 2002.

Pollan, Michael. *The Omnivore's Dilemma: A Natural History of Four Meals.* New York: Penguin, 2007.

Postman, Neil. *Technopoly: The Surrender of Culture to Technology*. New York: Knopf, 1992.
Prakash, Madhu Suri. "What Are People For? Wendell Berry on Education, Ecology, and Culture." *Educational Theory* 44, no. 2 (1994): 135–57.
Prakash, Madhu Suri, and Gustavo Esteva. *Escaping Education: Living as Learning within Grassroots Cultures*. New York: P. Lang, 2008.
Rilke, Rainer Maria. *Selected Poems of Rainer Maria Rilke*. Translated by Robert Bly. New York: Harper & Row, 1981.
Salisbury, John of. *The Metalogicon: A Twelfth-Century Defense of the Verbal and Logical Arts of the Trivium*. Translated by Daniel McGarry. Philadelphia: Paul Dry Books, 2009.
Salvucci, Emiliano. "Selfishness, Warfare, and Economics; or Integration, Cooperation, and Biology." *Frontiers in Cellular and Infection Microbiology* 2, no. 54 (May 1, 2012): 1–12.
Sayers, Dorothy. "The Lost Tools of Learning." Great Books Tutorial, 1947. http://www.gbt.org/text/sayers.html.
Schreck, Jane Margaret Hedahl. "Wendell Berry's Philosophy of Education: Lessons from Port William." PhD diss., University of North Dakota, 2013. http://gradworks.umi.com/35/87/3587458.html.
Shakespeare, William. *King Lear*. In *The Riverside Shakespeare*, edited by G. Blakemore Evans and J. J. M. Tobin. Boston: Houghton Mifflin, 1997.
Shirky, Clay. "Why I Just Asked My Students to Put Their Laptops Away. . . ." *Medium*, September 9, 2014. https://medium.com/@cshirky/why-i-just-asked-my-students-to-put-their-laptops-away-7f5f7c50f368.
Shiva, Vandana. *The Vandana Shiva Reader*. Culture of the Land: A Series in the New Agrarianism. Lexington: University Press of Kentucky, 2014.
Smith, Alexander McCall. *The Good Husband of Zebra Drive*. New York: Anchor Books, 2008.
Smith, James K. A. *Imagining the Kingdom: How Worship Works*. Grand Rapids, MI: Baker Books, 2013.
Smith, Kimberly K. *Wendell Berry and the Agrarian Tradition: A Common Grace*. Lawrence: University Press of Kansas, 2003.
Smith, Merlin G. "The Farm." *The Echo of Spring Arbor University Seminary* 6 (1927): 93.
Snider, Susannah. "3 Must-Know Facts about For-Profit Colleges, Student Debt." *US News & World Report*, October 1, 2014. http://www.usnews.com/education/best-colleges/paying-for-college/articles/2014/10/01/3-facts-for-students-to-know-about-for-profit-colleges-and-student-debt. Accessed August 25, 2015.
Sommerville, C. John. *The Decline of the Secular University*. Oxford: Oxford University Press, 2006.
Steiner, George. *Martin Heidegger*. Chicago: University of Chicago Press, 1991.
Sunflower Project. 2011. https://www.youtube.com/watch?v=Ok40wF-f5Hc&feature=youtube_gdata_player.

Tolkien, J. R. R. "Mythopoeia." In *Tree and Leaf,* 85–90. London: HarperCollins, 2001.

Truman, Cheryl. "Wendell Berry Pulling His Personal Papers from UK." June 2010. http://www.kentucky.com/2010/06/23/1319383/wendell-berry-pulling-his-personal.html.

Tuan, Yi-fu. *Cosmos and Hearth: A Cosmopolite's Viewpoint.* Minneapolis: University of Minnesota Press, 1996.

"Unambitious Loser with Happy, Fulfilling Life Still Lives in Hometown." *The Onion,* July 24, 2013. http://www.theonion.com/articles/unambitious-loser-with-happy-fulfilling-life-still,33233/.

Wallis, Bryan. "More Real than Real: The Weird Localism of Ralph Eugene Meatyard and Wendell Berry." *Australasian Journal of Ecocriticism and Cultural Ecology* 2 (August 4, 2013): 75–95.

"Warren Wilson College." http://www.warren-wilson.edu/work/. Accessed July 23, 2014.

Weil, Simone. *Awaiting God: A New Translation of* Attente de Dieu *and* Lettre à un Religieux. Translated by Brad Jersak. Abbotsford, BC: Fresh Wind Press, 2013.

"Welcome to the Work Colleges Consortium!" http://www.workcolleges.org/. Accessed July 23, 2014.

Wellmon, Chad. *Organizing Enlightenment: Information Overload and the Invention of the Modern Research University.* Baltimore: Johns Hopkins University Press, 2015.

"We over Me Farm." Paul Quinn College. http://www.weovermefarm.com/. Accessed March 17, 2015.

Whitney, Elspeth. *Paradise Restored: The Mechanical Arts from Antiquity through the Thirteenth Century.* Philadelphia: American Philosophical Society, 1990.

Wilson, E. O. "My Wish: Build the Encyclopedia of Life." Ted, March 2007. http://www.ted.com/talks/e_o_wilson_on_saving_life_on_earth/transcript?language=en#t-1215000.

Wirzba, Norman. "An Economy of Gratitude." In *Wendell Berry Life and Work,* edited by Jason Peters, 142–55. Culture of the Land: A Series in the New Agrarianism. Lexington: University Press of Kentucky, 2010.

———. *Living the Sabbath: Discovering the Rhythms of Rest and Delight.* The Christian Practice of Everyday Life. Grand Rapids, MI: Brazos Press, 2006.

———. *The Paradise of God: Renewing Religion in an Ecological Age.* Oxford: Oxford University Press, 2007.

"Work Education." College of the Ozarks. http://www.cofo.edu/Page/Students/Work-Education.96.html. Accessed July 23, 2014.

Zaraska, Marta. "Is Lab-Grown Meat Good for Us?" *The Atlantic,* August 19,

2013. http://www.theatlantic.com/health/archive/2013/08/is-lab-grown-meat-good-for-us/278778/.
Zencey, Eric. "Rootless Professors." In *Rooted in the Land: Essays on Community and Place,* edited by William Vitek and Wes Jackson, 15–19. New Haven, CT: Yale University Press, 1996.

Index

affections. *See* desires

agriculture, 17, 32, 66, 78, 87, 129, 131, 158, 161; industrial, 12–13, 26, 29, 47–48, 80

Augustine, 18, 104, 107, 177, 216n29, 216n30

Berry, works of: *A Place on Earth*, 173; "American Imagination and the Civil War," 147, 152, 157; "Bellarmine Commencement Address," 228n54; "The Body and the Earth," 151–52; "Caught in the Middle on Abortion and Homosexuality," 13; "Christianity and the Survival of Creation," 77, 102, 125; "The Conservation of Nature and the Preservation of Humanity," 6, 7, 10, 102; "Discipline and Hope," 12, 38; "Feminism, the Body, and the Machine," 85; "Fidelity," 142–43, 146; "The Futility of Global Thinking," 13; "The Gift of Good Land," 13, 125, 129–31, 215n19; "God and Country," 125; "Going to Work," 221n67, 228n54; *Hannah Coulter*, 1–3, 10, 41, 43, 47, 121, 178; *The Hidden Wound*, 77, 103, 127; "Higher Education and Home Defense," 8, 34; "In Defense of Literacy," 30, 63; "Irish Journal," 225n67; "It All Turns on Affection," 7, 79–80, 96, 184, 209n7; *Jayber Crow*, 44–45, 96, 107, 167–76, 178, 180–82, 195, 197, 227n29; *Life Is a Miracle*, 10, 17, 101, 102, 121–22, 126–28, 130, 132, 136–38, 156–58, 179, 208n48, 213n37, 220n53, 228n54; "Local Knowledge in the Age of Information," 11–12, 77–78, 83, 105, 147–48, 155, 160–61, 220n53; "The Loss of the University," 28, 35–39, 64, 95; "The Making of a Marginal Farm," 103; "Major in Homecoming: For Commencement, Northern Kentucky University," 6, 185, 202n26; "Manifesto: The Mad Farmer Liberation Front," 189–90; *The Memory of Old Jack*, 70–72, 82, 212n10; *Nathan Coulter: A Novel*, 141; "Our Deserted Country," 149, 155, 164, 167, 188; "Paragraphs from a Notebook," 208n45, 216n31; "People, Land, and Community," 81–82, 156, 180; "Poetry and Marriage," 103, 126, 165; "Poetry and Place," 18, 123–24; "Pray without Ceasing," 96–100, 107; "Prayer after Eating," 84, 122; "Preface: The Joy of Sales Resistance," 17, 63–64; *Remembering*, 25–28, 41, 46, 47–50, 68, 70; "Solving for Pattern," 224n45; "Standing by Words," 18, 50–54, 57, 80–81, 120, 122–23, 131–32, 220n55;

Berry, works of *(cont.)*
"Think Little," 87–88; "Thoughts in the Presence of Fear," 11, 56; "Two Economies," 9, 38; "Two Minds," 227n33; *The Unsettling of America*, 6, 12, 35, 58, 78–81, 92, 151–52, 155, 159, 177, 188, 205n10; "The Way of Ignorance," 53, 132, 178–79, 220n53; "What Are People For?" 212n11; "Why I Am Not Going to Buy a Computer," 16, 109; "The Wild Birds," 141–46; "The Work of Local Culture," 17, 42, 100, 153–55, 157–58, 192; "Writer and Region," 209n49
boomers and *stickers*, 5–11, 20, 123, 127–30, 132, 141–42, 155, 167, 188, 197

Chesterton, G. K., 154, 208n46, 223n22
Christianity, 13–14, 31–33, 45, 78, 102, 124, 125, 128–30, 133
consumerism, xiii, 1, 6, 14, 30–31, 110, 208n45
cosmopolitan, 55, 146–52, 155, 162, 164
Cronon, William, 181–84, 210n22
curiosity and studiousness, 168, 177–78, 187

desires, 1–4, 6–11, 18, 27, 33–36, 43–45, 96, 117, 127, 134, 143, 145, 150, 165, 168–69, 171–72, 174–81, 186–88; and literature, 60, 67; and work, 70–72, 75, 81–82
Dreher, Rod, 43
dualism, 70, 73–78, 81, 131, 144

Eliot, T. S., 18, 106, 216n33

fidelity, 20, 37, 72, 91, 127, 133, 140–65, 191
Florida, Richard, 163

gratitude, 20, 91, 96, 116–39
Griffiths, Paul J., 34, 179–80, 227n26

Heidegger, Martin, 116, 122, 124–25, 219n21
hooks, bell, 43
hope, 1–3, 16–18, 36, 42–43, 71, 82, 96–97, 101, 114, 157–58, 191–93
Hugh of St. Victor, 73, 78, 80, 106, 210n28, 211n49, 217n36

Illich, Ivan, 106, 211n49, 217n37
imagination, 1–5, 8, 10, 18–20, 25–28, 36, 38, 40–43, 45–46, 51, 54, 59, 66–67, 68, 72, 75–77, 81–82, 87–88, 91, 110, 114, 134, 155–57, 167, 193, 199

Jackson, Wes, 13, 66, 158
Jacobs, Alan, 132

Kerr, Clark, 29

language: abstract, 19, 47–50, 82, 149; responsible, 36, 50–68, 110–11. *See also* liberal arts
Leithart, Peter J., 124
Lewis, C. S., 9, 35, 39, 120, 210n21
liberal arts, 29, 37–39, 54–62, 73, 76, 78–80, 181–83
literature, 20, 30, 37, 63–68
love, 2–4, 10, 20, 45, 50, 53–54, 67, 70–77, 81–83, 91, 95–96, 98–100, 108, 129–30, 143, 146, 150–56, 162, 166–90

MacIntyre, Alasdair, 4, 19, 31, 91–93, 204n55, 206n18, 207n34, 214n3, 214n8, 214n11
memory, 20, 42, 95–115, 116, 152–53, 181, 187, 191
Milton, John, xiii, 66, 134
"multiversity," 29–30, 34

Oehlschlaeger, Fritz, 211n39, 214n8

parochial, 146–48, 152–58, 163–64
practices: admitting ignorance, 135–36; advising, 135; attentive study, 186–88; cross-cultural study, 161–63; curriculum of questions, 185–86; disciplinary history, 111–12; imagining better stories, 40–43; institutional memory 112–14; learning from literature, 63–68; liberal arts, 54–62; living out questions, 43–46; local curricula, 160–61; local research, 136–38; lower tuition, 163–65; memorizing poetry, 110–11; physicality of intellect, 84–85; rooted faculty, 158–60; Sabbath, 133–34; technology reduction, 109–10; work, 86–88; work colleges, 85–86
Prakash, Madhu Suri, 32, 192, 206n20

quadrivium. *See* liberal arts

sciences, 9, 30, 35, 63–64, 111–12, 128, 130, 132–33, 136–38, 150, 178, 205n9, 222n21
Smith, James K. A., 4, 83, 92, 134
Snyder, Gary, 192

stickers. See *boomers* and *stickers*
studiousness. *See* curiosity and studiousness

temperance, xi, xii, 12, 32
Tolkien, J. R. R., 65–66, 154
tree of knowledge, 11, 19, 28, 35–39, 43, 47, 64, 79, 181
trivium. *See* liberal arts
Tuan, Yi-fu, 149–51, 219n29, 222n22, 224n50

universities: history of, 28–33; land-grant, 73, 78–79, 148, 160

virtue, xi, xiii, 4–5, 9, 16–17, 19–20, 31–32, 91–94, 166, 191–93. *See also* fidelity; gratitude; hope; love; memory; temperance
vocation, 8, 11, 44–45, 120, 128, 130

Weil, Simone, 186–88
Wellmon, Chad, 205n9, 207n30, 222n19
Wirzba, Norman, 124, 199, 203n29, 208n34, 214n50, 219n28, 219n34, 219n42, 220n59
work, 9, 15, 19, 36, 39, 42–43, 45–46, 70–88, 93, 100–101, 113–14, 127–31, 134, 156, 159, 164, 192–93

Culture of the Land: A Series in the New Agrarianism

This series is devoted to the exploration and articulation of a new agrarianism that considers the health of habitats and human communities together. It demonstrates how agrarian insights and responsibilities can be worked out in diverse fields of learning and living: history, science, art, politics, economics, literature, philosophy, religion, urban planning, education, and public policy. Agrarianism is a comprehensive worldview that appreciates the intimate and practical connections that exist between humans and the earth. It stands as our most promising alternative to the unsustainable and destructive ways of current global, industrial, and consumer culture.

Series Editor
Norman Wirzba, Duke University, North Carolina

Advisory Board
Wendell Berry, Port Royal, Kentucky
Ellen Davis, Duke University, North Carolina
Patrick Holden, Soil Association, United Kingdom
Wes Jackson, Land Institute, Kansas
Gene Logsdon, Upper Sandusky, Ohio
Bill McKibben, Middlebury College, Vermont
David Orr, Oberlin College, Ohio
Michael Pollan, University of California at Berkeley, California
Jennifer Sahn, *Orion* magazine, Massachusetts
Vandana Shiva, Research Foundation for Science, Technology & Ecology, India
Bill Vitek, Clarkson University, New York

www.ingramcontent.com/pod-product-compliance
Lightning Source LLC
Chambersburg PA
CBHW030105170426
43198CB00009B/500